THE HAPPY TABLE OF
EUGENE WALTER

THE UNIVERSITY OF NORTH CAROLINA PRESS   CHAPEL HILL

THE HAPPY TABLE OF

EUGENE
WALTER

Southern Spirits in Food and Drink

An Ardent Survey of Southern Beverages and a Grand Selection
of Southern Dishes Employing Spiritous Flavorings

Edited by Donald Goodman & Thomas Head

Designed by Courtney Leigh Baker and set in Whitman, Museo, and Nelly Script
by Rebecca Evans. The paper in this book meets the guidelines for permanence
and durability of the Committee on Production Guidelines for Book Longevity
of the Council on Library Resources. The University of North Carolina Press has
been a member of the Green Press Initiative since 2003.

Frontispiece: Eugene Walter, Mobile, 1995. Courtesy of Walter Beckham,
http://www.walterbeckham.com.

Library of Congress Cataloging-in-Publication Data
The happy table of Eugene Walter: Southern spirits in food and drink: an ardent
survey of Southern beverages and a grand selection of Southern dishes employing
spiritous flavorings / edited by Donald Goodman and Thomas Head.
p. cm.
Includes index.
ISBN 978-0-8078-3483-1 (hardback)
1. Cooking, American—Southern style. 2. Cooking (Liquors)—Southern States.
3. Liquors—Southern States. 4. Walter, Eugene, 1921–1998. 5. Cookbooks.
I. Goodman, Donald, 1947– II. Head, Thomas, 1942–
TX715.2.S68H366 2011   641.5975—dc22   2011009285

15 14 13 12 11 5 4 3 2 1

The following articles by Eugene Walter have been reprinted with permission in
revised form: "Soups for Grand Balls and Cotillions," *Alabama Magazine* (January–
February 1981); "Bring Back the Oyster Loaf," *Mobile Bay Monthly Magazine* (1987);
"Carnival," *Alabama Magazine* 56, no. 1 (January–February 1992); and "Testimonial
for Caramel Cake," *Alabama Magazine* 56, no. 6 (September–October 1992).

MIX
Paper from
responsible sources
FSC
www.fsc.org   FSC® C013483

For

Scott Gonzalez, Scott Peacock, and Scott Wilson,
who all three have a head for Ahead, a passion for Past,
and a nod for iron—skillet, scallion, and skirmish forever

Contents

Foreword

THOMAS HEAD

The Happy Table of Eugene Walter is the first totally new Eugene Walter cookbook in more than a decade. It supplements the food books Walter published during his lifetime: *American Cooking: Southern Style* (1971) for the Time-Life Foods of the World series; *Delectable Dishes from Termite Hall: Rare and Unusual Recipes* (1982); and *Hints and Pinches* (1991), a guide to herbs, spices, and condiments. *The Happy Table of Eugene Walter* is based on an unfinished manuscript found among his papers, supplemented by recipes published only in local Alabama newspapers and magazines.

If you have never heard Eugene Walter's voice, you are in for a treat. (A collection of his songs and his readings from his poems and stories is available on a CD called *Rare Bird*, from Nomad Productions in Fairhope, Alabama. A few sample tracks are available on the web: www.nomadmusic studio.com/rarebird.htm.) The first and most obvious thing you'll notice about this unique voice is that it's a very southern voice. Even after years of living in New York, Paris, and Rome, he never lost the accent of his native Alabama. And no matter where he lived, he never lost his appetite for his native food: searching out the ingredients for gumbo in New York, wishing for butter beans in Paris, growing greens on his terrace in Rome.

Walter grew up at a time in the South when cooking meant home cooking. Even though his grandfather was in the fruit and vegetable importing business, everyday cooking in the Mobile of his youth largely depended on what was fresh, local, and seasonal. You ate tomatoes when tomatoes were in season, peaches when peaches were in season. ("In Westchester County," he intones in the poem of the same name, they have seckel pear trees but do not make marmalade, confiture, or chutney. Instead, scandalously, "they let the fruit ripen and fall on the ground.") His work seems to have anticipated most of the food trends of our own time — eat fresh, eat local, avoid the seduction of the pre-made, pre-packaged, and pre-ground (particularly in the case of black pepper).

The recipes reflect a time when cooks, often far from grocery stores, were forced to be inventive — if you were out of an ingredient called for in a recipe, you substituted an ingredient you had. Eugene Walter knew that this sort of invention based on necessity is the soul of home cooking, and he encouraged it. "Do your own thing: invent!" he frequently coaxed.

He realized as well that the inventiveness of home cooks extended to the canned and packaged goods that were increasingly available as the twentieth century progressed. He referred to those who objected to the use of canned food as "food snobs," ignorant of the South in "the days before the refrigerator." He even depends on Campbell's soups for an occasional shortcut and affectionately calls them "Mr. Campbell's soups."

Another characteristic of Eugene Walter's voice that is distressingly absent from the food world today is that it is a cultivated voice — a witty and educated voice that he translated into captivating prose. Walter wrote beautifully, and the recipes are a joy to read. Walter was an autodidact without the brittle edge that often characterizes the learning of the self-taught. He never lapsed into pedantry — in fact, he preferred a good story to factual accuracy. His writing voice is more like the voice of a learned uncle who wants to teach in the most pleasant way possible. He doesn't talk down to his audience — he assumes, for example, that his readers know the difference between a pinch and a dash, between a dash and a splash. He encourages his readers to invent, to experiment, and above all to enjoy cooking, eating, and drinking.

Whimsy is a constant in Eugene Walter's work. The cat, independent and adventurous, and the monkey, relentlessly curious and always active, were his two favorite animals. Walter shared these characteristics with the animals, as did his approach to food and drink. Walter loved a good story and was always willing to interrupt his narrative to tell one. He also loved a good recipe or kitchen tale, and his recipes are studded with stories of the people behind them. His introductory essays and his headnotes to the recipes are always a delight to read.

Eugene Walter compulsively collected recipes — from family manuscripts, from friends, from magazines, from labels, from ads — and pasted them in a series of notebooks, categorized by subject, which were his main source of reference when he wrote. Many of these recipes are identified by the town in Alabama where they originated; many are identified by the names of the families that served them, some as illustrious as the Bank-

At home with his cat, Mobile, 1990s. Photo by Mark Miller; courtesy of Eugene Walter estate.

heads and Luces, some as eccentric as Miss Minnie J. Cox, who never entered a room without exhorting the company in a loud voice to "say a little prayer for Miss Minnie J. Cox."

The recipes in *The Happy Table of Eugene Walter* are valuable not only because they taste good but also because Walter preserved recipes from the many ethnic groups that have contributed to our modern culinary repertoire. John Martin Taylor and Damon Fowler have written eloquently about the many sources of Charleston and Savannah cooking. Modern Louisiana food writers like Donald Link and John Besh have increased our awareness of the many sources of Louisiana cooking — the Cajun and Creole traditions, Spanish, Italian, French, German, American Indian. Eugene Walter does the same for Alabama cooking, influenced not only by the traditions of the English settlers and enslaved Africans but by the Caribbean, France, Italy, and Germany.

Eugene Walter's decision to compile a cookbook in which all the recipes contain alcohol was also a part of his respect for the traditions of the region he wrote about. There's none of the frat-boy naughtiness that pervades many of the current crop of cooking-with-alcohol books. Many of these recipes, he explains, were neglected or, of necessity, went underground during the Prohibition era, and we are in his debt for rescuing them.

The book itself is an unexpected reward of a monumental effort to catalog Eugene Walter's papers. After his death in 1998, Donald Goodman, executor of Walter's estate, retrieved about 150 boxes of papers from his cluttered home. These boxes of papers proved to be a treasure trove of letters, drawings, photographs, clippings, financial records, recipes, and manuscripts dating from all periods of the life of this multitalented man. I was lucky enough to be asked to help Don Goodman catalog the contents of these boxes, and during the year we went through them, we found wonderful things. Like many intensely creative people, Eugene Walter had more ideas than he ever had time to turn into finished products. One discovery was the essay "What Is Southern?" by Edna Lewis, which was posthumously printed by *Gourmet* as the centerpiece of its January 2008 edition. Walter had tucked it away in a folder for future publication in a book that never materialized.

In another box, we found a proposal for a book that Walter never finished, a book with the very Eugene title "Dixie Drinks: And Sometimes We're Right Moderate. A History of Southern Beverages, and How to Prepare Such, with Forgotten Formulas for Home-Made Wines and Cordials and a Grand Selection of Southern Dishes Employing Spiritous Flavorings." That manuscript is the primary source for *The Happy Table of Eugene Walter*. Walter envisioned his proposed book as a work in three parts — a section on cocktails and how to make them, a section on homemade wines and liqueurs, and a final section of southern recipes that use alcohol. This book is in two parts, cocktails and food, because we never found a draft of the proposed section on homemade wines and cordials.

The book seems to have progressed only to the proposal stage. Parts of the manuscript were typeset, and it was prefaced by a description of the book directed to a prospective publisher. (All the alcohol vanishes in cooking, Eugene assured the publisher, so "I presume the book will be a favorite Christmas present for fundamentalists.")

In preparing this manuscript for publication, we have made a few changes for consistency and done a bit of editing on certain of the recipes in the interest of clarity, but for the most part, we strove to let Eugene Walter's unique voice shine through, both in the recipe directions and in the headnotes and accompanying essays. In a few places, where Eugene's stories are too good to leave out, we have included a couple of old favorite recipes printed in earlier books.

It is our hope that when you read or cook from this book, you will be able to hear the voice of Eugene Walter always urging you to "seek fresh, avoid chemicals, keep a light hand, rise to the occasion, try what you don't know, have fun." It's a voice that's much needed in today's food culture. From Eugene and from us, "Good eating, you-all!"

Preface

DONALD GOODMAN

I met Eugene Walter in 1994 when I went hunting for a new home in Mobile, Alabama. After our absence for a number of years, my wife and I were returning to Alabama and decided on living in the Deep South. A friend, Tom Westmoreland, insisted I meet Eugene Walter, a man I had never heard of. Tom said Eugene was known as a Renaissance man who had lived part of his life in Italy but had returned to his native Mobile in the 1980s. I phoned Eugene and a date was set for dinner at one of his favorite restaurants, Roussos, in downtown Mobile. Since Eugene didn't drive, I agreed to meet him at his house and provide transportation.

A knock at Eugene's door brought forth the sounds of a small dog barking, a terrier, I thought. The door opened and there stood Eugene, dripping wet, with just a towel around his waist. "You're early," he said. "Wait a moment and I'll be ready." I saw no dog but assumed it had been placed in another room. In a few minutes Eugene reappeared, and off we went to Roussos.

As we entered the restaurant, I was startled when Eugene barked like the dog I had heard at his house. We were promptly greeted by a friendly, smiling host and shown to a secluded table in a corner of the room. As we were seated, the waiter quickly secreted a pepper shaker from the table into his pocket and replaced it with a pepper grinder. This did not go unnoticed by Eugene, who told the waiter to "dispose of that dead dust." I was to learn that it was Eugene's mission to rid the world of bottled, ground pepper, wherever that dread dust was found. After an enlightening digression on the benefits of freshly ground pepper, Eugene insisted I try the crab claws, spinach Mornay, and, for dessert, tiramisu. After repeated visits with Eugene to Roussos, I learned that these dishes were some of his favorites.

With Coco the stuffed monkey, Mobile, 1979. Photo by Alan Whitman; courtesy of Eugene Walter estate.

Roussos was a Mobile institution that had been nearly wiped out by Hurricane Frederic in 1979. The restaurant on the causeway, a highway across Mobile Bay, had been destroyed by wind and water, so the family moved the business inland to the historic Fort Conde area of downtown Mobile. Eugene was a regular patron who had earned his own "table," where he entertained guests.

When we returned to his home on Grand Boulevard, I was invited in for a digestif. We were greeted by five cats. Several came to examine me while others observed from a distance. I could not miss a sofa just inside the door that had one side in shreds. "You'll have to excuse the cats. They're learning to upholster." I asked about his dog. "I don't have one of those creatures. My barking is a warning to strangers."

I was shown into a dimly lit "cat free" room that had walls covered with paintings and bookcases. On display everywhere were curios and objets d'art: metal sculptures; monkeys rendered in brass as well as ceramic; a stuffed monkey, encased in glass, the size of a child's teddy bear dressed in

DONALD GOODMAN

a brocade jacket and vest wearing a hat adorned with what appeared to be butterflies or flowers; and a windup automaton monkey dressed in a Dior gown, with a Marie Antoinette–style wig, playing a lute. Presiding over this, and so much more, was a life-size cardboard figure of Dolly Parton.

Our conversation began with inquiry into my Alabama roots, my astrological sign, and why I had decided to move to Mobile. When I told Eugene that my wife and I had lived for a few years in Gordo, Alabama, he was delighted with the sound of the town's name and wanted to know where Gordo was. After explaining that it was in west central Alabama, I told Eugene a story about asking for directions to a hardware store in a town adjacent to Gordo. "Go down this road, turn left and act like you're going to Gordo but then turn right, and you'll see the store." From then on, whenever Eugene and I were looking for someplace in our many scavenging trips together — Eugene had learned, growing up in the Great Depression, to hoard bits of this and that to be repurposed when needed; his house was filled with collections of foil, ribbon, fabric, knickknacks, bric-a-brac, and whatnots — Eugene would tell me to "act like you're going to Gordo."

During that first evening spent with Eugene in his "cat free" room, I fell under the spell of a master storyteller, a spell aided, no doubt, by the digestif he served. Our casual conversation covered people we knew in that southern tradition of searching for commonality among acquaintances and family. I soon learned that Eugene knew a vast number of common as well as famous people. These were all mentioned in the telling of the stories of his life. The southerners I know love a good story, and Eugene told the best. The notion of "being in the right place at the right time" truly applied to Eugene Walter.

Eugene was born in Mobile, Alabama, on November 30, 1921, in his grandmother's house. He reminded everyone that he was triple Sagittarius: The sun, moon, and his ascendant planet were all in the same sign at his birth. His first horoscope said he would never be rich but would travel and receive what he really wanted in life. And so it came to pass.

He was christened in the Catholic church with the priest pouring holy water over him while his grandfather Walter touched his lips with peach brandy — a reminder, as Eugene said, of the sacred and the profane.

As a gift, the Walter relatives in Germany sent Eugene a stuffed monkey, the same monkey I saw in the glass case in his house. I learned that this monkey accompanied Eugene in his journeys around the world, along with a shoebox of Alabama dirt he kept under his bed.

I asked Eugene once, "Of all the places you've lived, if you could return to live in one of them, where would it be?" Without considering, he replied, "The Mobile of my youth."

Eugene spent his early, formative years in his Walter grandparents' household. He was the first grandchild and was watched over by his grandmother when his parents were working or out and about. Eugene's grandfather Walter had an import business that provided his family dining table with yams from Puerto Rico, onions from Bermuda, and blood oranges from Italy, along with meats from up north along the Alabama River. A block of ice in a small, zinc-lined box served as the icebox that later, with electrification, would become the refrigerator. Street vendors passing by the house sold fresh foods that would show up the same day at table, incorporated into a meal. Days were spent on the porch shucking corn, snapping beans, and shelling peas. Although exposed to his grandmother's kitchen, Eugene said he didn't learn to cook until after he moved away from home.

He began making up poems as a young child before he was able to read or write. He claimed to have learned French by listening to his grandmother when she exchanged gossip with neighbors, spoken in French so that young Eugene wouldn't be privy to the latest scandal. Encouraged by his grandmother, Eugene learned to read "gamboge," "ultramarine," and "rose madder," the colors in his watercolor box, before he learned to read his elementary school primer. When he mastered the task of putting pencil to paper, Eugene began his long career as a writer.

As young boys, Eugene and Truman Capote, who was then known as Buddy Persons, were members of the Sunshine Club. The club was sponsored by the *Mobile Press-Register* newspaper to encourage children to write stories, the best of which would appear in the paper. On Saturdays, Buddy Persons would come down from Monroeville to Mobile so that he could attend movies. As one of Eugene's stories goes, he and Buddy were waiting on the sidewalk to enter the movie theater when an older boy in a group of youngsters started picking on the diminutive Buddy. Buddy lowered his head and rammed the older boy full on. This incident led the others to give Buddy the nickname Bulldog. Buddy would go on to win second prize for his story "Old Mrs. Busybody," but it was never published because an aunt felt the story would scandalize Monroeville, since it was based on an eccentric character known by everyone in the city.

Eugene continued writing short stories and poetry. His early work was published in the *Public School Courier* in 1933 and in Murphy High

School's *Murphy Hi-Times* from 1936 to 1938. In his lifetime, his writing appeared in a number of literary journals in both Europe and America. His observations on society and life in general were published in newspapers and magazines in Rome, London, New York, and his native Mobile. His awards included the Lippincott Prize for his first novel, *The Untidy Pilgrim*; a Sewanee-Rockefeller Fellowship for *Monkey Poems*; the Prix Guilloux for translation; and an O. Henry Citation for his story "I Love You Batty Sisters."

An early creation was Eugene's alter ego, Dr. Sebastian Willoughby. In his writing, Eugene used various pseudonyms, but it was Willoughby who accompanied Eugene throughout his life. It was Eugene's establishment of the Willoughby Institute that supported the arts and first published some of Eugene's books. Eugene's most amusing character was his personal secretary, Angela Garvey. It was Garvey (Eugene) who responded to publishers wanting to know when a book draft would be submitted or to the power company's insistence on trimming the trees in Eugene's yard.

While in high school, Eugene met a friend of his grandmother's, Hammond Gayfer, who was a patron of art, music, and theater in Mobile. It was through Gayfer's friend Aimee King that Eugene was introduced to the Children's Theater of Mobile. He designed sets for productions including *Kai Koshru*, *The Sleeping Beauty*, and *Snow White and the Seven Dwarfs*. With King's and Gayfer's encouragement, Eugene organized a marionette company and toured it throughout the Gulf Coast region. With Mobile being the original home of Mardi Gras in the United States, the annual celebration of the holiday with its parades, floats, and masked balls attracted Eugene's talent. He designed costumes and tableaux for the various secret societies. In 1937, at the age of sixteen, Eugene had a one-man show in Mobile of his paintings and theatrical designs.

After high school, Eugene joined the Civilian Conservation Corps in Mississippi, where he worked as a highway sign painter. His favorite sign was "Soft Shoulder."

Eugene, inducted into the army in 1942 for service in World War II, was sent to New York to train as a cryptographer. There is an infamous story told by Eugene of his meeting Tallulah Bankhead when she was starring in *The Skin of Our Teeth* on Broadway. At the end of the play, Eugene asked to be allowed to go to Bankhead's dressing room to congratulate her on her performance. After being turned down, he told Tallulah's assistant to let her know a fellow Alabamian from Mobile wanted to see her. He was then admitted to her room, where Tallulah was undressing behind a screen.

After some small talk, Tallulah offered Eugene a memento. She let out a small groan and said, "Here, dahling. Take these," handing Eugene a few pubic hairs.

After his Broadway adventure, Eugene was assigned to the Andreanof Islands in the Aleutians. His creativity could not be stilled, and he worked on props, costumes, and scenery for the Army Air Force Theatre production of *Room Service*. While stationed in this most isolated of places in the world, he saw Gore Vidal, who was also serving in the war. Vidal's ship had docked at the islands, and Eugene saw him in passing. He could not have realized that later in life, they would be neighbors in Rome.

After the war, Eugene returned to Mobile, where he worked with the Mobile Chamber Orchestra, the Mobile Opera Guild, and the theatrical group the Joe Jefferson Players. His friends urged him to seek fame and fortune in the world outside his hometown, so he moved to New York and took an apartment in Greenwich Village. As fate would have it, across the way from him was Anaïs Nin, and in a basement apartment was Andrew Warhola, later to be known as Andy Warhol. Eugene collaborated with Nin and her husband, Ian Hugo, on the film *The Dangerous Telescope*.

While living in New York, Eugene worked during the day at the Chaucer Head Book Shop and later for the Foreign Exchange section of the New York Public Library. He built marionettes designed by Kurt Seligmann at the Knickerbocker Music Hall. In his spare time at night, he worked on costumes and sets at the Cherry Lane Theater and other off-Broadway sites. He attended classes at the New School and the Museum of Modern Art and studied drawing with Pavel Tchelitchew. When Dylan Thomas was in town, Eugene threw a party attended by José Garcia Villa and Jean Garrigue. It was Garrigue and Villa, along with Howard Moss, Robert DeVries, Marie Donat, and others, who helped Eugene stage the first known "happening" in the garden of the Museum of Modern Art. Despite all these activities during his years in New York, Eugene professed to feeling isolated, lamenting that, unlike in his hometown, people in New York didn't make eye contact.

In 1951, he moved to Paris, where Marguerite Caetani sought Eugene's assistance with her multilingual literary journal, *Botteghe Oscure*. It was during his first year in Paris while working for Caetani that Eugene met George Plimpton, who was working to get the *Paris Review* up and running. Eugene wrote a short story, "Troubadour," for the first issue, published along with stories by writers Terry Southern and Peter Matthiessen. Eugene served as a founding and contributing editor for the journal. His

At Greenwich Village party (in white shirt holding cigarette), 1950s.
Photo by Ottomar; courtesy of Eugene Walter estate.

first novel, *The Untidy Pilgrim*, had been submitted by a friend in New York for publication by Lippincott and won the Lippincott Prize for best first novel. The book he considered to be one of his best works, *Monkey Poems*, was published in Paris in 1953 by Finisterre.

With time on his hands, Eugene studied at the Alliance Française and the Sorbonne. He met Alice B. Toklas and delighted in the fact that she had a small mustache, the ends of which he thought she waxed. They exchanged recipes, books, and gossip for the few years Eugene was in Paris.

Caetani tired of shuttling between her office in Rome and meetings with Eugene in Paris. In the mid-1950s, she convinced Eugene to move to Rome and assist her as editor of her journal. After an impoverished start living in a tiny cottage in Rome, Eugene moved into a multistory palazzo. On the bottom floor, a fellow southerner, Leontyne Price, rented an apartment. Eugene lived on the top floor and kept a flower and vegetable garden on his terrace.

Eugene met Federico Fellini at a marionette performance that Eugene and a friend staged. Fellini's interest in marionettes had led him to Eugene, which in turn led Eugene to a job as an assistant to Fellini. Eugene was cast as the American journalist in Fellini's film *8 ½*. He also played the mother superior in Fellini's *Juliet of the Spirits*. As an assistant, Eugene worked as a script translator, translating from Italian to English. Italian film directors sought money from all sources to produce their films, and having a script in English made it easier for foreign investors to understand what they were investing in.

The 1960s was the golden age of filmmaking in Rome, with the studio Cinecitta at its center. Eugene soon became a sought-after translator and later said that he translated "hundreds" of film scripts. He also acted in "hundreds" of films, from Blake Edwards's *The Pink Panther* to Lina Wertmuller's *The Belle Starr Story*. If a film was in production in Rome, Eugene would seek a role, no matter how large or small. He collaborated with Nino Rota on the song "What Is a Youth" for Franco Zeffirelli's *Romeo and Juliet*, with Eugene providing the lyrics and Rota the music. The song became an international hit.

In addition to his screen performances, Eugene was cast as a mime in Hans Werner Henze's opera *Der Junge Lord*. He also collaborated with composer John Eaton on *The Lion and Androcles*, with composer Gail Kubrik on *Household Magic, or The New Southern Grimorium*, with composer Alfredo di Rocco on *Alice in the Wonderland*, and with composer Donald Ashwander on *Ouijie in the Tree*.

"Entrance of Alice B. (to music of
tambourines and canary birds)," Walter
sketch of Alice B. Toklas. Courtesy of
Eugene Walter estate.

In Rome, 1970s. Courtesy of
Eugene Walter estate.

In order to keep himself busy in Rome, Eugene wrote a weekly column for the *Rome Daily American* under the title "E.W.E.W.," or "Eugene Walter Every Week." He attended the Istituto Dante Alighieri to study the Italian language.

When Isak Dinesen came to Rome, Eugene met her as she stepped off the train. She was quoting one of Eugene's poems as they met. Eugene composed a marionette comedy for Dinesen's arrival, titled *Tania-Tania and Clara, Too!*

When he had the money, Eugene Walter entertained lavishly. Practically anyone and everyone who was in arts and letters in society came to Eugene's apartment during the 1960s and 1970s. Actors, artists, writers, musicians, dancers, and those famous for being famous all dined at Eugene's table. When the cupboard was bare, he improvised. One night, entertaining guests with little to serve, he ran out to a local bakery and bought a small assortment of breads that he toasted, smeared with peanut butter, and topped with a dill pickle and bacon. The party was a huge success. I thought the combination sounded dreadful until I tried it. It's pretty good. It helps to understand that part of the charm of dining with Eugene was the entertainment: Eugene. He could converse wittily and intelligently on any subject. A free hand with the wine helped. When in Rome, it was said you must have two audiences: one with the pope and one with Eugene Walter.

Muriel Spark, a friend of Eugene's, said that in Rome, Eugene's apartment was "the nearest thing to a salon." Dishes served in most southern households were exotic foods when prepared and served by Eugene to friends from around the world who knew little about the Deep South. He scoured the markets of Rome in search of the foods and spices needed for a meal. Eugene always served some dish to surprise and delight his diners. There might be a vegetable pudding studded with Vienna sausages standing on end or marshmallows roasted over the table candles.

Those on both sides of the Atlantic who met Eugene passed along their stories of the fantastic meals he prepared and served at his parties. Due to his reputation as a gourmet and accomplished writer, Time-Life Books contracted with Eugene in 1970 to write *American Cooking: Southern Style*, one in a series of books Time-Life produced on regional cooking. James Beard and Michael Field served as consultants, with Eugene providing the text. Eugene was sent to the United States, a car and driver provided, and off he went on a tour of the South. The resulting book was a best seller.

On the porch in Mobile, 1990s. Courtesy of Eugene Walter estate.

Although it has been out of print for years, it continues to be a much sought-after rare book.

In the 1970s, a political activist group known as Brigate Rosse, or Red Brigade, staged a number of street demonstrations in Italy. Eugene found himself in the middle of one such demonstration while walking through Rome and had a tooth knocked out by a policeman chasing one of the demonstrators. In 1978, the Red Brigade kidnapped Aldo Moro, a former prime minister, killed him, and left his body in the trunk of a car parked on Via Caetani, a street next to Eugene's residence. There had been talk among the expatriate community that Rome was becoming too dangerous. With the murder of Moro, Eugene decided it was time to get out. As Eugene put it, "I wonder what they're doing in Mobile?"

DONALD GOODMAN

Eugene packed up and, with his cats, boarded a steamer to Mobile. Friends met him at the dock and arranged for him to live in donated housing. Confounded by a Mobile that had changed so much it was barely recognizable, Eugene nevertheless settled in, only to be nearly wiped out, along with the rest of the city, by Hurricane Frederic in 1979. Magnificent oak trees that had lined the streets of Mobile were uprooted. Most of the city was without electricity; rooftops were extensively damaged. It wasn't the homecoming Eugene had expected.

Eugene had been away from Alabama for almost thirty years and had been forgotten or was unknown by most of the population. Dr. Leah Atkins, director of the Center for Arts and Humanities at Auburn University, organized "A Celebration: Eugene Walter, Renaissance Man" to recognize Eugene in his hometown and state and as a thank-you for his ongoing championing of the South. After his return to Mobile, Eugene wrote and published *The Likes of Which*, *The Pokeweed Alphabet: Or, a Child's Garden of Vices*, *Delectable Dishes from Termite Hall: Rare and Unusual Recipes*, *The Byzantine Riddle and Other Stories*, *Monkey Poems and Semilikewise*, *The Pack Rat and Other Antics*, and *Lizard Fever: Poems Lyric, Sardonic and Elegiac*. He had a weekly radio show on WHIL, Mobile's public radio station, and continued his observations on life in columns for the *Mobile Press-Register* and *Azalea City News and Review*. He also fought the "daily-ness of life" through his exuberant support of the arts and artists. At the time of his death, he had ideas for new projects, including the novels "Adam's House Cat," "The Blockade Runners," and "History of Mobile." Two cookbooks were planned, "The Dainty Glutton's Handbook" and "The Ginger Fiend's Cookbook."

Eugene was a force of nature, "a thing let loose," as he described his life. When asked what he was working on, he would say, "I'm a busy, busy boy." And busy he was. In addition to all his publications, Eugene maintained a correspondence with hundreds of friends and acquaintances. His files boasted more than 600 folders containing letters from individuals he corresponded with, including Daisy Aldan, Ernest Hemingway, Patricia Highsmith, Tab Hunter, Allen Ginsberg, Butterfly McQueen, Ned Rorem, and the artist known as Zev.

As with all strong people, Eugene was loved by many and loathed by others. I count myself as one who loved him and was honored to be considered a friend. If I could sit at his table with a glass of wine and listen to one more story . . .

At Renaissance Man celebration, Mobile, 1987.
Courtesy of *Mobile Press Register*.

Acknowledgments

Thanks to the late Michael Batterberry, John T. Edge, John Edgerton, Mike Cavanagh, and Mary Beth Lakin for supporting this project. Our gratitude to Eliot Hyche for his invaluable help in preparing the manuscript. Rebecca Florence, Jo Ann Breland Lord, Charlie Smoke, and Gabrielle Gutting were very helpful in providing research. We thank Elaine Maisner and the staff of the University of North Carolina Press for their guidance and assistance in bringing the book to print.

O for a beaker full of the warm South
Full of the true, the blushful Hippocrene,
With beaded bubbles winking at the brim,
And purple stained mouth.
—Percy Bysshe Shelley, "Ode to a Nightingale"

Author's Preface

This book has two parts: Part I, Drinks, formulas for the many mixed drinks enjoyed in the South; and Part II, Victuals, a rich choice of dishes I've collected for years, including spectacular cakes, cookies, puddings, creams, sorbets, and so on, which call for a cup of whiskey, a cup of rum, a bath of port or Sherry, splashes of wine or brandy. In Part II, too, are found many wonderful dishes that were almost lost during Prohibition and the Depression.

Naturally, we make the point that most alcohol vanishes in cookery, so one gets only the rich, worldly taste of the fermented grains and fruits. Sometimes the alcohol is burned off by flaming, in which case you might have to heat the liquor slightly to get it to catch fire.

THE HAPPY TABLE OF

EUGENE
WALTER

In Mobile, 1987. Courtesy of Mary Alma Durrett.

Introduction

Ever since I was a teenager, I've been fascinated by the differences between dishes prepared by cooks in houses next door to one another, differences between county to county or state to state, and even differences between versions of the same dish prepared by two members of the same household or members of different generations. One of the great delights of studying cookery and family traditions of "special dishes" in the South is one's growing awareness of a kind of sweet crankiness governing exchange of recipes. My grandmother used to say that if you wanted to get anywhere near somebody's "special" recipe, you'd have to ask seven members of the family on the same day, in quick succession, so nobody had a chance to discuss it with anybody else. Quite often, it is not a conscious exclusivity about Great Aunt Lily's muffin formula or Uncle Philidor's breakfast cake but simply an assumption that any cook would know to toss in a hint of mace or that bit of grated citrus peel.

"Season well" is one of the most staggering phrases that occur in old recipes, jotted on the backs of envelopes or on battered tablets in a kitchen drawer. If you assembled some twenty good southern cooks to a Geneva-like conference to define "season well" in relation to hundreds of dishes, you'd end up with a twenty-year conference and a forty-volume encyclopedia. There's a whole world of southern muffins and cookies and bread for breakfast, for snacks, for ravening children crashing in from school, for readers who've finished an Agatha or a Simenon at some wee small hour and need nourishment. Most of these recipes are very simple, but ah! what individual variations exist.

The South, whether rich or poor, black or white, town or country, has always been serious about food. Part of that is climate, of course, and perhaps, as well, a more various set of settlers than those who settled the North. I leave that question to historians and statisticians. If one remembers that Alabama is roughly the same geographical area as Greece with all of its islands, one would expect a great diversity of cookery, and there is just so. But there is also a surprising unity at last, as in all the South. The Gulf Coast gumbo is fairly exotic to the mountaineers of north Alabama, but then they have their versions of burgoo and stew. I think I may safely say that the common factors in the wildly diverse culinary regions of Gulf Coast and upcountry are corn, greens, beans, cornbread and biscuits, and pickles and relishes. Game and fish, of course. Odd to consider to what extent rabbit, domestic duck, and guinea fowl have all but vanished since about the beginning of World War II. Nor do squirrel and possum grace Alabama tables to the extent that once they did.

During the Depression years, especially from about 1931 to 1937, there were many wild and weird pastimes in the South, echoes of that odd and wonderful southern spirit that was crystallized during the Reconstruction period. There was a sense of make-do, a humorous patience, a sense of improvisation. People raised in that spirit, as was I, will always bend down to pick up a penny from the sidewalk, even a bit of copper wire. Unless you lived through it, you cannot make any sense of what it was all about. Consider, for instance, Tacky Parties, where everyone wore the oldest and shabbiest clothes they had, mismatched shoes, torn shirts, faded dresses, unbelievably battered headgear. Whoever had the worst won the Tacky Prize. There was a miniature golf course in every block, ten cents a game. There were Progressive Parties, where one had drinks at one home, first course at another, main course elsewhere, and so on. There were kite-flying contests, yo-yo contests, one-foot races, trained chicken meets! Well, everybody was dead broke and trying not to notice.

Perhaps the most amusing department of all southern kitchen studies is the endless array of chicken recipes, and the debates, discussions, disagreements, and family feuds on just what is really the true southern fried chicken. In Alabama, there are basically two sides to the question: Either you coat the chicken pieces with very light batter and deep fry them, or you toss them in a bag full of flour and whatever you favor, black or red pepper, a pinch of this or that, a little salt, then sauté the pieces in a proper sautoir (high-sided skillet or pan) in mostly bacon fat with a little butter to give the right color. This being the individualistic South, there are some fairly exotic variations. Around Huntsville, a couple of young hostesses have lately been offering a daring innovation that has pleased all who have tried it.

1 fryer chicken, 2 to 3 pounds,
   cut into pieces

1 lemon

1 garlic clove

1 cup mayonnaise

2 cups saltine cracker crumbs

1 mild onion, such as Vidalia

Bacon fat and corn oil for frying

Rub your chicken pieces all over with half a lemon, then with a frayed garlic clove. Smear mayonnaise well over pieces, then dip into mixture of cracker crumbs with a little grated mild onion or shallots. Fry slowly, turning often, in mostly bacon fat with a little corn oil added.

Another variation, which won its cook a first place in a national chicken cookery competition, had the chicken pieces nicely buttered and then dipped into finely chopped pecan meats. Nothing new under the sun! An eighteenth-century English visitor to the South described how the Indians cooked turkey over the campfire, turning often. The bird was smeared with boar fat and coated with finely chopped "Illinois nuts" (pecans).

The array of dishes featuring corn, lye hominy, hominy grits, and that encyclopedic lineup of puddings, breads, soufflés, muffins, pones, and succotashes is bewildering. One thing is certain, though: From Muscle Shoals to Bay Minette, almost all agree that one doesn't put sugar in cornbread or pones. That's a Yankee aberration.

And everybody knows that you can, in an emergency, make cornbread with cooking oil for shortening, but that for the true and satisfying taste, there is only bacon fat strained through a cloth.

"We eat everything of the pig except the squeal" is one of the most famous southern dictums, as is "You can't make an omelet without breaking some eggs," which probably goes back, at least, to Cro-Magnon days. There are certain customs and beliefs common to all the South and strictly adhered to in Alabama: For a real feast, you must have two kinds of meat and two kinds of bread, and there must always be more than enough food to serve the number of guests.

Greens! A humble and constant presence in any account of food in the South. Not many collect "fence corner greens" any more, save in truly rural Alabama: dandelions, wild sorrel, pokeweed, all that. But, in the everlasting returning cycles of life, dandelion greens have begun to turn up in the snobbiest and most right-out-of-*Gourmet*-magazine salads at yuppie, with-it, and trendsetting tables. But southern preparations for turnip greens, collard greens, and mustard greens, along with cabbage, go on forever.

Nothing irritates me more than the phrase "soul food," a catchall label for the simpler and more traditional southern dishes. In the late 1940s and 1950s, the big record companies began to divide black music into two categories: dance band and show music on the one hand, and blues, gospel, and ballads on the other. Pop music and soul music. Nightclub music and revival tent music. Later, some smart aleck or other, with imprecise reasoning, decided to split southern food into rural, po' folks, mostly black cooking and fancy, citified, mostly white cooking. All wrong! There are as many social classes and degrees of culinary sophistication among blacks as among whites in the Deep South, and what I was served in a soul food restaurant in New York makes me gag even in recollection. I mean soggy, thick cornbread made with probably Wesson Oil and dreary, long-dead greens so swimming in pork fat that my teeth and tongue were wearing thick silk pajamas after one spoonful, and no flushes of beer made it possible to taste the other dishes that followed. Soul food, indeed!

I remember two delightful messes of greens. Once I went with a hunting party to Mt. Vernon, Alabama. I was after wildflowers; they were out to shoot Bambi. The midday meal was prepared by an ancient humorous black woman who served up a grand repast on a table covered with colored comic sections from the Sunday paper. The food had been cooked in the fireplace, whether in pots hanging from hooks or sitting in the embers. The steaming mixed greens (mostly turnip and mustard) were flavored with cubes of lean bacon, onions, and one or two not-so-hot red peppers. They were delicate, not at all greasy, and infinitely satisfying. They had simmered on the hearth all morning and were tender but not disintegrated. Years later, I was invited by the Conrad Aikens to a private club in Savannah where a silver tureen of turnip greens was served in triumph. This time, bits of ham and of ham fat had been included. Most delicate, it could have been brought forth at a Paris table with Tabasco on the side. I questioned the chef, who laconically replied, "Low fire, slow cookin'." And that's the title of a cookbook I have in progress.

Well, greens, ah, yes. So many Alabama dishes have a double personality: simple for everyday or homefolks, fancy for guests or on Sunday and holidays. For instance, a great many serious eaters feel strongly that the turnip leaf and the turnip root are two different items and should be prepared separately, even if you are serving them in the same dish. I have heard serious discussion as to whether the roots should be served on top of the greens, or alongside the greens, or in a separate dish.

Let's look at two versions of such, the everyday and the Sunday.

WEDNESDAY GREENS

Bacon or fatback	Pinch of red or cayenne pepper
1 bunch turnip greens with turnip roots	1 onion
Salt	Sugar

In your big pot, brown as much bacon or fatback as you like. Pour off all but a tablespoon of fat (save it, naturally!), then put in your turnip or mixed green leaves, which have been washed many times, then torn up, not cut. Put in a pinch of salt, red pepper, and some finely chopped onion. Add a little water and let this simmer forever. Boil your turnip roots with a pinch of sugar and a pinch of salt. When fork will just pierce, drain, peel, slice, or cube, then keep hot until you serve them on top of greens.

Now the Sunday version.

SUNDAY GREENS

Bacon or fatback	1 bunch green onions
1 onion	Water
2 ham hocks	Sugar
1 bunch turnip greens with turnip roots	2 tablespoons butter
Salt	2 tablespoons heavy cream
Pinch of cayenne pepper	Pinch of powdered mace

Put a small piece of fatback or bacon in the big pot. In this case, brown your chopped onions and put in some ham hocks and the torn-up greens, flavoring with salt, cayenne pepper, and a few chopped green onions. If you're serving fresh radishes, chop their greens and toss in. Almost cover with water and cook over low flame, stirring occasionally. Simmer the turnip roots in water with a pinch of sugar and a pinch of salt just until fork will pierce. Peel and cube, butter well, add a couple of tablespoons of heavy cream, and flavor with a good pinch of powdered mace. Serve alongside the cooked greens.

In north Alabama, greens are often served with a good handful of sippets over them. These cubes of stale bread fried in bacon fat with a couple of unpeeled garlic toes in the skillet with them are usually known by their French name of croutons, but the ancient English name is sippets. Very fine they are with any dish of greens or any clear soup.

Mention of mace brings up the subject of spices and of Mobile as spice port, of folks coming by riverboat to shop in Mobile, and of how even the poorest backwoods farmer managed to have a little of the "Christmas spices" (cinnamon, cloves, nutmeg, mace) at some time or other, while more solvent households employed a full orchestration of aromatics that dazzle even now.

"Bring back the Funny Greek!" was a hoary joke way before the War Between the States. It meant, "When you go down to Mobile, don't forget to bring home a portion or so of fenugreek [Greek hay]," a mild, pungent, savory flavoring that went into every known stew and was one of the basics in gumbo until it vanished from sight during World War I.

In the subtropical climate of much of the Deep South, critters need plenty of salt (they sweat out all their body salt) and plenty of sugar (for energy — and for sheer greedy-guts pleasure) in the long, hot, still days. A favorite restorative luncheon dish way back when was a pound cake or un-iced yellow cake served with any one of a dozen or so traditional sauces. The cake was always *chilled*; the sauce not.

The joys of the Deep South culinary palate, enough to fill some twenty volumes without thinking twice (Dear Readers, send me every pumpkin fritter recipe you have gleaned from Granny or Auntie!), and the infinite requirements of the southern palate have occupied me long, startled me often, delighted me ever.

"Mr. Turnip and Miss Nutmeg, a marriage made in heaven (but secretly she has many lovers—Mr. Spinach, Mr. Rutabaga, indeed a long list!)," Walter sketch. Courtesy of Eugene Walter estate.

On Recipes & Measurements

An aside to cooks: No one has ever questioned or expressed uncertainties to me about the use of "pinch," "dash," and so on as measurements. In the long run, I feel that "pinch" is much more precise than the "⅛ of a teaspoon" employed in more prissy-proper recipes. The great southern cooks, well aware of differences of altitude, climate, temperament, astrological signs, mood, degree of appetite, type of stove, kinds of kitchen equipment, and, most of all, the eaters for whom they cook, would never specify precisely such a measurement. They know what is meant by splash, dribble, dollop, lump, squirt, and hint, the difference between a dusting and a topping, between a dash and a pinch. Above all, they know that recipes are to be *interpreted* and so read a recipe rather as Wanda Landowska might read a page of Scarlatti for the first time or as Van Cliburn might peruse a newly discovered Mussorgsky prelude. Above all, the serious cook knows who is coming to table, whether a ladies' luncheon of reducers; a gang of greedy-guts teenage boys; the steak-and-potato set in need of introduction to, say, a grits-cheese-and-garlic soufflé; thin Aunt Mayhem in from gardening, ravenous and tucking in; or fat Uncle Picky, soaked in rum and taking only little forkfuls.

The best advice to cooks is, I feel, *seek fresh, avoid chemicals, keep a light hand, rise to the occasion, try what you don't know, have fun* . . . and good eating, you-all!

PART ONE
DRINKS

The Cocktail, or I Feel Better Already

Every culture, from the most primitive to the most developed, has its repertory of remedies, tonics, and pick-me-ups based on fermented juices, saps, and grains, many going back to remotest antiquity, back and beyond all written languages.

Any historic collection of potables lists a bewildering infinity of names for these "mixed" drinks: juleps, cobblers, daisies, eye-openers, "cups," punches, wassails, soothers, gloom-chasers.

But the concept of the "cocktail" and the name itself are American developments. The British Isles enjoy many mixed drinks that might qualify as cocktails save for the fact that they are served at room temperature. The American cocktail is always ice-cold, served in ice-cold glasses.

Antoine Amédée Peychaud escaped from a slave uprising in the Caribbean and landed in New Orleans, then under Spanish rule, in the mid-1790s, bringing with him in his flight a few clothes, a pair of pistols, a few gold and silver coins . . . and a kind of household record book that contained formulas for traditional remedies and pick-me-ups. He set up a pharmacy (really an apothecary shop) where he concocted and sold, among other things, a bitters, the formula for which is still a closely guarded secret; the label tersely mentions "herbs and spices."

Like all reputable pharmacists, Peychaud prescribed all manner of tonics and remedies and enjoyed particular success with a drink to prevent malaria. The concoction was something like half a cup of brandy and a tablespoon of bitters with a little light molasses or sugar syrup. The brand name of cognac employed was Sazerac, not made now for many decades.

After Peychaud's death, a certain John Schiller, at Schiller's Sazerac Coffee House in New Orleans, continued to serve the highly popular drink. Schiller's successor, Thomas Handy, continued but replaced Sazerac brandy with rye whiskey. Over the years, as bourbon moved from peasant or po'-white-trash status to more socially acceptable classification, bourbon replaced whiskey, and what we have is the Sazerac cocktail we know today.

Like the julep, making the drink is something of a ritual. It starts off with soaking a sugar cube in Peychaud's bitters, shaking up the drink, then pouring it into a glass that has been rinsed out with absinthe. Well, absinthe, made of the wormwood plant, was a drink that was banned in 1912 because drinking large quantities led to aberrations, fits of violence, hysteria, visions, and even death. An anise-flavored spirit is employed now. Herbsaint, manufactured in New Orleans, little known outside of the Deep South, is a delightful imitation absinthe flavored with anise. The French manufacture several absinthe-inspired spirits, as do the Swiss. Pernod is usually employed today in the Sazerac cocktail, when served outside the Gulf Coast regions.

Even if you have never tasted Peychaud's bitters, you honor him every time you say the word "cocktail." Everybody knows what an old-fashioned eggcup looks like: a rimmed half-cup the size of an egg perched on top of a mirror-image, slightly bigger half-egg base, created to serve soft-boiled eggs, which once were accompanied by all manner of gravies, melted cheese, and butter-and-chives sauce to dribble over the egg once the eater had removed the top bit of shell and spooned up a bit of the soft inside. The soft-boiled egg, alas! has vanished into the world of the forgotten and obsolete, chased thither by the specter of salmonella and other mass-production villains. But Monsieur Peychaud measured his brandy-and-bitters drink in such an eggcup, called in French a *coquetier*. We'd say jigger or slug or dolloper. Well, those English in New Orleans, quick to enjoy anything spiritous, heard the Creoles speak of going by Peychaud's place, *pour un coquetier*, and transliterated the word into some rather crazy sound-alikes: cockletwilly, cocotilly, cacoutille, questantell, and — the version that really caught on and joined the English language — cocktail.

In the 1890s, a New Orleans saloon-keeper thought up a kind of frothy cocktail that became known as Ramos' Gin Fizz. The formula was a dark secret, but the known ingredients were gin, egg white, cream, sugar, orange blossom water, lime and lemon juice, and soda water. This drink required energetic and thorough shaking in order to achieve the smoothness and fizziness that made it distinctive. So successful was Mr. Ramos's beverage, which became the main attraction of his bar and other bars he soon owned, that he hired a whole corps of energetic young men to do nothing but shake fizzes. A visitor to New Orleans during Carnival in 1915 reported, in awesome tones: "A platoon of grinning young waiters, with white jackets and perspiring foreheads, seemed almost a variety show act as they furiously shook their cylinders of fizz, sometimes to one side, sometimes to another, sometimes simultaneously tossing the container to the shaker next to them, never dropping them, never breaking the rhythm of their frenetic gymnastics."

Ramos' Gin Fizz is very cool and refreshing, much appreciated in the subtropical Deep South, quite often served before breakfast as Yankees might serve orange juice or grapefruit juice. The Fizz is quite common at brunch as well.

Planter's Punch goes back to the 1830s, maybe even earlier. It started out as first-quality rum blended with lemon or lime juice, but now there are literally hundreds of versions. A version that sprang up in Natchez just after World War II called for one-quarter part bourbon and one-quarter part dark rum to one-half part light rum.

If some of these southern drinks have remained more or less confined to southern regions, one southern invention has become universal; one can find it in Singapore and in the grander touristy hotel bars of London and Paris. This is the Old-Fashioned, and even folks who have never tasted such are acquainted with the "old-fashioned" glass. This cocktail was the invention of a bartender at the Pendennis Club in Louisville, Kentucky. It seems there was a retired Civil War general who hated the taste of bourbon, if such a thing can be believed, nor was he overfond of drinks that were too sweet. What finally pleased him and, incidentally, his friends and eventually the nation was bourbon flavored with simple syrup, diluted with pure spring or branch water and a dash of bitters, and garnished with a cherry, a slice of orange, and a twist of lemon.

In the 1800s and perhaps earlier on, in the Carolinas, Kentucky, Tennessee, and north Georgia, there was a midmorning drink known as Cuff and Buttons served under the chinaberry or magnolia tree or on the veranda. Later, this drink, in a very slightly different version, was bottled as Southern Comfort. It is still very popular, served over cracked ice as a cocktail or served straight, un-iced, as a digestif. It is basically bourbon flavored with ripe peaches and a very little sweetening. A few old-fashioned households in the South, for summer parties or wedding receptions, let chopped ripe peaches and a little dribble of dark molasses soak overnight in enough bourbon to cover, stirring constantly. The mixture is strained, added to four times more whiskey and a couple of drops of spring or branch water, and then served very cold.

Coca-Cola, when first created in 1886 by that pharmacist in Atlanta, had a wonderful flavor and contained "stimulants" that are now, I believe, forbidden by law. Coca-Cola became the basis for dozens of drinks made with rum especially but with rye and bourbon, too. Alas, what is sold as Coca-Cola today is rather blah.

There is a whole world of toddies and cough syrups that exist in old family records and kitchen account books, most never published. One delightful one is called Stop-the-Sniffles. This is simply chopped crystallized ginger with a little grated orange peel and a couple of mashed cloves, soaked in best bourbon and strained only when ready to be served very hot before bedtime. The same mix, diluted with spring or branch water and served over cracked ice, is a delightful before-meal cocktail. The sugar from the crystallized ginger is quite enough sweetening.

Someday, if I live long enough and manage to get permission to prowl through old household archives, and have time to do so, I'd like to do a collection of about a thousand of these remedies and tonics in a thick book with red-and-gold binding, titled "I Feel Better Already." As dear Gertrude might say, "A cocktail is a cocktail is a cocktail is a cocktail." Even when pretending to be something else.

Bourbon

When the name "Bourbon" is mentioned, most Europeans and Latin Americans automatically have a subconscious kind of slide-show of formal gardens, kings named Louis, Marie Antoinette, and the shadow of the guillotine. North Americans, instead, salivate thinking of the highball, the toddy, and the julep.

Yet few Americans know anything about bourbon whiskey, what it is and why we have it. It can be called bourbon only when made in the United States of America. Our Congress officially designated it as "a distinctive product of the United States," and it is accorded the same international protections given Scotch and cognac by the fourteen-nation Federation Internationale de Vins and Spiriteaux, which lays down the law quite firmly on what may be called what in the world liquor market.

Bourbon outsells blended whiskeys and Scotch by millions of gallons in the United States. There are 200 brands, apart from the thousands of private brands now on the open market. Cultists pretend to recognize the differences, but the famous anecdote of the young man clerking in a liquor store says it best: "Sure, I can tell the difference the morning after. If it wasn't a good bourbon, I'll know it."

Madeira, cognac, and the superior forms of rum, especially the white, were the snob drinks in early America. It was the Reconstruction period that made bourbon whiskey synonymous with the South. Gin, that Dutch distillation based on juniper berries and angelica, originally created to quell the menstrual pains of nuns, was big news during the Prohibition period (1919–33). Gin was in, simply because it was colorless and could be served in water glasses or sit on the bathroom shelf disguised as rubbing alcohol or mouthwash. But bourbon whiskey is, indeed, our national drink today.

Bourbon takes its name from Bourbon County, Kentucky, which used to be much bigger, covering most of the north- central part of the state. It was later divided up. And what is Bourbon County today has no distillery of any kind!

The name whiskey (whisky in the British Isles), from the Scots words *Uisge beatha* (from Gaelic *Usque baugh*) meaning "water of life," is subject to a vast body of legend and folklore in both Scotland and Ireland. It is mostly from the Scots that we have our lore.

The Scots and Irish settlers in America brought both their skill in whiskey-making and their unbelievable thirst. Under Washington's presidency, in 1791, the federal government levied a tax on whiskey that caused an irate insurrection, known later as the Whiskey Rebellion, and was the reason that great numbers of New Englanders of Scots and Irish background moved to the wilds of Kentucky and Tennessee. They found that the rich fields gave a high yield when cultivated in corn, so they began to make their whiskey of this rather than the rye or barley they'd preferred before. There was a benign fate at work, perhaps, for the clear water bubbling from the limestone rocks had a high calcium content, which added a taste that went well with the corn.

The ruddy caramel color and the smoky taste of bourbon have a background in legend, too. Often repeated is the tale of the farmer who put barrels of whiskey underground so they could age in his barn. After the barn burned down, he dug up the barrels, tasted the brew with some hesitation, gave a shout of joy, and immediately invited neighbors from miles around. Most historians today say that the first barrels available to the first distillers were those used to ship fish. The insides of the barrels were burned to remove the remaining smell and taste of fish. Whatever the truth, by law, bourbon whiskey cannot be called thus unless produced in white oak barrels that have been charred. The barrels must only be used once.

In one telling of the origin of bourbon, Reverend Elijah Craig, a Baptist minister, is given credit for distilling bourbon whiskey in 1789. This fact shakes members of Fundamentalist cults in the South, who claim that whiskey was invented by the devil. Some of the terms printed on whiskey labels have been so long accepted that few are really able to explain what they mean.

"Sweet mash" and "sour mash" are terms used to describe two different yeasting processes. Sweet mash is created with only freshly developed yeast as fermenting agent. Sour mash is the result of some new yeast and a mixture of leftover yeast from each preceding batch. This last is the method used in bourbon.

"Bottled in bond" (certified by the familiar green stamp) means that the whiskey in the bottle is 100 proof, is at least four years old, and was bottled under government supervision and that all the whiskey in the bottle was produced by the same distiller during a single year. The phrase does not guarantee flavor, aroma, quality, and the like.

"Proof." Ah, here we get into one of those international confusions like inches and meters, ounces and liters! The old English "proof" means the concentration of alcohol in a beverage that will allow gunpowder, soaked with it, to burn with a steady flame. A weaker mixture makes the flame smolder or go out; a higher content can lead to conflagration, even explosion, and the services of the fire department. The French system is simply to measure the percentage of alcohol by volume, expressed in degrees: 100 degrees means 100 percent alcohol. Our 100 proof actually means 57.1 percent alcohol. With the fact that the U.S. gallon is somewhat smaller than the British and, more than that, 175 degrees British proof is 200 degrees U.S. proof, it might be best simply to draw the curtain on these matters and go on to the controversy that has engendered more controversy than perhaps even the Civil War.

The mint julep, a very cold drink served in a frosted silver or glass tumbler, is made with either sugar or sugar water, either crushed or uncrushed mint, and the very best bourbon whiskey. It is delightfully refreshing and a known cure for headaches, crankiness, and fatigue. It would take some 500 pages to relate the different recipes, anecdotes, myths, and legends associated with this drink, but at least a few pages are devoted to it in the next section.

As a last word on bourbon, it should be noted that it is a highly popular pre-dinner drink in England. The English writer Alec Waugh has gone on record as insisting that it arouses the appetite while not anesthetizing the taste buds, as gin is said to do, or leaving a strong aftertaste, as in the case of many wines and aperitifs.

Juleps, Mint or Otherwise

Maryland Julep (circa 1790) • Bluegrass Julep (circa 1912) • Ladies'
Julep • The Milton Makeover (from Milton, Florida) • Russian Julep

The mint julep has become, in about two centuries, a kind of symbol of the
South, and everybody enjoys the drink, but no two southerners will finally
agree on the exact details of preparing the real, the authentic, julep. Like
all elements of southern civility or savagery, the julep has been exposed
to the humor, crankiness, and hectic participation, the sardonic hold-
back, the final fervor that flavors all things southern. I call it "the mists of
change, the change of mists." If I were really wealthy, I'd create a bar with
a bartender named Misty and a bar list with 200 versions, at the least, of
the julep.

Mrs. Frances Trollope, mother of the novelist Anthony Trollope, arrived
from England in 1827. She traveled quite a bit, taking notes, settled in St.
Louis and tried to run a shop, and antagonized the locals with her acid
comments on American manners and customs. Later, back in England,
she published her book *Domestic Manners of the Americans*, which irritated
most Americans even more, although many agreed with her about women
nursing their babies in the orchestra sections of theaters, and even more
about public spitting. Although spittoons were everywhere, men (and
some old women) would spit a mouthful of snuff or tobacco or whatever
in any convenient corner: The corners of public offices and theater or concert hall lobbies were brown and nasty. Naturally, the book was a best
seller. The British were fascinated by her ranting against drinking whiskey
and water for breakfast and queer combinations (to her) of food such as
ham with applesauce.

"Fat Cats drink juleps, and don't they JUST . . . !,"
Walter sketch. Courtesy of Eugene Walter estate.

One of the very few things Mrs. Trollope found to admire in America was . . . the mint julep. A few years after her return to Britain, she published her novel *The Old World and the New*, where she describes a pick-me-up served to some characters in a blazing Cincinnati summer:

It would, I truly believe, be utterly impossible for the art of man to administer anything so likely to restore them from the overwhelming effects of heat and fatigue, as a large glass filled to the brim with the fragrant leaves of the nerve-restoring mint, as many lumps of the solidly pellucid crystal-looking ice as it can conveniently contain, a proper proportion of fine white sugar (not beet-root), and then — I would whisper it gently if I knew how — a whole wine-glass full of whiskey poured upon it, to find its insinuating way among the crystal rocks, and the verdant leaves, till by gentle degrees, a beverage is produced that must create a delicious sensation of coolness, under a tropical sun, and a revival of strength, where strength seemed gone forever.

What, exactly, is the julep? That is a subject that, in the southern states, can initiate as many arguments, discussions, disagreements, and private opinions as the definition of what, precisely, is the true way to prepare fried chicken or a green tomato pie or crab cakes or . . . or . . . or . . .

How much Persian do you speak? More than you know! Azure, vermillion, zephyr, pajamas. And a julep (from the Persian *gulab*, for rose water) is what a Persian prince would sip on a warm evening as he sat in his paradise ("paradise" is from the Persian word for "garden"). His julep was purely and simply cool spring water flavored with the deliciously scented rose water, which is part of practically all sweet dishes in that part of the world — Turkish Delight, for example.

Most Mediterranean countries had echoes of the julep, but usually alcoholic — clear distillations of fruit or flowers diluted with cool water. Not syrups, but eaux de vie. The julep was undoubtedly introduced into the British Isles by English noblemen who had been received by Persian princes. Those British Isles have so many kinds of punches and wassails and mixed fruit and spirit drinks that it's hard to keep up with them. The julep was just one of a long list and probably came first to Charleston, South Carolina, if old household recipe books can be believed. Our early juleps were made of cognac; then, of best white rum flavored with rose water; or of simply rum in which rose petals had been soaked. Or of brandy and water flavored with fruit or flowers. Infinite variations.

Fine rum, Madeira wine, Amontillado Sherry, the best port, French cognac, and every tint of first-class Jamaica rum were the drinks of the aristocratic world, with the beers, ales, stouts, and whiskeys the beverages of the common man. It is likely that bourbon whiskey made its entrée into the white-columned mansions by way of becoming a basic part of the drink known as the mint julep.

The proper formula for preparing a mint julep is indeed a vexed question. In Maryland, rye whiskey is the only acceptable spirit for this drink; in Kentucky, where everybody (but everybody) traditionally drinks at least one julep during the Derby, only bourbon is acceptable.

Mr. Bill Samuels, Jim Beam's godson, head of Maker's Mark Distillery in Loretto, Kentucky, took an understandably lofty attitude toward most of the juleps served at the Derby, muttering something about "mint-flavored sorry whiskey" and laying down strict rules for making a julep. You must have well-aged, top-quality bourbon; purest cane sugar; good, fresh mint, preferably spearmint, but plucked two minutes earlier no matter what. The mint leaves must never touch the whiskey.

"At first we used cheesecloth to help extract the mint essence," he is reported to have said. "Then we tried very old damask napkins. But still tiny particles of mint would migrate into the liquid. We switched to Hanes Number Two white T-shirts. We wash them without soap, then roll up the mint leaves in the damp shirts. Twisting hard at each end of the shirt renders the mint juice without any particles."

Novelist and historian John Edgerton, who writes knowingly and wittily on southern culinary and Dionysian matters, says: "There are two aromas — bourbon and mint — that must be present in a julep that has found its equilibrium, and none must dominate or overwhelm."

For a very long time, the julep somehow did not emigrate. Oh, perhaps to the bar at the Astor Hotel, the Algonquin, the Plaza, but since World War II, the julep has turned up all over the world. A version that has both rum and cognac added over fresh pineapple has caused raised eyebrows and flipped wigs on the part of southerners visiting Manila. In the backwoods — or should I say backwaters — of those 2,000-odd Caribbean islands, there still turn up drinks called "joobies" or "goobies," which are based on flowers soaked in rum or brandy and are descendants of the original Persian or Arab beverages that made their way the other route, through Africa, and into New World fields of fermentation.

After trudging through untold acres of factual history, reportage, and comment and listening to countless verbal arias on the subject of the julep, one concludes that the majority opinion is that you must employ the very best well-aged bourbon whiskey, freshly plucked mint — preferably spearmint or a close cousin — and spring water. The water is important, since nowadays most American communities have such quantities of chlorine or who-knows-what in the water system that the truly delicate presence of the mint in the julep may be contaminated, indeed sabotaged beyond belief. Buy a good bottle of spring water from mountain springs.

A silver tumbler is what is shown as the trademark of the julep in the more slick, lifted-pinky food magazines, but real julep-drinkers like anything with a handle so that the heat of the hand doesn't too soon melt the important frosting. Old beer glasses with handles, tankards, are best, but a thick cut-glass tumbler supplies correct insulation, too. All, but all, agree on sugar of sugarcane origin, not beet. What is implicit in all this rink-dinky ritual is the true and important function of the julep as social lubricant.

There are dozens of formulas for ripe fruit, berries, or flowers soaked in best bourbon whiskey and served very cold over cracked ice. There are endless variants employing white rum, dark rum, and brandy. They are all good. Invent one of your own. A hint: Elder flowers when they first bloom, soaked in white rum sweetened with pale strained honey, are Very Good.

It would be helpful to glance at a few julep formulas of now and then and here and there.

MARYLAND JULEP (CIRCA 1790)

1 handful fresh mint

Confectioner's sugar

Brandy

Water

1 cup boiling water

French cognac

Gather the mint while the dew is on it, sprinkle with confectioner's sugar and a few drops of brandy and water, and bruise it gently until the mint oil begins to come. In bruising the mint, use a glass mortar and a wooden pestle. A pestle made of beech wood is best, but be sure whatever pestle used is wooden. Put the bruised mint in a glass and pour over it a cup of boiling water.

Let this sit for 15 minutes. Then strain the mint and pour the juice into a silver tankard that has been filled with crushed ice. Let this stand for a few minutes, then pour into it your French cognac that has been kept at a temperature of about 40 degrees and garnish the silver tankard with sprigs of mint.

Do not under any circumstances, other than a case of lockjaw, use a straw when drinking it, but drink from a tankard.

BLUEGRASS JULEP (CIRCA 1912)

½ cup spring water

½ cup granulated sugar

Handful of mint sprigs

Bourbon

Take a dipper of water from a limestone spring and dissolve enough granulated sugar in it to give a fine oily texture, then set it aside. Take a goblet of sterling silver (or, in an emergency, a tumbler of cut crystal) and a single medium-sized leaf of mint, selected for succulent tenderness and plucked from the living plant not more than 10 minutes before. Using the back of a sterling spoon, bruise the leaf gently yet purposefully against the inside of the goblet and heap full of fairly fine-cracked ice made from limestone spring water. Pour straight bourbon whiskey slowly into the goblet, letting it trickle through the ice at its leisure until the vessel is almost full. Set aside for 1 minute. Add the sugared water, a tablespoon or so, until the goblet threatens to overflow. Garnish the rim with 3 freshly picked mint sprigs. Do not stir. Let stand in a cool springhouse or icebox until the frosting on the goblet or tumbler is thick. Sip slowly; don't use a straw. Between sips, think of someone you love.

LADIES' JULEP

(Pour le matin apres le bal masque)

For ladies who are feeling delicate after a carnival ball or wedding party, or horse race, or visits from out-of-town cousins, the following julep-type freshener, from Monroeville, Alabama, is the perfect medicine.

1 cup rose petals	¼ cup cane sugar
1 ripe peach	White rum
1 piece crystallized ginger	Champagne sec

Pick petals from old-fashioned, strongly perfumed roses in early morning. Put them into a bowl with a very ripe peach chopped fine, 1 finely chopped piece of crystallized ginger, and a little cane sugar. Pour a cup or so of the very best white rum over this mélange. Let sit at least an hour or so. Strain and chill. Dilute with best French Champagne sec and serve in thoroughly chilled Champagne glasses. If this is before noon, serve very hot, buttered, coarse-ground grits on a dainty plate after one such julep, then serve several more juleps.

THE MILTON MAKEOVER (FROM MILTON, FLORIDA)

Sometimes, in late summer in very hot climates, mint just isn't there, so delightful variations of the mint julep have sprung up. This is one.

1 kumquat	Dark rum
1 tangerine	Lemon juice
1 orange	Candied orange peel or
Bourbon	crystallized ginger
Cane sugar	for garnish

Scrape only the outer skin of a few kumquats, tangerines, sweet oranges, or whatever combination of these you conjure into a good quantity of best bourbon. Add a dash of cane sugar. Let sit an hour or so, then strain and chill well. Add a dash of dark rum. Add 1 or 2 drops of lemon juice. Pour over cracked ice in chilled mugs or tankards, garnish with 1 thin strip of candied orange peel or crystallized ginger, and serve after putting into icebox at least 15 minutes.

RUSSIAN JULEP

2 cups fresh mint leaves

Warm water

Cane sugar

1 quart vodka

Soak mint leaves in a little warm water with as much or as little cane sugar as suits you. Strain this liquid into a quart of vodka; chill well. Serve in chilled glasses.

Eggnog

Allison McGregor's Eggnog • Brandy Posset • Eggnog, 1939 • Banana
Eggnog • Eggnog • Mary Scruggs's Eggnog • Georgia Eggnog

One of the endless discussions in the South deals with the question of
what is the authentic recipe for eggnog. Eggnog is the subject of as much
dispute and disagreement as mint juleps. The variants in recipes are endless, but in both these fields, there seem to be two basic schools of thought.
For mint juleps, the basic question is, Do you crush the mint manually, or
do you let the ice do the crushing in the julep? When it comes to nogs, the
disagreement centers around whether we are speaking of something one
drinks or of a lush, slurpy concoction that one eats with a spoon.

The dispute then moves to the proper time to serve it. On Christmas
Eve? New Year's Eve? Or the evening of Christmas? Or all day Christmas
for those who drop in?

The correct answer in both cases seems to vary by century and by lo-
cation. Earlier versions seem to fall in the "drink" camp. [Editor's note:
Due to the possibility that eggs could be contaminated with bacteria, eggs
labeled as "pasteurized" should be used in the following recipes.]

Allison McGregor's Eggnog is a Virginia version of a recipe handed down from her eighteenth-century Scots great-grandmother named Alysoun McGregor.

Note that this is a drink. The recipe is for a single serving and must be multiplied as required. It is served in goblets or small tankards rather than in the usual punch cups or wine glasses.

1 egg yolk	¼ jigger dark rum
1 teaspoon sugar	1 cup cold milk
2 jiggers dry Spanish Sherry	Powdered nutmeg
¾ jigger cognac	Powdered cinnamon

For each portion, put egg and sugar into serving receptacle and shake or whip well, then add spirits (and some ice, if you like). Shake well, then add milk and dust top with both nutmeg and cinnamon.

BRANDY POSSET

In Elizabeth Raffald's cookbook *The Experienced English Housekeeper* (1780), the kitchen Bible in many Virginia, Carolina, and north Georgia households right up till the War Between the States, there is a recipe for a posset, but we'd call it a nog.

1 quart cream	Whole nutmeg
Stick of cinnamon	½ cup sugar
6 egg yolks	1 cup brandy

"Boil a quart of cream over a slow fire, with a stick of cinnamon in it, take it off to cool, beat the yolks of six eggs very well, and mix then with the cream, add nutmeg and sugar to your taste, set it over a slow fire, and stir it one way, when it is like a fine thin custard take it off and pour it into your tureen or bowl, with a glass of brandy, stir it gently together, and serve it up with tea wafers around it."

The great Eva B. Purefoy, genial hostess and kitchen monarch of the Purefoy Hotel in Talladega, Alabama, noted the difference between a thick
modern and a liquid "old-time" eggnog.

1 dozen eggs, separated	¼ cup dark rum
1 cup sugar	1 quart whipping cream
1 pint bourbon whiskey	Whole nutmeg

Beat egg yolks well, about half an hour if hand beater is used. Gradually
beat in half the sugar. Gradually add whiskey very, very slowly, beating
constantly. Add rum slowly. (Some omit the rum and add a little more
bourbon.) In a separate bowl, beat egg whites stiff, beat in remaining
sugar, and fold in whipped cream, then fold into egg yolk mixture. If an
old-time thin eggnog is desired, add 1 quart of milk to this same recipe.
Without milk, this serves about 12. Sprinkle with grated nutmeg if
desired.

BANANA EGGNOG

Mrs. Purefoy always liked to serve the children some kind of facsimile of
what the adults were drinking. This is her famous children's eggnog.

1 fully ripe banana	or
1 egg	2 tablespoons chocolate syrup
1 cup cold milk	or
2 tablespoons finely chopped	2 tablespoons ginger syrup from
pineapple with juice	the Chinese jars

Slice banana into bowl and beat with rotary eggbeater or electric mixer
until smooth and creamy. Add stiffly beaten egg white, then separately
beaten egg yolk, then milk, then pineapple or chocolate or ginger syrup.
Keep beating until well mixed. Serve cold. This is delicious and nutri-
tious. Good, with lots of squirts of bourbon, for the elderly.

EGGNOG

From *The Dixie Cookbook*, still used today, published in Atlanta in 1885 by the publishing house of L. A. Clarkson. The authors are not listed by name but are referred to as a bevy of "southern ladies."

½ cup sugar

6 eggs, separated

1 quart heavy cream

½ pint brandy

Whole nutmeg

"Stir half a cup of sugar (white), yolks of 6 eggs well-beaten, into one quart of rich cream; add half a pint of brandy, flavor with nutmeg, and lastly add the whites of the eggs well whipped. M.H."

One favorite recipe for eggnog uses white rum and adds a good dash of powdered ginger, but the grated nutmeg is usual on top when serving.

MARY SCRUGGS'S EGGNOG

Mrs. Mary Williams Scruggs of Mansfield, Louisiana, received her ancient formula for eggnog from her father, who was born in 1853. Mrs. Scruggs, always happy to share her recipes, insisted that "real eggnog is always eaten with a spoon, not sipped."

Mrs. Scruggs remembers how all the menfolk gathered in the kitchen to beat and whip with old rotary beaters (this being before electric kitchen instruments) and, naturally, to sample the bourbon employed in the recipe. Cut-glass bowls and cut-glass cups, always. And freshly ground nutmeg, please! Here's her basic recipe, easily doubled.

12 tablespoons sugar

12 eggs, separated

12 tablespoons bourbon

½ pint whipping cream

Whole nutmeg

Add 1 tablespoon sugar for each yolk and beat until yolks are lemon-colored and very thick. Add 1 tablespoon best bourbon whiskey for each yolk when yolks are halfway beaten. Whip egg whites until stiff, whip cream until stiff, and fold all together. Add grated nutmeg on top of each serving.

24 eggs, separated

3 cups bourbon

2 quarts whipping cream

1 ½ cups plus ½ tablespoon sugar

Nutmeg to taste

Beat egg yolks at medium speed on mixer until they are pale and fluffy. Add bourbon, a few drops at a time, never stopping beating. You can do this the day before and keep covered in fridge.

Whip cream till it stands in peaks, add 6 tablespoons sugar, and fold in egg yolks. Beat egg whites till they are dry and have lost their shininess completely before you begin to add the rest of the sugar. Add remaining sugar to egg whites about 1 tablespoon at a time; go on beating after all sugar has been added. Fold the whites into the cream and yolk mix, continuing to blend and fold until thoroughly mixed and smooth. Serve from silver or crystal punch bowl into tall glasses; eat with iced-tea spoons. Put nutmeg on top of each serving, using whole nutmeg and grater. This will serve about 2 dozen.

Punch

Eugenia Sledge Punch • Ginger Cup • Burgundy Cup •
Sherbet Punch • Pineapple Punch • Alba Club Punch • Bombay
Punch • Southern Wedding Punch • Summer Punch • Chatham
Artillery Punch • Class Reunion Punch • Sunday School
Punch (Demopolis, circa 1880) • Merry Mabel

Champagne, Punch, & Wine

Any book about southern drinking habits must, if it is not to be ridiculed by old families in those so-called dry counties, occupy itself, if only in passing, with the theme of Champagne. That sparkling white wine in symbolic, bosomy bottles from that section of France is the very symbol of happiness, gaiety, erotic games and pleasure, poetry, art, the best of Europe imported into the New World, nostalgia, healthful cooking, the afternoon nap, unflappable tempers, and civilization.

I shall be totally misunderstood. I should never have written the preceding paragraph if I am to be acceptable to three-fourths of the United States.

When I write "erotic," I don't mean "dirty sex," I mean the Greek god of Love, and in this case, I am thinking of the courtly parlor games of tease-coquetry and verbal jousting, which are typical of all CIVILIZED warm-climate countries. Come with me to Lecce, to Sicily, to Pelos, to Malaga, to Charleston, to Mobile.

I remember moments, when I was a little brat, about 1926, when a company near my grandfather's produce firm down on the waterfront of Mobile used to ship Champagne, each bottle insulated in a Sunday section of the *Mobile Register*, to old families in the driest sections of Alabama, "dry" even before Prohibition, "dry" even as I sit here now. All that hellish inheritance of the Whiskey Rebellion. When I asked what those bottles, being carefully packed into Heinz soup and Miss Louc canned vegetable cartons, contained, Mr. S., the shipper, who'd had the bottles from French freighters, gave a smile, which was a masterpiece of our (French) southern hypocrisy, ruffled my hair, and said, "Medicine." He was correct, of course. Somewhere upstate, amidst joyless cults, more cultivated families still drank Champagne at christenings, at funeral feasts after Mama's funeral, after the birth of the first male child.

Well, let's take a look at the history of those sparkling wines from the Champagne province in northern France. We first read enthusiastic accounts of them in the thirteenth century. Yes, I did say thirteenth. We forget that what are called the Dark Ages weren't all that dark, just as we forget that the United States, known as a democracy, isn't all that democratic. That much of Africa, felt to be "backwards," has for millennia studied herbal medicine and basic psychology.

Dom Pérignon was the cellar master of the abbey of Hautvillers in 1668 and had theories about wine-making, about controlled fermentation, all that. He used stoppers made of corks rather than the then-traditional plugs of oil-soaked rags to contain the delightful bubbly nature of his fine white wine. When his experiments came to fruition, he bubbled with joy (excuse the term) and according to legend is reported to have shouted to the other monks to come at once. "Quickly!" he cried, "I am drinking stars!" That's been the reaction to Champagne ever since.

In international anonymous wine tastings, American Champagnes always rank high. This country makes the whole range of sparkling wines, from sweet to very dry. Try them all, I say, since they're affordable in comparison to imported French Champagnes. Remember that if you have that secret southern love (prominent in educated southerners, unknown in the let's-burn-everything-down cults) for all things French, the grapes and the know-how involved in American Champagnes are all from France. Not imitations. The reason Champagne is expensive is that it is aged in bottles, not in casks. Traditionally, the grapes are picked 100 days after the vines have bloomed. The wine is allowed to ferment in big casks over a winter, then it is ritually blended and put into bottles. The final fermentation in bottles is what makes Champagne different from all other wines and requires trained attendants and attention that makes the brew expensive. After years of aging, each bottle is opened with expert care as each little explosion blasts out the sediment. Then the range of flavor is determined and the final bottling takes place. Laws, regulations, traditions, emotions, philosophical opinion, all enter into the final categories of Champagne: nature (driest of all), brut, secor (dry), semi-doux, doux.

The number of punches and cups traditional in southern society is astronomical. Among the little side dishes placed near the big punch bowl we find toasted pecans flavored with white pepper, tiny thin sandwiches of smoked salmon, and, in recent years, smoked catfish fillets. Olives, never! I remember two Mobile Junior League ladies discussing a party by a very charming Pittsburgh colleague who'd moved to town and distinguished herself by energetic fund-raising. But after one of her Champagne-punch parties, a lady eyeing the serving table looked at her friend, raised her eyebrows, and said in a single word that summoned more than a century of tradition, nay snobbism, "Olives . . ."

During the truly heinous warmth of July and August, I often keep glasses in the refrigerator and bring them out a minute or so before I am going to pour any wine. White wine should always be slightly chilled, and chilled is the operative word: not glacier-ized or Arcticked. The ice bucket is what I prefer. Put in the ice and the bottle about fifteen minutes before going to table. Bottles are always stored on their side, of course. Makes a great difference. And even the simpler table wines are really better if they're not bounced, juggled, tossed, or rolled before being opened. Open reds an hour before serving so they can bloom. Open whites when you put them in the ice bucket. As Voltaire said, respect for wine is respect for God and the law.

Many traditional southern punch recipes, essential for celebrating everything from weddings to birthdays, depend on a bottle of chilled Champagne.

EUGENIA SLEDGE PUNCH

Block of ice

3 oranges, peeled and sectioned

1 lemon, peeled and sectioned

1 to 2 cups fresh fruit in season:
  peaches, apricots, ripe wild
  persimmons, plums, whatever,
  peeled, seeded, smashed

A few long, thin slices of
  cucumber rind

1 bottle Champagne

2 jiggers cognac

2 jiggers Benedictine

Mint sprigs or lemon balm

Put block of ice in big punch bowl, or if you're without such, use a baby tub. Pour in everything else slowly. Adorn each glass, when served, with mint sprigs or lemon balm.

GINGER CUP

½ cup candied ginger, chopped

1 bottle white rum

Block of ice

1 bottle cognac

Dry Champagne

Grated orange peel and mint sprigs
for garnish

Soak ginger overnight in refrigerator in rum. Put block of ice in punch bowl or baby bathtub. Slowly pour the rum and ginger and the bottle of cognac over it. Fill the punch bowl to the brim with dry Champagne. Add lots of grated orange peel and mint sprigs before serving.

BURGUNDY CUP

1 bottle best Burgundy wine

1 cup sugar

½ cup brandy

1 quart sparkling water

2 bottles Champagne

Block of ice

Mix wine with sugar, then pour everything slowly over big block of ice.

SHERBET PUNCH

1 quart sherbet (orange, lemon,
lime, or pineapple)

1 bottle sauterne

2 bottles Champagne

Put sherbet in middle of chilled punch bowl. Pour chilled sauterne and Champagne around it, not over it. Put a little glop of sherbet in each serving.

PINEAPPLE PUNCH

2 fresh pineapples

Sugar to taste (2 cups, more or less)

Juice of 1 lemon and 1 orange

3 1-liter bottles chilled Chablis

1 ½ jiggers brandy

3 bottles chilled Champagne

1 ice ring (use a ring mold such as you
use for mousses or gelatin desserts,
fill with water, and put into freezer
till solid)

Peel and core pineapple and cut into small, bite-size pieces. Mix with sugar, fruit juice, 2 bottles of Chablis, and brandy. Marinate overnight. When ready to serve, mix with the third bottle of Chablis and the Champagne in chilled punch bowl. Float ice ring on top of punch.

ALBA CLUB PUNCH

8 ripe apricots

2 cups ripe strawberries

1 quart white rum

1 cup light brown sugar

Dash of Peychaud's bitters

3 bottles chilled Champagne

Peel apricots; remove stem caps from strawberries. Mix fruit, rum, sugar, and bitters. Allow to marinate several hours or overnight, then put into chilled bowl and pour in chilled Champagne.

BOMBAY PUNCH

Oh, yes, this is the punch on those verandas in Kipling's India, Victoria's India, after the polo match. It was customary to sink a punch bowl into a big tub of ice and pour in all the thoroughly chilled ingredients. Cut the grapes in half and float on top of the punch.

1 liter sweet Sherry

1 liter brandy

½ cup maraschino liqueur

½ pint Cointreau

4 bottles Champagne

2 liters sparkling mineral water

3 to 4 bunches seedless grapes

SOUTHERN WEDDING PUNCH

4 cups apricot nectar

4 cups pineapple juice

4 cups guava nectar

2 cups white rum

Block of ice

6 cups chilled Champagne

Mix first 4 ingredients in big pitcher, cover, and refrigerate until very cold. Can be prepared a day ahead. Put ice in bowl; let sit to chill bowl. Pour off water; put in another chunk of ice if first has melted too much. Pour punch in; add the very cold Champagne. Stir a little. Serve. About 20 cups.

SUMMER PUNCH

The following is a good punch to serve to a crowd that needs livening up; it doesn't seem alcoholic.

8 cups orange juice

6 cups vodka

1 ½ cups grapefruit juice

¼ cup fresh lime juice

¾ cup fresh lemon juice

⅓ cup sugar

50 ice cubes

1 orange, seeded, sliced thin

1 lemon, seeded, sliced thin

1 pint strawberries or cherries or purple
  grapes, all seeded, cut in half

Mint sprigs

Put first 6 ingredients in chilled punch bowl; stir till sugar has dissolved. Add ice cubes and fruit and stir gently. Put ice in punch cups, ladle punch, and serve. Some like a sprig of mint in each glass. Punch is sometimes made with gin.

The famous Savannah charmer Henrietta Waring gave me this formula from her grandfather and said that way back when, it had been described as having "the perfume and lightness of a meadow in Spring." She also supplied the information that this punch is the very one that "knocked out Admiral Dewey on his visit to Savannah."

Juice of 2 dozen oranges

Juice of 2 dozen lemons

1 pound green tea in 2 gallons
    cold water (let stand overnight,
    then strain)

5 pounds brown sugar

3 gallons scuppernong wine

1 gallon St. Croix dark rum

1 gallon Hennessy cognac

1 gallon best bourbon

Crushed ice

2 quarts cherries

1 gallon Gordon's gin

12 bottles Champagne

Mix juices and tea first, preferably in a cedar tub, then add sugar and liquors. Let this lovely mix set a week or two or longer, covered. When ready to serve, add crushed ice, cherries, and 12 bottles of very cold Champagne. Stir well.

This punch has strong elements but it's that lemon that counts and somehow unites the other flavors.

2 lemons

¼ pound sugar

2 borage sprigs

Few leaves of lemon balm

1 ½ pints ice water

½ bottle Madeira

¼ pint good brandy

1 bottle Champagne

Grate 1 lemon finely into sugar. Slice other lemon really thin, removing pith, and add to sugar mix, then add herbs, water, Madeira, and brandy. Mix till sugar dissolves.

Chill at least an hour, longer's better. Add chilled Champagne just before serving. About 15 servings. If you make twice this, forbid tape recorders.

SUNDAY SCHOOL PUNCH (DEMOPOLIS, CIRCA 1880)

Block of ice

1 quart boiling water

2 teaspoons black tea

Orange and lemon peel

2 cups sugar

1½ cups orange juice

½ cup lemon juice

Tart apples

1 pint ice-cold water

1 pint Muscatel

1 pint best white rum

Place block of ice in punch bowl; decorate rim with flowers. Pour boiling water over tea and citrus peels; steep a few minutes and put in sugar and juice. Place stars and crescent moons cut from tart apples in bowl cavity hollowed on top of block of ice. Strain steeping mixture, add 1 pint ice-cold water, and then add wine and rum. Pour mixture slowly over block of ice. Chill glasses. Provide chairs.

MERRY MABEL

1 cup syrup from preserved ginger
   or honey

1 cup light rum

1 cup fresh orange juice

2 blocks of ice

¼ cup chopped candied ginger

Cognac

2 to 3 bottles Champagne, chilled

Place preserved ginger syrup or honey, light rum, and orange juice into blender. Blend on low speed until ingredients are mixed. Put 1 block of ice into your punch bowl. When bowl is chilled, toss out ice and water and put another big block of ice in middle of punch bowl. Pour mixture over ice and add chopped candied ginger. Add splash of best cognac, then pour in 2 or 3 bottles of very cold Champagne.

Be ready with your pitch pipe; there will be singing.

Iced Tea and Coffee

When is iced tea iced, yes, but tea, no?

On the Gulf Coast, many ladies, of the old school of ladylike behavior, will openly sip tall glasses of bourbon and spring water on their own front porches or when in company of men, but when lunching in a restaurant with other ladies, no. Which is why one often sees ladies sipping what seems to be iced tea in restaurants. Iced tea is never taken with food in most households. It's a midmorning or midafternoon refreshment during warm weather.

Ladies lunching in restaurants sip a tall glass of what seems iced tea but is really about three-quarters of a cup of best bourbon, diluted with a bit of Perrier or San Pellegrino and colored (that is to say, disguised) by a good splash of amaretto. Looks like iced tea but tastes much better and does much more for you.

All the southern ports were coffee, tea, and spice ports, although World War II wiped away many of the old waterfront companies. There was a time when Mobile smelt staggeringly good, what with the various kinds of coffee being roasted. But there was also a cookie company downtown, and the combination made everybody drool and rush out for a cuppa half a dozen times a day. New Orleans still has its coffee traditions, and a section of Magazine Street in the Vieux Carre still smells like heaven.

Most southerners prefer a strong, dark brew. There are certain traditional types who like a good cup of coffee to help them sleep. Their reasoning goes like this: The dark, black coffee has a longer roast that cooks off more of the caffeine. But more than that fact, they insist on scrupulously clean pots for making coffee. Many southern households have two coffee pots. At the end of the day, the pot is scrubbed hard and set to air. The coffee pot that was airing today is used tomorrow morning. Coffee must be freshly ground just before being cooked. Some prefer mountain water, some local spring water. In Paris, when I was a student, I knew a number of Brazilian students who would fill a saucepan with mineral water from central France; into it, when it boiled, they'd hold a boiled-clean white tennis sock filled with fresh ground coffee. After roughly a minute, the sock was removed and the coffee served. Pot and sock were scrubbed and boiled and aired for a day. Tomorrow's brew employed a second pot, another sock.

Once you're swept into this Latin coffee tradition, you understand the old proverbial dictum that says that coffee must be "black as the Devil, strong as Death, sweet as Love, and hot as Hell."

Hot Drinks

Café Brulot • Winter Day Coffee • Hot Buttered Rum • Mulled
Wine • New Orleans Variation of Mulled Wine • Cider Bishop

CAFÉ BRULOT

Mark Twain felt strongly about New Orleans coffee and had superlatives
for the famous after-dinner concoction Café Brulot. There are countless
versions of this beverage.

1 orange	Cointreau or Grand Marnier
Cloves	1 cup brandy
Cinnamon	1 pot strong, hot coffee

Take thin strips of peel from orange and place in bowl. Remove pith,
seeds, and membranes from orange and place flesh in bowl. Season with
cloves, cinnamon, and a splash of Cointreau or Grand Marnier. Heat
brandy and put into bowl. Set on fire and tilt bowl back and forth until
flames subside, then pour in very strong, hot coffee. Mix and serve at
once.

WINTER DAY COFFEE

1 vanilla bean, split lengthwise

1 cup ground, well-roasted
  coffee beans (black)

10 cups water

⅔ cup whipping cream

3 tablespoons sugar

Bourbon

Sugar and ground nutmeg to taste

Scrape vanilla seeds into the coffeepot; add the bean. Brew up your coffee with the 10 cups of water. Whip cream until it forms soft peaks, then gradually add 2 tablespoons sugar; beat till stiff. Discard vanilla bean. Pour coffee into cups, add bourbon and sugar to taste, and top with cream and nutmeg. Good for cold, rainy-day gossip sessions.

HOT BUTTERED RUM

On cold nights, hot buttered rum is a great drink and positively remedial for folks with colds, influenza, or fatigue or after visits from cousins.

8 cups apple cider

6 tablespoons fresh lemon juice

15 whole allspice berries

10 whole cloves

2 cinnamon sticks, broken into small bits

5 teaspoons dark honey

4 tablespoons best unsalted butter

2 cups dark rum

Boil first 6 ingredients about 5 minutes. Remove from heat, add butter, stir till melted, strain into 8 warm mugs, and divide rum among them.

MULLED WINE

1¼ cups light corn syrup

1 cup water

6 whole cloves

4 whole allspice

1 cinnamon stick

2 cups dry red wine

1 cup fresh tangerine, satsuma,
  or orange juice

½ cup fresh lemon juice

Combine syrup, water, and spices and heat to boiling point, stirring the while. Boil 10 minutes. Let stand 1 hour; strain. Combine this mix with wine and juices. Heat and serve at once.

NEW ORLEANS VARIATION OF MULLED WINE

1 cup light corn syrup

¼ cup syrup from preserved ginger

1 cup water

6 whole cloves

4 juniper berries, cracked

4 whole allspice

1 stick cinnamon

1 ½ cups dry red wine

1 cup apple juice or cider

¼ cup fresh orange or tangerine juice

Prepare exactly as in Mulled Wine recipe above. Both recipes serve 4 tipplers.

CIDER BISHOP

There are several drinks with "Bishop" in the title, usually hot, spicy wine punches. This is different, usually served at Christmas or New Year.

1 orange stuck with 20 cloves

2 teaspoons honey

1 quart hard cider

Good splash of brandy

Preheat oven to 425 degrees. Put orange in hot oven and roast until cloves are powdery. Take out and cut orange in quarters and place in top of double boiler with honey and cider. Heat the mixture over hot water, blending it for about 20 minutes. Pour into warmed mugs and top with a good splash of brandy. Don't be stingy.

Hangover Cures

Black Velvet • Bloody Mary • Brandy Alexander • Hangover
Punch • New Orleans Remedy • Demopolis Morning-After Punch •
Carib Cure-All • Black Strap • La Mechante

What gentlemen feel when they've imbibed slightly too much the evening before and are awakening with throbbing temples and a heightened sensitivity to certain sudden noises has had many names through the centuries. "Rumstroke" was an early name for the unhappy moment, and "effects" was a favorite expression. "The morning after" is still current, although less frequently employed than "hangover," which, according to *Partridge's Dictionary of Slang and Unconventional English*, found its way into common usage about 1910.

Ladies, who were supposed to sip daintily and never really "drink," never, of course, had hangovers, or didn't before the liberation of the 1920s Jazz Age. They stayed in their rooms, and it was reported in hushed tones that they were "feeling delicate" or "having a difficult moment." The Demon Rum, often mentioned in direst tones by temperance workers, became a comic hero for live-it-up youths after World War I. "I danced with the Demon Rum" and "The Demon Rum laid me low last night" were popular expressions, while "Had a bit too much" was understood by all for centuries.

Sensitivity to light and noise brought forth many jokes as old as time. "The cat woke me up, stomping across the bedroom." "Dry leaves were screeching across the porch." "The sunshine was pounding through my window." "The clock was bombing in my bedroom."

Many are the remedies. Most agree on rest, darkened rooms, lots of liquids, hot soups, and especially, of course, "a hair of the dog that bit me."

In Greenwich Village, 1950s. Courtesy of Eugene Walter estate.

Delightful that French onion soup spiked with a splash of cognac helps, but a jigger of the cognac downed in one gulp is what multitudes swear by. Four parts sweet vermouth with one part of the Italian bitters called Fernet-Branca, shaken with ice and a twist of lemon peel, seems to help many.

A rather Spartan cure for a hangover that is employed by older military gentlemen and seems to me to be rather a show-offy concept is the raw egg with a dash of Lea and Perrins, gulped right from the eggshell. Very cold sauerkraut juice, sometimes with tomato juice added, sometimes vodka, always lemon juice and salt, is very helpful.

Ladies often recommend very cold buttermilk or vanilla ice cream, while some swear by warm milk and aspirin. Others claim very cold yogurt (real yogurt, not pasteurized) is the only thing, while certain Anglified ladies call for very hot tea with honey, lemon, and cognac.

No matter what remedy you choose, remember to recline in cushions, contrive total silence, and eat something simple as soon as your head stops throbbing. Cornbread, grits, oatmeal, boiled barley, baked potatoes all help. Lots of water!

BLACK VELVET

David Embury, writing on hangover remedies, highlights the drink known as Black Velvet, saying, "The combination of champagne and stout sounds terrifying — something like molasses and horseradish. Actually, it is excellent." He prepares it like this . . . and here follow other tried-and-trues for the throbbing moment.

4 parts well-chilled English stout
4 parts extra-dry Champagne (brut)

Pour stout into very cold Champagne glasses, then add Champagne without mixing. Serve at once.

BLOODY MARY

2 parts tomato juice

1 part vodka

1 lemon

1 teaspoon Lea and Perrins
Worcestershire sauce

Freshly ground black pepper

Combine tomato juice with vodka. Add juice of half a lemon, Lea and Perrins sauce, and freshly ground black pepper. Pour over crushed ice in a cocktail and shake briefly, making as little racket as possible. Pour through strainer into iced glasses.

BRANDY ALEXANDER

Heavy cream

Crème de cacao

Cognac

Combine equal parts heavy cream, crème de cacao, and cognac into a cocktail shaker. Add crushed ice; shake well. Strain into very cold glasses.

HANGOVER PUNCH

1 egg

1 cup milk

2 ounces whiskey, rye, bourbon, or Scotch

Sugar

Nutmeg

Combine raw, pasteurized egg, milk, and whiskey with sugar to taste. Put into shaker with cracked ice. Shake well, strain into tumbler, sprinkle with nutmeg, and serve at once.

NEW ORLEANS REMEDY

Heavy cream

Milk

Sugar

Peychaud's bitters

Add 1 part heavy cream to 2 parts milk; heat just to boiling. Add sugar to taste and a generous splash of Peychaud's bitters.

DEMOPOLIS MORNING-AFTER PUNCH

1 pot strong pekoe tea

Bourbon

Molasses

Grated orange peel

Grated lemon peel

Peychaud's bitters

Stir equal parts strong pekoe tea with bourbon whiskey. To each cup add a tablespoon of molasses, a little grated orange and lemon peel, and a splash of bitters. Serve very hot.

CARIB CURE-ALL

Champagne sec

Lemon juice

Grenadine

Angostura bitters

Combine very dry, very cold Champagne, lemon juice as you like, lots of grenadine, and a good splash of bitters; mix well in shaker with cracked ice, strain, and serve in cold glasses.

BLACK STRAP

This is a hangover remedy that had a flare of popularity as a before-dinner cocktail along the Gulf Coast around the turn of the last century.

2 jiggers old Jamaica rum

2 tablespoons ice water

Peychaud's bitters

Fresh pineapple, sliced, for garnish

Shake together rum, water, and Peychaud's bitters. Pour over cracked ice and garnish with a slice of fresh pineapple.

LA MECHANTE

Another hangover soother that took on a life of its own as an appetizer was La Mechante. In New Orleans, those who drank this version of the martini cocktail liked to add 1 or 2 capers to the glass when serving and always a drop or two (drop, not splash) of the juice from Zatarain's capers from New Orleans. This juice is a delightfully spicy vinegar. Ice-cold white vermouth with a splash of this juice is a nice aperitif, too.

Wild or garden sorrel

2 parts best English gin

1 part white French vermouth

Capers for garnish

Soak a handful of sorrel in gin and vermouth. Garnish with capers. Serve very cold.

PART TWO

VICTUALS

Cocktail Snacks and First Courses

Mock Caviar • Devilish Eggs • Deviled Eggs • Goober Toast •
Chicken Liver Pâté • Ham Pâté • Chicken Liver and Ham Pâté • Galvez
Crackers • Brandy Ball • Cheese Spread • Baked Grapefruit

There's a whole world of cold soups, savory light appetizers, and little appetite-arousers that existed in the old days along the Gulf Coast. When one studies the few remaining handwritten cartes de jour from the hotel dining rooms, especially the beach hotels such as at Coden and Baldwin County, one seems to find a kind of series of invitational tidbits to begin meals in hot weather, especially at midday.

Imagine sitting down, in July, to a cup of very cold white soup, with a buttermilk base, flavored, as the case might be, with celery, or watercress, or horseradish, or nasturtium stems and green seeds, or chives and shallots, or fresh corn kernels and slivers of baked ham, most of these with a dash of dry Sherry or Madeira, often a hit of Peychaud's bitters. Nobody seems to have a recipe for it, but there was a luncheon cold soup in the 1920s, in full mockery of the law and Prohibition dullards, which was a cold potato soup flavored with chopped capers and a splash of dry vermouth and English gin. This was called Flapper Soup.

First the soup, then a small plate with two or three small portions of delightful surprises. A deviled egg (there are hundreds of versions of this), a thin slice of baked ham rolled up around a filling of cottage cheese and chopped watercress with a bit of Creole mustard, cold boiled first baby turnip roots dressed with a saltless mayonnaise heavily charged with nutmeg, a ripe but not soft peach sliced with paper thin slices of purple onion in a vinaigrette sauce. And what about the endless variety of olive dishes? Provençal olives, kalamata olives, mild California olives, black or green, in an infinite set of variations.

Relaxing at Termite Hall, Mobile, 1987.
Courtesy of Joyce Fay.

MOCK CAVIAR

2 cups mild California black olives, finely chopped

2 teaspoons fresh garlic, chopped (if you don't have fresh garlic, then, instead of the sourpuss type that has been sitting in storage or shop for a lifetime, use the white parts of green onions)

2 teaspoons grated lemon peel

Splash of gin or vodka

3 ½ tablespoons best olive oil

A few fresh rosemary or sage leaves, chopped

Few drops of Tabasco

Freshly ground black pepper

Mix first 7 ingredients well. You can do it in a processor if you like, but then it's mush. Add freshly ground black pepper, taste to see if it needs a few grains of salt, then chill well and serve with small hot biscuits or saltless crackers.

DEVILISH EGGS

It was that delightful, humorously cranky old Mobile lady Miss Minnie J. Cox (she lived on Broad Street a few feet from the canal full of crayfish that ran down the middle of the street) who shook her head furiously when she explained, "Deviled eggs and devilish eggs are as different as Mae West and Zasu Pitts. Don't forget it!" At that point, in the 1920s, Zasu Pitts was a sensitive beauty who'd starred in Eric von Stroheim's silent film *Greed* while Mae West was a larky vaudeville and Broadway star much in the news since the police closed her latest stage show. Miss Cox was famous for saying very seriously, "Say a little prayer for Miss Minnie J. Cox," whenever she entered or left a gathering. I thought of her years later when reading Anton Chekhov. There's that moment in *The Cherry Orchard* when the governess Charlotte enters a crowded, noisy family reunion, pauses in the door to the parlor, and says to nobody listening: "My little dog eats nuts."

For a front porch or backyard cocktail party, these eggs, garnished with fresh watercress flavored with lemon juice, celery seeds, and dried dill, alongside mild black California olives that have soaked a few days in their own juice along with halved garlic toes, grated lemon peel, and chopped celery leaves, flanked by fresh, warm cheese straws, will cause Yankees to move South to stay and propose business deals or marriages to natives.

6 hard-boiled eggs, chopped small	1 teaspoon Dijon or Creole mustard
1 ½ teaspoons minced mild onion	(or the new Dijonnaise)
3 strips of bacon, fried crisp then	2 tablespoons mayonnaise
crumbled fine	Drop or 2 of Tabasco, according to
Pinch of salt	how devilish you are
At least ½ teaspoon freshly ground	1 heaping cup grated Parmesan or
black pepper	finely shredded Cheddar cheese

Mix together everything but cheese until creamy. Form into little balls or little quail-egg-size mounds. Roll in cheese. Put in covered receptacle and put into fridge until serving. Makes about 24 to 27 appetizers. Old-fashioned hostesses usually serve hot, thin halves of buttermilk biscuits on which to place these devilish eggs.

DEVILED EGGS

Among the easiest and quickest appetizers or snacks for those unexpected relatives or friends or for midnight whoop-de-doos after the theater or a concert are these deviled eggs.

Put eggs in cold water, bring to boil, boil five minutes, immediately put in cold water, and change water every few minutes. Peel eggs and slice a tiny slice of white off opposite sides lengthwise. This is so eggs will sit, not frisk on the plate. Cut eggs in half lengthwise. Mash yellows with a can of Underwood Deviled Ham, a bit of minced onion (or garlic), a good dash of Tabasco, salt, a little freshly ground pepper, and a dash of milk, or cream, or mayonnaise. Pile filling neatly in half-whites, then sprinkle generously with mild paprika and top each half with a caper or a radish slice or half a cherry tomato. Arrange on plate and put in fridge to chill.

Deviled Egg variants: All manner of stuffings are welcomed in deviled eggs. For instance: finely chopped dark meat of chicken or turkey flavored with chopped green onion, horseradish sauce, and mayonnaise. Tuna fish with chopped capers and chives and a good splash of Tabasco. Mild pickled red peppers chopped and mixed with chopped ham, chopped boiled shrimp, or boiled veal; or catfish, mayonnaise, chopped mild onion, same mustard aforementioned, and a dash of red hot pepper. Invent your own!

While eggs are chilling, prepare Goober Toast (recipe follows).

Spread whole-wheat or rye bread slices or English muffin halves with a thin, even layer of unsalted butter; a not-quite-so-thin, even layer of Creole or Dijon mustard or the new Dijonnaise; and a generous layer of good American peanut butter. Put into 375-degree oven until peanut butter looks like it wants to splutter. Remove, put ice-cold slices of kosher dill pickles on top, and serve at once with cold beer.

CHICKEN LIVER PÂTÉ

3 to 4 stalks celery

Salt and freshly ground black pepper

A little grated lemon peel for broth

1 pound chicken livers, cleaned and
    trimmed

1 cup unsalted butter

⅓ cup Calvados or applejack
    (hard not soft) or cream Sherry

¼ cup finely chopped onion

2 teaspoons dry mustard

1 small garlic toe

Pinch of cayenne pepper

Good pinch of freshly grated
    nutmeg

Pinch of cloves

½ cup dried white raisins

Make broth of celery with leaves, coarsely chopped, a dash of salt and pepper, and lemon peel. Bring to boil over high heat. Add livers, let come again to boil, and turn down fire to medium. Cook 10 minutes, drain, and discard celery. Combine chopped livers, butter, Calvados (or applejack or Sherry), and flavorings. Process in food processor or chop and bash until smooth. Add raisins and mix well. Pour into crock (about 3 cups), cover with plastic wrap, and refrigerate. Let firm up 4 to 6 hours in fridge. Let stand at room temperature about an hour before serving.

    Serve with Melba toast, crisp crackers, or toasted fingers of English muffin. Radishes go well alongside or watercress dressed with salt, celery seeds, and lemon juice.

HAM PÂTÉ

1 1/3 cups finely ground ham

2 tablespoons mayonnaise

2 teaspoons Creole or Dijon mustard
   or Dijonnaise

1 teaspoon prepared horseradish

2 teaspoons dry Sherry

Salt to taste (probably won't need it)

Freshly ground black pepper

Mix everything; put into oiled mold and into fridge. Serve with crackers or toast triangles. Depending on whether your taste is for sweet or sour, serve peach pickles or dill pickles. Warm toasted pecans are good with this, too.

CHICKEN LIVER AND HAM PÂTÉ

You can adjust the recipe according to quantity required.

1 cup chicken livers

2/3 cup cooked ham

1/2 cup unsalted butter or fat

2 slices bacon

Port

Salt and freshly ground black
   pepper to taste

Mace

Powdered ginger

1 envelope Mrs. Knox unflavored
   gelatin

1/3 cup cold water

1 1/3 cups cream

French cognac

Go over the livers carefully; with your kitchen scissors, snip off bits of ventricle and fat. Chop the livers very small. Messy, but the only way. Ham should be chopped fine, too. In your heavy skillet, melt butter and add a bit of finely chopped bacon. Omit bacon if ham is very salty. Add chicken livers and turn until brown and done. Add ham, stir, and mix well. Add splash of port, stir, and mix well. Flavor with salt, freshly ground black pepper, a dash of mace, and a dash of powdered ginger. Soak gelatin in cold water. Heat cream and add gelatin; stir until melted. Put in a splash of best French cognac; stir well. Combine liver mixture with gelatin mixture. Have a buttered dish ready and put your pâté mixture into it. Chill until firm.

3 tablespoons peanut butter

1 tablespoon nut or corn oil

5 tablespoons yogurt or 4 tablespoons
   buttermilk

½ cup whole-wheat flour

½ cup yellow cornmeal, slightly
   moistened with milk

Pinch of salt

Preheat oven to 400 degrees. Beat thoroughly together ingredients in order listed. Let dough sit 5 minutes or so. If dough is then too sticky to roll out easily, add a little more flour, a tablespoon at a time, till you can form a soft ball of the dough. If dough is too stiff, add more yogurt or buttermilk. You can add to dough sesame seeds or 1 tablespoon dried and pounded basil, thyme, dill, or oregano, as you like.

Lightly flour a board and knead dough enough to form a ball; cut into 3 sections, dust with flour, and carefully roll out each section into a sheet ¹⁄₁₆ of an inch thick. Keep dusting the rolling pin. Now, according to weather, altitude, and temperature, you might want to cut out your crackers with a cookie cutter before the dough is rolled so thin. Then roll crackers out flatter, so they will be crisp crackers, not doughy biscuits. Sprinkle more sesame seeds. Prick each cracker with a fork. Place on a lightly greased cookie sheet and let them dry a bit, then bake crackers from 5 to 8 minutes. They burn easily, so check often; hover over oven. When they're golden, they're done. Let them cool thoroughly. Store in airtight container if not devoured immediately. If humidity gets to them, just crisp them up in a 200-degree oven. These are delightful with all manner of soups, vegetables, and salads.

½ cup sesame seeds
  (or celery seeds)
2 cups crumbled Roquefort
  or Gorgonzola

1 8-ounce packet cream cheese
1 garlic toe, finely chopped
2 tablespoons snipped parsley
3 tablespoons brandy (cognac's best)

Set seeds aside. Beat remaining ingredients until smooth and well mixed. Cover and refrigerate overnight or at least 6 hours. When ready to serve, shape mixture into a ball, roll in seeds, and put on serving dish with watercress, parsley, and inner leaves of celery. Serve with crackers or fingers of pumpernickel bread alongside.

About that cheese: We always say Cheddar when we write down recipes like this, but it is not that great English cheese to which we refer. That is served at cheese time after a meal, with very fine wine. What this dish calls for is what we used to call, in old southern recipes . . . rat-trap cheese. That is, any of the deep yellow or orange-colored cheeses from Wisconsin, Oregon, Minnesota, New York State, etc., which has a delightful musty-musky cheese flavor all its own, perfect for serving alongside apple pie, for toasted cheese sandwiches, absolutely required for genuine potatoes au gratin. Avoid like the plague those dire synthetic cheeses that become ropey when heated and plug up both children and adults.

1 pound American rat-trap cheese
  (sharp Wisconsin or New York),
  chopped into little bits
6 scallions, chopped
2 tablespoons finely chopped chives

1½ teaspoons Creole or Dijon mustard
2 tablespoons unsalted butter
2½ tablespoons dry Sherry
Dash of Tabasco
Dash of cognac

Blend or whip all together till smooth. Put in small bowl and refrigerate. Bring to room temperature before serving, surrounded by small hot biscuits, freshly made whole-wheat toast, or crackers.

This is very good as an opener for a game or fish dinner. Or Thanksgiving. You'll need half a grapefruit for each diner.

½ grapefruit

2 tablespoons corn flakes

2 tablespoons brown sugar

Good dash of powdered cinnamon

Splash of sweet Sherry or white port

2 tablespoons melted butter

Preheat oven to 400 degrees. Remove seeds from grapefruit, core, and loosen sections. Crush corn flakes and add brown sugar, cinnamon, wine, and melted butter. Top grapefruit half with this mixture and bake 10 minutes.

Soups

MRS. CHIN'S BROTH

One of the lost worlds of Mobile cookery is the pantheon of soups. Everybody loved soups and vied to surpass each other in cooking them. After the ball or after the parade or even on just one of our damp, chilly nights, nothing is better: a good filling soup, a salad, cheese with either a ripe pear or apple, and never mind dessert . . . serve a thimble of orange liqueur with the coffee. For many years, in Mobile, a delightful and gifted Chinese family named Chin ran a family business with branches all over the city: the Sam Joy Laundry. Mrs. Chin was a great cook, and when giving recipes, she always claimed that this broth was the basis for over half of her dishes.

5 to 6 pounds chicken wings, back, legs
8 big slices of ginger root about ⅛ inch thick, flattened with a wooden mallet
½ teaspoon grated lemon peel

¾ cup Scotch whiskey
Salt
6 quarts water
Handful chopped chives
Little bit of freshly ground black pepper

Cut the chicken into small bits; remove fat and skin. Blanch the chicken in a big pot of boiling water, drain, and rinse in cold water. Wash out your pot very well and put into it the chicken, ginger, lemon peel, Scotch, salt, and 6 quarts of water. Bring to a boil, skimming off the foam that rises, then simmer 3 hours, skimming off the foam now and again. Strain the soup through a triple thickness of rinsed and squeezed-out cheesecloth. Let it cool completely, best in fridge, then remove fat from top. Serve with a sprinkling of chives and pepper to taste. This can be kept 3 or 4 days in fridge or frozen. Makes about 12 cups. Good just as it is, served hot, or in countless variations, or as basis for sauces and gravies.

Do your own thing: invent! Add baby okra and simmer till okra is tender; add dash of Tabasco. Add slivers of ham, turkey, chicken, whatever, chopped inner celery leaves, and ribbons of carrot. Add baby shrimp and, when serving, top with a glop of sour cream flavored with dried dill. Add chopped green onions, then a handful of pearl barley; cook till done. Add greens, shredded, like sorrel, dandelion, mâche, baby lettuce, etc. Serve with dandelion flowers on top.

ONION SOUP

1 stick unsalted butter

10 onions, sliced

2 quarts water

1 quart rich beef stock

2 cups dry white wine

2 slices untoasted French bread

Salt and freshly ground black pepper to taste

1½ cups freshly grated Parmesan cheese, plus extra for each bowl

1 small piece toasted, buttered French bread for each bowl

Melt butter in skillet and sauté onions slowly, stirring, till they are golden and almost transparent. Then add water, stock, wine, and untoasted French bread, torn up. Add salt, pepper, and grated cheese and simmer 30 to 40 minutes. In each bowl, place a piece of toasted, buttered French bread topped with more cheese. If you like, you can sprinkle chopped chives on top of all.

CREAMED CARROTS SOUP

A good cream soup for cold weather.

1 bunch (about 8 medium) carrots,
    scraped, cut into ½-inch thick
    coins
2 cups mild onions, sliced
Water
½ teaspoon salt

1 can (10 ¾ ounces) condensed
    cream of potato soup
1 teaspoon grated orange peel
1 teaspoon dried dill
Good splash of Madeira or Sherry
Salt and mace to taste

Place sliced carrots and onions in a pot, cover with water, add salt, and bring to a boil. Reduce heat to simmer and cook carrots and onions about 15 minutes. Drain. Puree carrots, onions, cream of potato soup, orange peel, and dill in food processor or food mill. Stir while heating, then add wine a minute before serving. Add salt and mace to taste.

JASPER EGGPLANT SOUP

This recipe comes from a member of the Sledge family in Jasper, Alabama; it is said to have been a favorite of Tallulah and Eugenia Bankhead, whose mother was a Sledge.

½ cup olive oil
1 heaping tablespoon unsalted butter
2 ½ pounds young eggplants,
    peeled, cut into inch-long pieces
1 mild onion, finely chopped
4 stalks celery, finely chopped
1 carrot, finely chopped
2 to 3 shallots or spring onions,
    finely chopped

4 big garlic toes, smashed
4 cups chicken broth
1 cup freshly grated Parmesan cheese
2 cups heavy cream
½ cup dry Sherry
Salt and freshly ground black pepper
Pinch of allspice
1 cup chopped fresh basil leaves

Melt oil and butter in heavy big pot over low heat and put in eggplant, onions, celery, carrots, shallots, and garlic; stir now and then until all are tender. Add broth, bring to a boil, and simmer over low heat an hour. Put through sieve or puree in processor until very smooth, then put into another pot and stir in cheese, cream, and Sherry. Bring to a boil and add salt, pepper, and allspice; simmer 5 minutes. Stir in basil before serving in hot cups. Makes 8 cups for a starter or 4 bowls for a course. Pretzels good alongside, or cracklings.

BLACK BEAN SOUP

4 carrots, chopped

2 onions, chopped

1 garlic toe, minced

2 tablespoons olive oil

2 tablespoons ground cumin seeds

Good dash of cayenne pepper

1 ½ teaspoons ground coriander seeds

2 16-ounce cans black beans with their liquid

4 cups beef broth

½ cup long-grain rice

Generous ½ cup Sherry

Salt and freshly ground black pepper to taste

Sour cream

Crisply fried bacon, crumbled

Fresh coriander (cilantro) leaves

Cook carrots, onions, and garlic in oil over moderate heat, until soft, stirring constantly. Stir in cumin, cayenne pepper, and coriander and cook mixture, stirring, for about 1 minute. Add beans, their liquid, and broth; bring to a boil, then simmer for 15 minutes. Add rice; simmer 15 to 20 minutes or until rice is tender. Puree half this mixture and stir back into the half that is not pureed. Season with Sherry, salt, and freshly ground black pepper to taste. Ladle soup into heated bowls, top with dollop of sour cream, and sprinkle generously with crumbled bacon bits and fresh coriander (or parsley). Serves 6.

CARIBBEAN GARLIC SOUP

This is often served on Ash Wednesday before a grits or cornmeal soufflé.

6 big fresh garlic cloves, peeled

2 cans condensed beef broth

1 cup dry Sherry

2 cups water

4 small slices French bread

¼ cup unsalted butter, softened

2 ½ tablespoons grated Parmesan
cheese

Simmer garlic in broth about 15 minutes or until soft. Remove garlic and set aside. Add Sherry and water to broth; simmer on low. Meanwhile, toast bread on one side under broiler. Remove and spread butter on untoasted sides. Mash garlic and spread on butter. Sprinkle with cheese. Broil about half a minute or until bubbly and brown. Place slice of bread in each serving bowl, ladle hot soup over, and serve at once. Serves 4.

NIP AND SNIP SOUP

The soup can be prepared in advance, the garnish just before serving.

¾ stick unsalted butter

1 big purple onion, finely chopped

1 pound turnip roots, peeled
and chopped

1 pound parsnip roots, peeled
and chopped

½ cup best dry Sherry

4 cups chicken or beef broth
(add a little grated lemon peel
if beef)

Salt and freshly ground pepper

Pinch of celery seeds or dried dill

For garnish:

Oil for frying

1 leek, lower part only, cut into
¼-inch slices

1 beaten egg

Flour

Salt and freshly ground pepper

⅓ cup chopped fresh chives
or sorrel

Toasted sliced almonds

Paprika

Melt butter in big pan over medium heat. Cook onion slowly till golden. Add roots and stir well; add Sherry and reduce heat to low. Place a sheet of foil right on top of vegetables, then cover pot with a tight lid. Steam till tender; add stock by spoonfuls if vegetables dry out. Cook about 45 minutes. Puree vegetables with remaining stock; taste for flavor, adding to your taste a little salt, freshly ground pepper, or celery seeds or dried dill.

When ready to serve, prepare garnish. Heat 1 inch of oil in heavy medium-sized pan to 375 degrees. Separate leeks into rings. Dip leeks first into egg, then into flour seasoned with salt and pepper. Shake off excess flour. Fry leeks until golden, about 45 seconds. Take up with slotted spoon and dry on paper towels. Bring soup to simmer. Taste for seasoning. Garnish each bowl with leeks, chives or sorrel, almonds, and a dash of paprika.

CAROLINA SHRIMP BISQUE

2 tablespoons olive oil	3 ½ cups milk
½ pound unshelled shrimp	1 teaspoon Worcestershire sauce
1 garlic toe, minced	1 tablespoon light olive oil
½ cup cream Sherry	¼ teaspoon grated lemon peel
1 stick unsalted butter	A few celery seeds
3 ½ tablespoons flour	Salt and freshly ground black pepper
¼ teaspoon Tabasco	to taste

Heat oil in skillet; cook shrimp with garlic about 2 to 3 minutes, depending on size. Put aside to cool. Shell shrimp, cut into small pieces, and marinate in Sherry about half an hour. In top of double boiler or in pan set over simmering water, melt ½ stick butter. Whisk in flour and Tabasco and cook up this white roux 2 to 3 minutes. Add milk a little at a time, always whisking energetically. Bring to boil, then lower heat and simmer 5 minutes until it thickens. Stir in the Worcestershire and everything else except shrimp. Cook covered over low heat, stirring now and then, for 15 minutes. Add cooked shrimp. Divide bisque among 4 warmed soup bowls, and then put a nice dab of butter on top of each. You might like to sprinkle a little chopped French sorrel on top, or a few chopped capers, or dill.

4 tablespoons butter

1 cup finely chopped mild onions

1 cup chopped celery with about
    ½ cup of inner leaves

1 red or green pepper (red is prettier
    in this dish), chopped

3 tablespoons flour

2 cups chicken stock

2 cups water

1 broken bay leaf

Handful dried basil

Dash of dill seeds or dried dill

2 cups milk

2 cups fresh, frozen, or canned
    corn kernels

¾ cup dry white wine

2 dozen shucked medium oysters,
    with about ⅓ cup of their liquid

1 cup boiled rice or pearl barley

1 cup white lye hominy

Salt and freshly ground black
    pepper

Melt butter over medium heat, then sauté onions, celery, and red or green pepper a few minutes. Sprinkle in flour and continue cooking about 10 minutes or until flour begins to brown lightly. Add stock, water, and flavorings. Simmer on low 35 to 45 minutes. Add milk and corn. Heat without boiling 10 to 12 minutes. Before serving, add wine and cook 3 minutes, then add oysters, oyster liquor, rice or barley, and hominy. Heat 6 to 7 minutes, until oysters puff up and edges curl. Serve at once, adding salt and pepper to taste. Serves 6 to 8.

A sprinkle of chopped parsley or dill and a dash of mild paprika dress up the portions. Remove bay leaf before serving the chowder. Heated white cornbread with chive-filled unsalted butter is nice alongside.

The old Little Theatre in downtown Mobile presented a famous production of *Peer Gynt* in the mid-1930s with the full Grieg score wired in from a nearby bigger auditorium, since the Little Theatre orchestra pit was too small for a full symphonic ensemble. The family of the Norwegian Captain Knudsen designed authentic Norwegian costumes and served this Norwegian soup after dress rehearsal; ever since, the recipe changes hands locally under the name Peer Gynt Soup.

2 tablespoons unsalted butter

3 big carrots, peeled and diced

1 medium onion, chopped

1 medium ripe tomato, seeded and
   chopped

2 tablespoons flour

1½ cups water

½ cup dry white wine

¾ pound tiny cooked shrimp

1 cup half-and-half or light cream

Dash of Tabasco

Salt and freshly ground black pepper
   to taste

Bit of dill if you like: 1 tablespoon
   chopped fresh or 1 teaspoon
   dried

In big casserole, combine butter, carrots, onion, and tomato. Cook covered over low heat, stirring now and then, till carrots are tender. Blend flour into mix; stir in water and wine. Simmer till bubbly. Stir in shrimp and mix well. Over lowest heat, stir in cream. Add seasonings, whisk very well, and serve hot. Serves 4.

THE COLONEL'S CHOWDER

4 tablespoons unsalted butter

1 cup finely chopped mild onion

2½ cups canned cream-style corn

⅓ cup best bourbon

¼ teaspoon grated nutmeg

1 teaspoon salt

Freshly ground black pepper to taste

3 to 4 drops Tabasco

½ cup chicken stock

½ cup heavy cream

Melt butter in heavy soup pan and cook onion until transparent. Stir in corn. Heat bourbon in small pan. Remove from heat, set on fire, let flame a second or so, and then pour over corn mixture. Stir in everything else, heat well, and serve hot.

This soup was traditional as a picker-up at intermission of grand balls or cotillions.

1 ½ cups coarsely ground [cooked] white meat of chicken or other fowl

3 tablespoons ground, blanched almonds

4 ½ cups chicken stock

2 cups medium cream

Yolks of 3 eggs

Tarragon

Salt and freshly ground black pepper

Splash of dry Sherry

Parsley

Add meat and almonds to stock, saving a little meat aside. Bring slowly to boil. Place in double boiler and stir in cream. When heated, pour over egg yolks, lightly beaten, stirring constantly. Return to double boiler; cook carefully until soup thickens. Add tarragon, salt, and pepper; stir in a little dry Sherry. Serve topped with some ground white meat mixed with chopped parsley.

TUSKEGEE PEANUT BISQUE

3 cups milk

½ teaspoon chopped onion

Salt and freshly ground black pepper

1 tablespoon flour

1 tablespoon water

½ cup peanut butter

Crushed peanuts, paprika, and celery leaves for garnish

Splash of dry vermouth

Heat milk to a simmer; add onion, salt, and pepper. Mix flour and water to a smooth paste and stir in peanut butter. Add mixture to milk, stirring until all is smooth. When serving, garnish with crushed peanuts, a dash of paprika, and chopped celery leaves. A splash of dry white vermouth well mixed in at the end is very tasty.

BAYOU STREET BEER SOUP

¾ cup unsalted butter

¼ cup grated celery

¼ cup grated carrot

¼ cup grated green pepper

¼ cup grated onion

⅓ cup flour

4 cups chicken broth

1 teaspoon salt

¼ teaspoon white pepper

Dash of mace

3 cups (about ¾ pound) grated
sharp Cheddar cheese

1 bottle (12 ounces) light beer,
at room temperature

Melt butter in soup pot. Add celery, carrot, green pepper, and onion.
Cook over low heat until soft, stirring frequently. Add flour and blend
in, then add broth, salt, pepper, and mace. Cook, stirring, until soup
thickens. Strain soup, puree vegetables, and return to soup pot. Over low
heat, add cheese a little at a time, blending until melted. Blend in beer.
Heat thoroughly. DON'T boil. Serves 6 or 4 healthier appetites.

WINTERTIME SOUP

4 tablespoons unsalted butter

½ cup chopped leeks, white part

½ cup chopped carrots

½ cup chopped celery

4 tablespoons flour

4 cups beef broth

1 12-ounce bottle beer

1 pound firm white cheese, shredded

1 pound rat-trap cheese (orange),
shredded

Pinch of cayenne pepper

2 cracked juniper berries

Salt and freshly ground black pepper
to taste

Fresh chives, chopped

Crisp-fried bacon, crumbled

Melt butter in heavy soup pot. Cook leeks, carrots, and celery over low
heat, stirring constantly, about 4 minutes. Add flour and cook, stirring,
another 2 minutes. Add broth and beer. Bring slowly to simmer, about
15 to 20 minutes, stirring now and then. Over low heat, add shredded
cheeses, whisking all the while, until smooth. Add seasonings. Cook over
low heat until well-heated but DO NOT BOIL or soup will separate. When
serving, sprinkle with chives and bacon. Icy beer alongside.

HASTY SOUP FOR UNEXPECTED GUESTS

2 cans Mr. Campbell's consommé

2 cans field peas with their liquid

1 teaspoon tomato ketchup

½ teaspoon grated lemon peel

2 tablespoons dry Sherry

Inner celery leaves or parsley or chives

Salt and freshly ground black pepper
    to taste

Heat first 4 ingredients just to boiling point, turn fire low, and stir in dry Sherry. Serve at once in hot cups or bowls, sprinkling chopped inner celery leaves or parsley or chives over. Add salt and pepper to taste.

CREAM OF PEANUT SOUP

This, with a good salad, cheese, and fruit, makes a grand luncheon.

¼ cup unsalted butter

1 cup chopped celery

1 onion, chopped

2 tablespoons flour

7 cups chicken or beef stock
    or broth

1 cup creamy peanut butter

Freshly ground black pepper

Pinch of savory or 1 teaspoon
    Dijon or Creole mustard

1 cup light cream

Splash of dry Sherry

Inner celery leaves

Paprika

Melt butter, toss in celery and onion, and cook until tender, not browned. Add flour; stir till all's smooth. Gradually add broth and let come to a boil, at which point add peanut butter and seasonings; simmer 15 minutes. Add cream and Sherry at last minute; leave on fire long enough to heat well. Sprinkle chopped inner celery leaves on each serving, with a spot of mild paprika. Yum!

MISS NANA'S OYSTER SOUP

¾ cup finely chopped onion

¾ cup chopped green pepper

1 ½ tablespoons melted unsalted
   butter

2 ½ cups milk

1 8-ounce package cream cheese,
   softened

2 ½ cups chicken broth

1 generous pint fresh oysters,
   drained

Freshly ground white pepper

Pinch of dried dill

Salt to taste

Splash of dry Sherry (about
   1 tablespoon)

Inner celery leaves for garnish

Sauté onion and pepper in butter. Add milk and cream cheese and cook over low flame, stirring till smooth. Add broth, oysters, and seasonings and cook 8 to 10 minutes or until edges of oysters curl, then add Sherry and cook 1 minute longer. Serve at once, sprinkling chopped inner celery leaves on top.

Note: Sometimes, instead of salt, crumbled, crisp bacon was added to the soup at the end. Very good.

GAZPACHO

This is something that definitely requires a blender. Put your cutting blade into blender jar.

4 tomatoes, peeled and quartered

3 green peppers, cored and quartered

1 small onion, peeled and quartered

2 garlic cloves, peeled

1 large cucumber, peeled, seeded,
   and diced

½ teaspoon salt

½ teaspoon chili powder

½ cup pure olive oil

¼ cup lemon juice

3 cups tomato juice

¼ cup dry Sherry

½ cup sour cream

1 teaspoon freshly ground pepper

A few inner celery leaves, chopped

Process tomatoes, green peppers, onion, garlic, and cucumber separately. Chop each on medium-low speed. Pour into large jar. Add salt, chili powder, olive oil, lemon juice, tomato juice, and Sherry; stir to blend. Chill. Serve cold with topping of sour cream, pepper to taste, and celery leaves.

HASTY LUNCHEON

1 can Mr. Campbell's cream of
   potato soup
1 can Mr. Campbell's chicken broth
½ cup chopped green onions
½ cup chopped inner celery leaves
2 cups milk

1 can small shrimp
2 ½ tablespoons dry Sherry
Mild paprika
Croutons
Salt and freshly ground pepper
   to taste

Mix first 7 ingredients and bring to a simmer, stirring occasionally. Serve in well-heated bowls, sprinkled with mild paprika and croutons. Add salt and pepper to taste.

MOBILE GUMBO

Although gumbo is kin to bouillabaisse and many Scandinavian and Mediterranean and African dishes, it truly is a Gulf Coast invention, based on such elements as the gumbo filé (the Indians' powdered, dried sassafras leaves) and the African use of okra (known also as *gombaud, cornes grecques*) as a way of making a smooth and rich consistency in a stew of seafood or poultry or meat and wild game.

Most cooks add some chopped ham to their gumbo. You can add crab meat, chicken, turkey, beef, pork, or mutton according to your taste and your leftovers. Almost EVERYBODY prefers a really good turkey gumbo with lots of meat to that dreary carcass brought to table on Christmas Day.

Two books you should consult: the Junior League of Baton Rouge's *River Road Recipes* and Lafcadio Hearn's *La Cuisine Creole* of the late nineteenth century. Most libraries should have these.

If you are using anything wild for your gumbo (duck, hare, venison, etc.), it is usual to marinate it in dry red wine before cooking.

2 cups chicken stock	Pinch of dried dill
2 cups water	Pinch of thyme, fresh or dried
1 large onion, chopped	1 ½ pounds raw shrimp
2 celery stalks, chopped	½ cup all-purpose flour
6 garlic cloves, minced	¼ cup bacon or ham fat
1 green bell pepper, chopped with seeds removed	¼ cup unsalted butter
	1 cup diced onion
2 bay leaves	1 cup diced celery
½ tablespoon grated lemon peel	Olive oil
½ teaspoon freshly ground black pepper	2 cups sliced fresh okra or canned
	Dash of Tabasco

Pour stock and water into a pot. In a skillet, sauté onions until golden with celery, garlic, and bell pepper. Add this mixture to the pot along with bay leaves, lemon peel, freshly ground black pepper, dried dill, and thyme. Bring to a boil, then reduce to a simmer. When this has simmered about 15 minutes, drop in your shrimp. Cook small shrimp 2 to 3 minutes, big shrimp 5 to 7 minutes. Turn off heat, cover, and let sit until room temperature.

Meanwhile, brown the flour in bacon or ham fat with the unsalted butter. Most people like this roux a rather dark brown. Remember that roux goes on cooking a minute after you remove from heat, so take off fire JUST BEFORE it's the color brown you want. Keep stirring with a wooden spoon the whole while it's cooking.

Strain and save broth, saving shrimp and discarding vegetables. Clean shrimp when at room temperature.

In the pot the shrimp was cooked in, sauté diced onions, celery, whatever you wish in your gumbo, in a little olive oil. When vegetables are translucent, add strained shrimp broth, sliced okra (or canned, with all the gooey juice), and the roux, plus a little grated lemon peel and a dash of Tabasco. Place pot over low heat to keep warm. Just before serving, add the shrimp. Mobile Gumbo is piquant but not as hot as N'Orleans or 'Cajun (Acadien).

A Green Gumbo for Lent or for the days after overstuffing (Christmas, Thanksgiving, weddings, birthdays, etc.) is delightful with coarsely chopped mild white fish (or catfish) fillets added 10 minutes before removing from fire. Also, fresh oysters or clams can be added and cooked just ten minutes. Some cooks like to add green peas or red beans for color contrast. Some cooks make green tomatoes a chief element in Green Gumbo with added dill.

DON'T BE SHY! EXPERIMENT! TERRIFY THE NATIVES!

1 bunch green onions, chopped

1 bunch leeks, chopped

1 bunch chives, chopped

2 garlic cloves, minced

4 tablespoons unsalted butter

2 cups chicken, seafood, or
    beef stock

2 cups water

1 bunch bitter greens (sorrel, collards,
    dandelion, etc.), chopped

1 bunch small carrots, turnips, or
    radishes with their leaves, chopped

½ tablespoon grated lemon
    peel

2 bay leaves

3 capers, chopped

3 celery stalks with inner leaves,
    finely chopped

Dash of fenugreek

Dash of marjoram

Cook green onions, leeks, chives, and garlic in unsalted butter until golden. Put into soup pot chicken, seafood, or beef stock and water. Add some bitter greens and carrots, turnips, or radishes (with their leaves), then add grated lemon peel, bay leaves, capers, celery, fenugreek, and marjoram. Bring pot to a boil, then reduce to simmer for 40 minutes. Remove bay leaves.

Serve with wild or brown rice sprinkled with crumbled, crisp bacon. Put an array of pepper sauces and the pepper mill on the table when gumbo is served.

Meat and Relishes

Cotton Belt Brisket • Barbados Stew • Polish Paint Stew • Gdansk
Beef Goodie • Mrs. Alan Alda's Pepper Steak • Carbonnade of Beef •
Hamburgers with Tequila • Caribbean Flank Steak • Memphis Marinade
for Broiling Beef • North Georgia Barbecue Sauce • Smears for Roasts •
Marinades by Dr. S. Willoughby • Wine Sauce (Sauce Madere) • Veal
Cutlets, Italian Style • Stuffed Breast of Veal • Plaquemine Pork Cutlets •
Italian Pork Chops • Blount County Pork • Braised Pork • Country Ribs •
Kentucky Pork Roast • Point Clear Roast Pork • Cooked Marinade for
Venison • Shanks in Stout • Lamb Chops with Mint Julep Sauce • Quick
Mint Sauce • Mobile Lamb Stew • Roast Lamb with Banana Croquettes •
Baby Lamb Chops with Tarragon • Carrot Relish • Cranberry Fig
Relish • Dutch Relish • Kumquat Relish • Happles

COTTON BELT BRISKET

2 cups dry red wine

2 medium onions, sliced

4 shallots or green onions, minced

6 parsley sprigs

2 teaspoons dried thyme

Pinches or hints of these as you like:

    2 to 3 cloves, allspice,

    1 to 2 cracked juniper berries,

    marjoram, celery seeds

1 ½ teaspoons salt

¾ teaspoon freshly ground black
    pepper

3 pounds beef brisket

4 cups beef stock

Combine wine, onions, spices, salt, and pepper in big glass bowl. Pierce meat with fork in many places, put into marinade, and refrigerate, turning now and then, about 48 hours. Heat meat, marinade, and stock to boiling; reduce heat at once. Simmer uncovered until beef is very tender, 3 to 4 hours. Put meat on serving platter and keep warm. Boil up liquid in pot until reduced by about a third, roughly 10 minutes. Strain liquid; spoon off top grease. Slice meat thinly and pour cooking gravy over it.

Hot buttered grits or cornmeal mush or rice goes well with this.

BARBADOS STEW

½ cup all-purpose flour	2 cups chopped green bell pepper
1 tablespoon salt	1 bay leaf
1 teaspoon freshly ground black pepper	2 teaspoons Tabasco or Trappey's pepper sauce
2 pounds boneless beef chuck, cut into 1-inch pieces	3 tablespoons tomato paste
¼ cup vegetable oil	1 teaspoon sugar
1 big garlic clove, crushed	2 tablespoons dark rum
2 ½ cups chopped onion	12 stuffed green olives, sliced thin
	1 ¼ cups tomatoes, peeled and diced

Mix together flour, salt, and pepper. Dredge the meat chunks in this, shaking off excess. In a deep pot, heat the oil over medium heat till it is hot but not smoking. Brown the meat in batches, turning; drain on paper towels. Put garlic, onion, and pepper into pot and cook until soft, stirring now and again. Add bay leaf, Tabasco, tomato paste, and sugar and simmer, covered, about 15 minutes; stir often. Add meat and cook, covered, 1 ½ to 2 hours, stirring now and again, until meat is tender. Now add rum, olives, and tomatoes; simmer 15 minutes more. Serve over boiled rice or pearl barley that has been liberally doused with turmeric (curcuma) while cooking. Pickled green beans or okra are good alongside.

Variations: You might wish to add, according to your taste, 1 teaspoon grated lemon peel, a pinch of thyme, and, instead of the olives, some chopped celery and capers.

POLISH PAINT STEW

2 pounds chuck steak	1 cup dry red wine
2 strips bacon	1 cup beets, cooked and diced
2 onions, finely chopped	1 teaspoon dried dill
1 garlic toe	Cracked black peppercorns
3 tablespoons unsalted butter	½ cup cream
2 cups beef stock or broth	Splash of brandy

Cut chuck steak into bite-size pieces. Place bacon, cut up fine, with onions and garlic into a stew pan with unsalted butter. Brown bacon, onions, and garlic, then put in meat and brown it. Add enough stock or broth to cover, plus a good cup of dry red wine. Simmer for an hour or so until beef is tender. Then add beets, dill, peppercorns, cream, and brandy. Heat up well; serve with boiled pearl barley and a salad dressed with Dijon or New Orleans mustard and grated onion peel, lemon, and oil.

GDANSK BEEF GOODIE

2- to 3-pound chuck roast	1 cup water
Olive oil	1 tablespoon sugar
Horseradish	1 teaspoon salt
Mustard	1 teaspoon lemon juice
Tomato paste	2 pounds new potatoes
Onion powder	Honey
Garlic powder	White wine
Unsalted butter	2 tablespoons unsalted butter
2 large white onions	1 stick unsalted butter, melted
2 whole cloves	Cumin seeds

Marinate chuck roast smeared with olive oil, horseradish, mustard, tomato paste, onion powder, and garlic powder overnight in refrigerator. Preheat oven to 450 degrees. Remove roast from marinade. Slice thickly and place in open baking pan, each slice buttered with unsalted butter. Cook 10 minutes in oven at 450. Turn heat down to 350, pour in marinade juices, and cover loosely with aluminum foil.

Slice root end off onions; stand in a deep baking pan with whole clove stuck in top of each onion. Stir together water, sugar, salt, and lemon juice. Pour over onions. Place next to roast or on rack above. Cook roast and onions for an hour or so or until just right. While onions and roast cook, place new potatoes in a pot on top of the stove, cover with water, and boil 30 minutes or until fork just pierces. Leave in pot while roast finishes cooking. When done, remove roast and allow juices to settle. Sprinkle onions with honey and white wine; put a tablespoon of butter on top and leave in oven about 10 more minutes. Drain potatoes; pour melted butter over and sprinkle with cumin seeds. Let everybody add his or her salt at will. Coarse sea salt is great with beef like this.

MRS. ALAN ALDA'S PEPPER STEAK

2 pounds best steak, cut 1-inch thick	A few drops of juice from pressed garlic
2 tablespoons peppercorns	3 tablespoons beef broth
Salt to taste	3 tablespoons cognac
3 tablespoons unsalted butter	Watercress or parsley for garnish
1 tablespoon minced parsley	

Pat steaks with paper towels to dry. Crush peppercorns coarsely and rub and press them into both sides of the steak. Let stand at room temperature several hours. Preheat grill. Broil 3 to 4 inches from heat until brown; turn and grill on reverse about 5 minutes for very rare, longer for medium, more for well-done. Transfer to heated platter at once; salt to taste. Pour juices from broiler pan into small skillet and add butter, parsley, garlic juice, broth, and cognac. Cook over medium heat until sauce is reduced by one-half. Pour over steak. Garnish and serve. For 4 normal, 2 gluttons.

CARBONNADE OF BEEF

This seems perhaps a great quantity for the usual dinner party, but as in all classic slow-cooking stews, gumbos, etc., somehow they work better cooked in generous amounts. You can always freeze half of it in plastic containers.

Now remember, you're the boss in your own kitchen, and recipes are for your interpretation, they are not congressional laws, so think seriously about the spices and aromatics. I love that mysterious "je ne sais quoi" that the juniper berries give the dish. A lady in Marseille adds quite a bit of fresh basil to her carbonnade. Concentrate, levitate, spice it up! to your own taste.

10 small new potatoes	2 cans (bottles) beer, Dutch if possible
4 sliced yellow onions	½ teaspoon dried or fresh marjoram
1 stick butter	½ teaspoon dried basil
4 pounds round steak	1 garlic toe, minced
Flour	Handful parsley, chopped
2 ½ tablespoons best gin, Dutch if possible	1 to 2 crushed juniper berries
	Salt to taste
2 cups beef stock	Freshly ground black pepper

Cut potatoes in quarters, chop onions coarsely, and brown potatoes and onions in butter; put aside. Cut beef into serving-size bits, sprinkle with flour, then pound with heavy wooden mallet, making flour penetrate into meat. Brown meat in butter in hot skillet, high flame. Heat gin separately, ignite, pour over meat, and stir well together. Put meat and drippings in big casserole, add all else, and simmer slowly for 2 to 3 hours. If you like, you can thicken sauce with a flour and butter roux.

HAMBURGERS WITH TEQUILA

½ cup tequila	2 crushed bay leaves
2 tablespoons olive oil	Pinch of thyme
½ cup minced celery	Freshly ground black pepper
½ cup minced onion	Pinch of salt
4 tablespoons tarragon vinegar	1 pound ground chuck

Mix all ingredients except meat over low flame; don't simmer. Then chill in icebox. Shape ground chuck into patties. Brush marinade frequently over hamburgers while cooking them. (Tough beef can be marinated in this overnight for stew; steaks are delicious broiled with this marinade.) Try dressing any fresh fruit salad with tequila, honey, and almond extract; you'll be pleasantly surprised. Use honey instead of sugar, of course, and not too much.

CARIBBEAN FLANK STEAK

1 generous cup red Burgundy

½ cup red wine vinegar

½ cup fresh orange juice

4 tablespoons best gin

1 garlic toe, smashed

2 small onions, chopped

1 small carrot, scraped and sliced

3 bay leaves, torn in half

1 teaspoon peppercorns, smashed

1 teaspoon grated lemon peel

Good pinch of dried marjoram

Pinch of rosemary

1 ½ teaspoons celery seeds

3 ½ pounds flank steak

Olive oil

Coarse salt

Mix all but steak, oil, and salt in shallow dish or baking pan. Put meat in this marinade, turning several times, then let sit, loosely covered, overnight in fridge, or at least 3 hours in kitchen. Remove steak from marinade and pat dry with paper towels. Reserve marinade. Steak must be at room temperature, so let sit 20 to 30 minutes if it has been in fridge. Brush both sides of meat with oil, then sprinkle with salt. Broil steak about 4 inches from fire, turning once, about 7 minutes for rare. Slice steak diagonally into very thin slices. Heat ¾ cup of marinade and pour over steak.

A salad of watercress and inner celery leaves dressed with lemon juice, oil, salt, and pepper is good alongside. French or Italian bread, lightly toasted, for sopping, naturally. Save what's left of marinade. Simmer it 10 minutes and put in tightly closed jar in fridge. When ready to use on second round, add ⅓ cup Burgundy.

MEMPHIS MARINADE FOR BROILING BEEF

⅓ cup Creole mustard

⅓ cup best bourbon

¼ cup packed brown sugar

1 small onion, finely chopped

1 tablespoon Worcestershire sauce

2 garlic toes, minced and mashed
with a pinch of salt

¼ cup fresh lemon juice

¾ cup plain yogurt

2 tablespoons best olive oil

Whisk together all the ingredients, mixing well. Score both sides of your broiling meat with several ¼-inch-deep diagonal cuts; place in flat dish and pour marinade over meat, turning several times before covering and chilling in fridge overnight. Let meat return to room temperature before broiling.

NORTH GEORGIA BARBECUE SAUCE

This recipe serves for venison as well as beef. Use Angostura bitters if you can't get Peychaud's.

3 tablespoons Worcestershire sauce

1 ½ tablespoons Creole or Dijon
    mustard

1 cup onion chutney

1 ½ tablespoons Peychaud's bitters
    (from New Orleans)

1 ½ tablespoons honey thinned with
    warm water

1 pint best bourbon whiskey

You'll want any good big beef steak (a top sirloin is good). Mix all the sauce ingredients and put in meat to marinate at least 5 hours, overnight if possible. Barbecue meat as usual, turning, basting with sauce. Sauce can be used again if refrigerated. Judge quantities for making sauce; you need enough for meat to be completely inundated.

SMEARS FOR ROASTS

Most Gulf Coast traditional households have coatings that are spread on meat roasts before cooking—marinades, but what in local talk is a "smear." Roasts are "smeared," covered with a clean damp towel, and left for half an hour before being grilled or baked.

Every household has its private formula for a smear, maybe several smears, differing according to the meat. Almost all smears have bourbon as a kind of coordinator. Most ham or pork smears are sweet.

One famous Mobile cook prepared ham in this fashion: Cut some fat from the ham and melt it in frying pan. Smear ham all over with fat. The night before, or some hours before, make the smear mix and keep it in the fridge. This consisted of minced sweet onion, a bit of minced kumquat or orange peel, a good glop of unrefined honey or molasses, a dash of Tabasco, and freshly ground black pepper, all well mixed. A half cup of best bourbon was mixed in, and this smear was spread all over the roast before it went into the oven.

A well-known local cook always wowed her dinner guests with pork roast cooked with this smear: smooth peanut butter mixed with Dijon or Zatarain's Creole mustard, molasses, a dash of powdered ginger, and crushed juniper berries, all mixed with a good half-cup of bourbon.

The original sense of the word marinade is "to pickle in brine" and referred to the fish preserved in this fashion. But since early times, there have been pre-cooking baths of wines or oils with various herbs or spices employed. Sylvia Humphrey, the well-known food editor, says, in an essay on this tradition: "Marinades, the beauty baths that touch up cheap cuts of meat and leftovers, have become popular when there are no longer any cheap meats. But the principle works even with expensive meats. Although marinades will make nearly anything tender, they also season foods in a most pleasant way. The most expensive of meats, the filet of beef, can profit from a marinade, not to tenderize this tender-as-butter cut of meat, but to enhance the flavor of one of the most tasteless."

Basically, a marinade is a mixture of oil, acid (lemon, wine, or vinegar), and spices and/or herbs, in which meat or fish soaks for a few hours or overnight. The acid breaks down the fibers, tenderizing the flesh, while the oil carries into it the savory seasonings.

Usually the marinade is strained and used to baste the flesh when it is later cooked, or used at the end, to make gravy. However, in South America, the Caribbean, Charleston, and the Scandinavian countries, corbina, bass, or salmon is prepared as seviche, where the marinade serves to "cook" the fish employed. The fillets of fish are simply put to soak in lime juice with paper-thin onion slices, or lemon, or combination of lime, lemon, and orange, or white wine vinegar, overnight. Dill goes with the salmon; cracked white peppercorns go into most of the fish marinades. Wine is the essential ingredient in many of the baths for cheaper cuts of meat but goes into dozens of marinades for different purposes. Leftover roast beef soaked in a good dry red wine before going into a stew with onions, celery, and carrots has a new and delightful flavor, nothing like yesterday's spare roast.

The consensus among great cooks everywhere is that seafood requires very little time in a marinade. Delicate fish are actually pre-cooked in this way, so that you can cut down the actual cooking time. Meat should be soaked in a pot close to its own size, with a weight employed to keep the meat submerged. The bigger the cut, the longer the soaking time. A ten-pound roast needs overnight. Remember that the strength of the vinegar increases with time; use much less for a long marinade. Wine is better. But remember that red wine often darkens pale meat or fish.

As Dr. Sebastian Willoughby. Courtesy of Eugene Walter estate.

Yogurt is another good tenderizing agent: Marinate mutton or lamb chops in yogurt with some garlic and dill. A wonderful marinade for a leg of lamb is thus: Make slits all over the leg and insert slivers of raw garlic and onion. Smear the meat with a mixture of Dijon or Creole mustard, dry red wine, freshly ground black pepper, rosemary, a bit of brown sugar, a little salt, and about two tablespoons pure olive oil. Turn and turn the meat in this mixture. Roast in a hot oven, basting with (unstrained) marinade. When meat is done, keep hot and scrape up all the gunk in the pan, adding more wine and a dash of bitters. Reduce to make your gravy. Have lots of crusty bread for dipping.

A wonderful hors d'oeuvre: brussels sprouts cooked till just pierceable in water with sugar and salt. Cool, cut precisely in halves, sprinkle with lemon juice, and let sit a few minutes while you mix some yogurt, prepared horseradish, dill, and a pinch of salt and pepper. Mix all together and let stand. Sprinkle with chopped parsley or chives or both when ready to serve. A good French dressing can be employed to marinate any leftover cooked vegetables to transform them completely.

Don't forget dessert marinades. Ripe peaches marinated in white port, chilled, served with either a sprig of mint or a slice of crystallized ginger, is a perfect sweet course. But after pork or lamb, try surprising your guests with tart apple slices soaked in lemon juice, sweet white wine, and crème de menthe. The color is outrageous, the taste reassuring. If you really want to scare your in-laws, soak the apple slices in a blue-colored Triple Sec or the purple liqueurs, such as Parfait d'Amour, made from passion vine fruit. Well, dears, have a good soak!

WINE SAUCE (SAUCE MADERE)

Sauce Madere is an ancient classic in the French cuisine; it survives today in the coastal regions of the South, especially Mobile, New Orleans, Savannah, and Charleston, although not called Madeira Sauce but simply Wine Sauce. For pork dishes, it is often prepared with tawny port instead of Madeira. In times past, and even well into the 1970s of the twentieth century, Madeira was what bank officials drank at their meetings, and under one of the old Mobile banks, in low-ceilinged, heavy brick arches that were once the foundations of Fort Charlotte, built when Mobile was British, were stored an unbelievable number of cases of fine Madeira.

½ cup plus 2 tablespoons Madeira

2 cups beef stock or broth

4 tablespoons unsalted butter

2 tablespoons flour

Salt and freshly ground black pepper

In a heavy pan, boil ½ cup fine Madeira until reduced by half. Add to this a very rich beef stock or broth and thicken with 2 tablespoons unsalted butter, which has been well blended with flour. Simmer 10 minutes. Season with salt and freshly ground black pepper. Just before serving, whisk in 2 more tablespoons Madeira and 2 more tablespoons unsalted butter. Simple as that. Transforms roast beef, filet mignon, and such into a religious experience.

Curious and puzzling that so few Italians came to the South in the old days. The few who did so were for the most part highly educated and highly trained artisans who carved the marble mantels and created wooden and plaster moldings and ornaments, including the ceiling rosettes from which descended the chandeliers. Since they were mostly north Italians, their cuisine was close to that of the south of France. Many Gulf Coast eggplant and tomato dishes that we are familiar with are Italian in origin but known to us under French names. This very dish was served at a banquet in 1849 at the Battle House Hotel in Mobile, prepared by a French chef. It was listed, naturally, as "Cotelettes de veau a l'Italienne."

Handful of unbleached flour

6 boneless veal cutlets, what the Italians call *scallopine*

½ stick unsalted butter

4 tablespoons first quality olive oil

⅓ cup dry white wine

6 tablespoons capers (the kind put up in vinegar, not those salt-preserved), drained, with vinegar saved for salads

Salt and freshly ground black pepper

Small bunch of parsley, well-washed, stems removed, leaves coarsely chopped

Flour the cutlets lightly. Melt butter and oil in medium-sized casserole. When butter is melted, put in the cutlets and cook 1 minute on each side over low heat.

Remove cutlets. Add wine to the casserole, cover, and simmer 5 minutes or so. Chop capers coarsely. Put capers in wine sauce, cook a minute or so, then put cutlets back in casserole and simmer all a few minutes. Taste for salt and pepper. Place cutlets on heated platter and pour sauce over; sprinkle all with parsley. Serves 6 dainty eaters, 4 greedy-guts.

STUFFED BREAST OF VEAL

2 pounds breast of veal

Salt and freshly ground black pepper

Dash of Worcestershire sauce

½ cup white wine

1 lemon, juiced (reserve ½ teaspoon for stuffing)

¾ cup bread crumbs

¼ cup milk

2 eggs

6 bacon slices

1 garlic clove, minced

1 tablespoon minced parsley

1 tablespoon minced costmary (mint leaves may be substituted)

2 tablespoons Madeira or cream Sherry

3 tablespoons unsalted butter

Get your butcher to cut a neat pocket in a 2-pound breast of veal. Preheat oven to 350 degrees. Sprinkle the meat with salt, freshly ground black pepper, Worcestershire diluted in white wine, and lemon juice. Stuffing: bread crumbs soaked in a little milk and lemon juice; eggs, slightly beaten; 1 slice bacon, finely chopped; garlic; parsley; costmary; and Madeira or cream Sherry. Add salt and pepper to taste. Mix all together; stuff pocket in meat. Roll the meat, tie it, and place in fairly tight oven dish so it won't have a chance to dry out. Put slices of bacon over it and a few dabs of butter; roast until tender, roughly 1 ½ hours.

PLAQUEMINE PORK CUTLETS

1 ½ pounds pork cutlets

Salt and freshly ground black pepper

3 ½ tablespoons unsalted butter

1 ½ tablespoons vegetable oil

1 big, ripe pear, cored and sliced thin

Good glop of fresh or dried thyme (about 1 scant tablespoon)

2 garlic toes, finely minced

2 tablespoons red wine vinegar

1 tablespoon molasses

¾ cup chicken stock or canned chicken broth

1 tablespoon cognac

Parsley and inner celery leaves for garnish

Pound meat flat, about ¼-inch thick. Season with salt and pepper. Melt 1 ½ tablespoons butter with oil over medium to high fire. Brown pork till just cooked through, about 2 minutes a side. Put aside and keep warm. Add pear slices to skillet; cook about 3 minutes, till beginning to brown.

Add thyme and garlic; cook a minute longer. Add vinegar, scrape up pan bottom, and cook 30 seconds. Add molasses, stock, and cognac; simmer till pears are tender and sauce reduced, about 3 to 4 minutes. Whisk in remaining butter. Put cutlets in pan and cook till heated through. Arrange meat on platter; pour sauce over. Garnish.

ITALIAN PORK CHOPS

On one of those gray winter days, this is the perfect dish. This calls for fairly thick, center-cut pork chops.

4 center-cut pork chops (with bones), at least an inch thick

Salt and freshly ground black pepper

2 tablespoons vegetable oil

1 small red onion, sliced thin

1 tablespoon Dijon or Creole mustard

½ small head savoy cabbage, cored and sliced thin

1 to 2 Granny Smith apples, peeled, cored, sliced lengthwise

1 cup beer

Pinch of dried thyme

2 to 3 cracked juniper berries

¼ cup chicken stock or canned chicken broth

Sprinkle chops lightly with salt and pepper. Heat oil in big skillet; cook chops over medium heat, turning once, till nicely browned, roughly 8 to 9 minutes. Take chops out, cover, and keep warm. Put onion in skillet and sauté about 2 minutes, then add mustard, cabbage, and apples. Sauté till cabbage starts to turn slightly brown, about 2 to 3 minutes. Add beer, bring to boil, and simmer 4 to 5 minutes. Return chops to skillet, covering them with cabbage mix. Add thyme, juniper, and stock. Bring to boil, cover, and simmer till chops are cooked through, about a quarter of an hour. Taste for salt and pepper. Serve at once. Hash browned potatoes good alongside. Serves 4 dainty eaters, 2 lumberjacks.

BLOUNT COUNTY PORK

4 smallish turnips, peeled, cut in halves

4 small yams, cut into ⅓-inch slices

8 tablespoons butter

1 ½ teaspoons dried thyme, crumbled

Salt and freshly ground black pepper

2 pounds pork tenderloins, dried with paper towels

2 tablespoons light molasses

2 tablespoons bourbon whiskey

Preheat oven to 425 degrees. Mix turnips and yams in big baking dish; top with 6 tablespoons butter and 1 teaspoon thyme. Season with salt and pepper. Bake till roots are tender, stirring occasionally and basting with the butter, about half an hour.

Melt 2 tablespoons butter in skillet over medium-high heat. Season pork with salt and pepper. Brown meat on all sides, then add pork to vegetable dish. In skillet, mix molasses and rest of thyme into drippings, then mix in bourbon. Spoon over pork and vegetables; roast about 15 to 20 minutes, turning occasionally. Divide roots among 4 serving plates. Slice pork, arrange on plates, and serve at once. A light, dry red wine with this. Serves 4.

BRAISED PORK

8 ounces thick bacon slices, cut into 1-inch pieces

2 pounds pork shoulder, trimmed and cut into 1-inch pieces

2 cups dry white wine

1 basket (about 2 dozen, give or take) white pearl onions, peeled

1 cup water

1 big carrot, cut into ¼-inch slices

Bouquet garni: 4 parsley sprigs, 2 thyme sprigs, 1 bay leaf, 8 whole black peppercorns, tied in bit of cheesecloth or thin white cotton

More minced parsley

Cook bacon in large Dutch oven over medium heat until just golden. Remove from pot and put in pork; brown in batches. Put bacon and all pork back into pot and add everything else save minced parsley. Simmer about 1 ½ hours or until tender. Remove bouquet garni. Divide meat and vegetables among 4 shallow soup bowls and sprinkle with parsley. Steamed new potatoes or small white cornmeal hush puppies are good with this dish. This serves 4 of average appetite. If you're having greedy-guts to table, better just double everything.

COUNTRY RIBS

2 pounds country ribs

1 cup red wine

2 tablespoons Dijon or Creole mustard

1/4 cup honey

1/3 cup cider vinegar

Dash of mace

1 onion, chopped

Several dashes of marjoram

Salt and freshly ground black pepper

Juice from lemon or orange

Put ribs to soak in a mixture of the wine, mustard, honey, cider vinegar, mace, onion, marjoram, and salt and freshly ground black pepper. Soak overnight or at least 4 hours. Preheat oven to 375 degrees. Dry ribs; save marinade. Put ribs in oven and after 20 minutes pour off fat and turn ribs. After 15 minutes pour off fat, pour marinade over meat, cover with foil, and cook 45 minutes at 350 degrees, turning and basting several times. Squeeze a little lemon or orange juice over ribs toward end of cooking. Add more wine if needed. Uncover for last 10 minutes so ribs will brown. Judge for yourself when done; meat must be tender, ribs of good color, and enough pan drippings left to make gravy.

KENTUCKY PORK ROAST

1/2 cup Creole or Dijon mustard

4 pounds pork roast

2/3 cup dark brown sugar

1/2 cup peanut oil

Generous 2/3 cup best bourbon
    whiskey

2 cups rich chicken stock

Salt and freshly ground black pepper

1/2 teaspoon dried thyme

1/4 teaspoon dried sage

1/4 teaspoon powdered mace

1 tablespoon chopped parsley

1 tablespoon flour

1 tablespoon unsalted butter

Preheat oven to 350 degrees. Smear the mustard carefully all over the roast, then roll it in the brown sugar. Heat oil in a heavy casserole and brown roast on all sides over moderate heat. Heat the bourbon slightly and pour over roast, saving out 1 teaspoon. Ignite the teaspoon of bourbon with a match, then pour into pot to ignite the rest. Add 1 cup of the stock in which you've mixed the salt, pepper, and herbs. Cover the casserole, put in oven, and let braise 1 1/2 to 2 hours or, if you are using meat thermometer, till it registers 160 degrees. Remove roast, put on hot platter, and keep warm. Put the rest of the stock in the pot and boil it over high heat, stirring and scraping up browned bits. Strain liquid into a saucepan; skim off fat. With your fingers, mix flour and butter together in a good *beurre manié*. Whisk this into sauce a bit at a time and cook until sauce is smooth and thick. Serve this with the roast.

POINT CLEAR ROAST PORK

An old family of French and Spanish origins had a private ceremony. When the long, hot summer ended and the first cool weather turned up in late October or early November, they served a luscious pork roast with a crust that was sweet-piquant, several kinds of greens on the side, and for dessert an apple pie that wasn't a pie but was a classic apple pie recipe with green tomatoes instead. Glasses of ice-cold anisette with a splash of ice-cold gin were served in ice-cold glasses in the parlor or on the front porch afterward.

1 5-pound boneless pork loin roast, rolled and tied

1 tablespoon plus ¼ cup unsalted butter

2 tablespoons flour

1 tablespoon dry mustard

1 tablespoon whole mustard seeds (or mix of celery seeds and mustard powder)

2 tablespoons Dijon or Creole mustard

1 tablespoon cracked black peppercorns

1 tablespoon cracked dried green peppercorns

1 tablespoon cracked white peppercorns

2 tablespoons light brown sugar

2 teaspoons dried thyme, crumbled

For gravy:

1 ½ cups apple cider

4 tablespoons applejack or Calvados

2 tablespoons flour

¾ cup chicken stock or canned broth

1 tablespoon cider vinegar

1 teaspoon Creole or Dijon mustard

Salt and freshly ground pepper to taste

Preheat oven to 475 degrees. Brown roast in 1 tablespoon butter, about 4 minutes per side. Remove; cool 10 minutes. In bowl, mix ¼ cup butter with flour, mustards, peppercorns, sugar, and thyme. Spread paste on top and sides of roast. Cook in oven 30 minutes, then reduce heat to 325 and roast 1 hour and 20 minutes for medium meat.

Place meat on cutting board and cover with foil. Put 2 tablespoons drippings from roasting pan in heavy small saucepan. Pour off remaining drippings from roasting pan and put aside for some other day. Heat roasting pan over medium-low heat. Add apple cider and applejack or Calvados and boil until reduced to about ¼ cup, scraping the browned bits. Next, heat saucepan of drippings over medium-low heat. Add flour and stir until light brown, about 2 minutes. Whisk in reduced cider and stock. Simmer, stirring now and then, until thickened, about 2 minutes. Remove from fire; stir in vinegar and mustard. Taste for salt; add if needed. Pepper, too.

Carve roast and serve with gravy in heated bowl. Heated French bread on side for sopping, *naturellement*.

COOKED MARINADE FOR VENISON

1 cup cooking oil	2 tablespoons salt
½ pound carrots, minced	1 teaspoon peppercorns
½ pound onions, minced	4 tablespoons brown sugar
2 ounces shallots, minced	3 to 4 stalks parsley
1 crushed garlic clove	2 rosemary sprigs
2 cups vinegar	2 thyme sprigs
2 bottles dry white wine	2 bay leaves
3 quarts water	2 cloves

Heat the oil and sauté the vegetables a little, then add vinegar, wine, water, salt, peppercorns, sugar, and herbs and spices. Cook 20 minutes, let sit for a quarter of an hour, then strain and let cool before marinating the haunch of venison or any very big cut of meat. The strained liquid is used to baste the cooking meat and, afterward, to make the gravy with pan juices or drippings. The great Escoffier recommends for a leg of mutton such a marinade but adds 1 tablespoon juniper berries, 1 quart less water, and 4 more cloves of garlic.

6 lamb shanks (roughly 6 pounds)

Salt to taste

Good dose of freshly ground
    black pepper

½ cup all-purpose flour

5 tablespoons vegetable oil

1 tablespoon bacon fat

5 cups chopped onion

4 cups beef stock or canned
    beef broth

1 12-ounce bottle stout

4 carrots, peeled, cut into 1-inch bits

4 to 6 turnips, cut into 1-inch bits

4 to 5 radishes, cut into 1-inch bits
    (long white ones if possible)

1 garlic toe, unpeeled

1 bay leaf

Drop or so of Tabasco

½ cup raisins

Season shanks with salt and pepper. Coat with flour. Heat oil and fat in large Dutch oven over high heat. Brown shanks well, in batches. With tongs or big forks, take out shanks and put in big bowl. Brown onions till translucent, about 5 minutes, scraping up bits from bottom of pan. Add what's left of flour; stir 1 minute. Put shanks and drippings back into Dutch oven. Add stock and stout. Cover; bring to boil. Reduce heat and simmer till meat begins to be tender, about 1 hour. Add root vegetables and flavorings; simmer uncovered till all is tender and stew thickens slightly, about 40 minutes. Spoon off fat from surface. Toss in raisins; simmer 10 to 15 minutes longer. This is best kept overnight and reheated the next day. Remove garlic when serving. Wild rice or yellow hominy alongside, or peas and rice. A salad of spinach and green onions is good after.

LAMB CHOPS WITH MINT JULEP SAUCE

1 ½ cups fresh mint leaves

3 tablespoons best bourbon
    whiskey

¾ cup sugar

⅓ cup white vinegar

12 4-ounce lamb chops

Salt and freshly ground black pepper
    to taste

4 ½ tablespoons unsalted butter

4 ½ tablespoons vegetable oil

Chop mint fine; mix with bourbon, sugar, and vinegar. Put in bowl, cover, and chill. Pat lamb chops dry and sprinkle with salt and pepper. Sauté chops in melted butter and oil over medium heat in heavy skillet, about 5 minutes per side for medium-rare, a minute longer if you prefer more done. Put 2 chops on each plate and pour sauce over. Brown rice is good with this, or boiled barley. Serves 6 polite guests, 4 greedy-guts.

QUICK MINT SAUCE

1 ½ tablespoons confectioner's sugar	½ cup vinegar
3 tablespoons hot water	⅓ cup fresh mint leaves, packed

Dissolve confectioner's sugar in hot water and let cool. Add good vinegar of your choice (some old books call for cognac or bourbon instead of vinegar) and mint.

MOBILE LAMB STEW

4 pounds lamb shoulder (with bones)	2 smashed, unpeeled garlic toes
1 ½ cups thinly sliced onion	Rosemary as you like (about
Light olive or nut oil	1 ½ teaspoons)
Flour	1 ½ cups chopped tomatoes
Salt and freshly ground black pepper	3 cups lamb or chicken stock
1 cup dry white French vermouth	

Lamb shoulder is often sold already cut for stew, or you can buy lamb shoulder chops. Cut off excess fat (chop and toss out for birds; they love it) and cut meat into chunks about 1 to 2 inches. Leave bones in; they give flavor to stew. Sauté onions to light brown, about 6 minutes in a tablespoon of oil. Put onion in casserole. Just before adding lamb pieces to brown, shake flour, salt, and pepper over them, then shake in colander to remove excess flour. Brown lamb bits a few at a time, then put in casserole. Wash out frying pan with vermouth, then pour it with the meat. Add garlic, rosemary, tomatoes, and enough stock to just cover ingredients. Simmer an hour to an hour and a half on top of stove or in 325-degree oven till lamb is tender. Pour stew into colander set over big bowl. Remove bones from meat and place meat in serving dish or casserole. Press all ingredients through colander into sauce. Degrease sauce. Pour sauce over lamb, taste for flavorings, and reheat to simmer before serving.

Plain boiled pearl barley is very good with this, or rice flavored with fenugreek seeds or turmeric. Note: Tomatoes must be ripe or you might want to use half fresh, half Italian canned tomatoes and a glop of tomato paste.

ROAST LAMB WITH BANANA CROQUETTES

1 leg of lamb	Flour
Salt	Bacon fat
Pepper	Hot water
1 onion, sliced in half	Dry red wine
Spicy mustard	Parsley sprigs for garnish

For croquettes:

Bunch of bananas	Peanut oil for frying
Lemon juice	Confectioner's sugar
2 beaten eggs	Cinnamon
2 cups bread crumbs	

Preheat oven to 450 degrees. Remove superfluous fat from leg of lamb and score the thin layer of fat on the outer side of the leg diagonally. Rub with salt, pepper, onion, and some hot mustard. Dredge well with flour and set pan in very hot oven to sear outside of meat. After 15 minutes, reduce heat to 325 and cook just under 2 hours. Baste frequently with bacon fat melted in hot water and a little dry red wine. When serving, place paper frill on leg and garnish with parsley sprigs and banana croquettes.

To prepare croquettes: Remove skin and threads from bananas; trim to cylinder-shaped croquette form, coating with lemon juice to prevent discoloring. Roll in egg, then in sifted bread crumbs. Fry in deep fat until lightly browned. Drain on paper towels, then dust with confectioner's sugar and a pinch of cinnamon.

BABY LAMB CHOPS WITH TARRAGON

8 to 12 baby lamb chops

3 tablespoons butter

½ cup dry white vermouth

1 teaspoon tarragon

2 tablespoons chopped parsley

Sauté chops in butter to preferred stage of doneness. Pour off some of the fat. Place chops on hot platter. Add vermouth, tarragon, and parsley to pan juices. Boil briskly, stirring constantly, until mixture is reduced by one-half. Pour over chops and serve at once. Serves 4.

CARROT RELISH

This is very good with wild game, turkey, ham, or roast beef.

4 carrots, chopped

1 tablespoon chopped candied ginger

2 mild onions, chopped

½ cup finely chopped celery heart

1 tablespoon grated orange peel

1 tablespoon orange juice

½ cup honey or molasses

1 tablespoon cider vinegar

Pinch of salt

Pinch of powdered cloves

½ cup raisins

Splash of bourbon or brandy

Stir together all ingredients, except for spirits, and simmer until liquid is reduced and carrots are soft. Add spirits and simmer a good minute longer. Let cool. Put in closed container and into refrigerator until ready to serve.

This is good with the eternal bird but even better with roast pork, ham, or veal.

1 ½ cups fresh cranberries	Good dash of freshly ground black
1 ½ cups finely chopped dried figs	pepper and half as much white
1 cup diced mild onion	pepper
¼ cup firmly packed dark brown	1 cup water
sugar	¼ cup red wine vinegar
1 tablespoon grated orange peel	¼ cup light molasses or sorghum

Combine all in heavy pan; bring to boil. Reduce heat and simmer, uncovered, for an hour or until thickened, stirring often. Remove from heat; let cool.

Can be refrigerated in airtight containers for up to 2 weeks. Serve at room temperature.

Serve with pork, lamb, or venison.

4 garlic cloves, minced and smashed	3 cloves
½ teaspoon salt	1 cup tawny port
1 ½ teaspoons minced candied ginger	1 ½ cups dry red wine
2 tablespoons light olive oil	1 tablespoon brown sugar
4 tablespoons unsalted butter	2 teaspoons grated orange peel
1 pound mild purple onions, finely	Salt and freshly ground black pepper
chopped (about 3 ½ cups)	

Mash the garlic, salt, and ginger into a paste. In big skillet, melt oil and butter. Cook garlic puree over low heat, stirring constantly, until perfume rises. Add onions and turn up heat a tiny bit. Cook until onions soften. Add cloves, port, and wine; bring to boil, stirring until thickening to a jam-like feel. Mash mixture with fork and season with brown sugar, orange peel, and salt and pepper.

KUMQUAT RELISH

3 tablespoons sugar

1 cup white port or any sweet white wine

1 ½ cups water

Good pinch of powdered cinnamon

Good pinch of allspice

1 cup chopped celery heart

½ cup chopped tart apple

½ cup chopped mild onion

1 ½ cups sliced kumquats

1 heaping teaspoon cornstarch

1 ½ tablespoons water

Splash of cognac

Combine sugar, wine, 1 ½ cups water, spices, celery, apple, and onion. Bring to boil; simmer uncovered about 20 minutes till liquid is reduced. Add kumquats and return to boil. Cover, turn down heat, and simmer 2 to 3 minutes. Mix cornstarch with 1 ½ tablespoons water. Add to kumquat mixture and bring to boil. Cook 1 to 2 minutes, stirring constantly. Add a splash of cognac. Cover and chill. Good with wild meat, guinea fowl, or turkey.

Nice served in small individual ramekins sitting right on plate.

Variations: Omit celery, apple, and onion and this is truly Big Yum served over buttermilk sherbet or vanilla ice cream.

HAPPLES

Prepare this dish for Christmas breakfast.

Jonathan or other tart, green apples

Honey

Rum, Sherry, or bourbon

Mace

Cinnamon

Crisp-cooked ham fat

Core but don't peel apples. Slice and put in wide, flat baking dish. Pour honey and a splash of rum, Sherry, or bourbon whiskey over; sprinkle with mace (a hint) and cinnamon (a bold statement), then bake until fork-able but not mushy. Sprinkle with LOTS of crisp-cooked ham fat and serve alongside plain scrambled eggs and hot biscuits.

Poultry

Brunswick Stew • Chicken Custard • Chicken with Sage
and Wine • Chicken Annecy • Yellow Rice • Prima Donna Chicken •
Chicken with Madeira • Spring Chicken • Barbados Chicken • Mark
and Clair's Chicken • Citrus Chutney • Chicken with Tarragon •
Quail with Sauce • Duck Breasts with Green Peppercorns • Braised
Duck • Turkey Tattle and Dressing Dope • The Day after Thanksgiving:
Cold Turkey Pâté • Turkey Casino

BRUNSWICK STEW

What is called Brunswick Stew on the Gulf Coast has as many different
versions, almost, as jambalaya. Originally made of squirrel and called simply Squirrel Stew, the rodents were soon replaced by guinea fowl, pheas-
ant, even young turkeys. Guinea hen's best.

2 small guinea hens, cut into
    serving pieces
2 teaspoons salt
Good dash of mild paprika
2 tablespoons vegetable oil
2 onions, sliced thin
1 mild green pepper, diced
3 cups water
2 cups canned tomatoes with
    their juice

2 tablespoons chopped parsley
Tabasco
½ teaspoon or more of paprika
2 bay leaves, torn in half
1 teaspoon grated lemon peel
2 cups whole kernel corn or
    ¾ cup uncooked barley
2 cups lima beans
Dash of dry Sherry

Sprinkle guinea hen pieces with 1 teaspoon salt and dash of paprika. In a big pan, heat oil and brown bird pieces on all sides. Remove guinea hen from pan, and add onion and pepper and cook until soft. Add water, tomatoes with juice, parsley, salt, dash of Tabasco, seasonings, and barley (if using barley). Return guinea hen to pan, cover, turn down heat, and simmer 30 minutes. Add corn and beans; cook 20 minutes longer. Pour in Sherry and taste for seasoning in last 10 minutes of cooking. Remove bay leaves.

Serve in flat soup plates with either rice or new potatoes. If using new potatoes, choose smallest, cut in half while hot, and drench with butter, salt, freshly ground black pepper, and dried dill. Let diners go ahead and dump them into stew.

CHICKEN CUSTARD

1 chicken (about 3 ½ pounds), cut into 8 pieces	3 parsley sprigs
1 teaspoon salt	¾ cup chicken stock or broth
½ teaspoon or more freshly ground pepper	12 small white onions, peeled, cross-cut in root end
Dash of ground mace	½ teaspoon sugar
8 tablespoons unsalted butter	¼ cup dry vermouth
1 teaspoon oil	½ cup chopped scallions
½ cup freshly chopped cooked ham	1 tablespoon chopped parsley
2 big carrots, peeled and chopped	4 eggs
1 clove	6 tablespoons all-purpose flour
1 medium yellow onion	1 teaspoon baking powder
	½ cup heavy cream

Sprinkle chicken pieces with salt, pepper, and mace; let stand at least 30 minutes. Heat 3 tablespoons butter and 1 teaspoon oil in heavy skillet over medium-low heat. Add ham and carrots; cook until carrots soften, about 5 minutes. Transfer mix to bowl and set aside. Melt another 3 tablespoons butter in same skillet, medium heat. Arrange as many chicken pieces as will fit in one layer in skillet, skin side down. Sauté until golden brown, 7 to 8 minutes. Turn pieces and repeat 5 to 6 minutes for other side. Put aside; brown remaining pieces and remove. Put in ham and carrot. Stick clove into middle of yellow onion. Add parsley sprigs and pour in stock, scraping pot. Return chicken to skillet. Heat over medium till boiling, reduce to simmer, and cook covered about 20 minutes.

Meanwhile, heat oven to 375 degrees. Butter a 2-inch-deep, 2-quart baking dish. Melt remaining butter in non-reactive skillet and add white onions; sprinkle with sugar. Sauté, stirring often, till onions are golden. Carefully pour vermouth into skillet; go on cooking onions uncovered, shaking skillet occasionally till liquid is absorbed and onions tender, about 10 to 12 minutes. Put chicken in baking dish, skin side up. With a slotted spoon, add ham and carrots to baking dish and then pour remaining liquid and onions over chicken. Sprinkle with chopped scallions and parsley. Remove parsley sprigs and yellow onion with clove.

In a blender, blend eggs, then add flour, baking powder, cream, and reserved pan juices and mix until smooth. Pour this custard mixture evenly over chicken; bake until custard is golden brown and puffed, about 30 minutes. Serve at once.

CHICKEN WITH SAGE AND WINE

4 tablespoons unsalted butter

1 3-pound chicken, cut as you please into pieces

6 fresh sage leaves or a scant teaspoon of dried sage

¾ cup good dry red wine

½ cup chicken stock

Freshly ground black pepper

Salt to taste

Fresh sage flowers for garnish, if you have them (better to remove flowers to keep plants sprouting throughout the summer)

Heat butter in heavy skillet. Chicken pieces, which have been washed and dried, must not crowd each other in pan. Cook on medium to high until chicken is rich golden brown, roughly 9 minutes. Be careful not to pierce flesh when turning. Cook other side about 7 minutes. Cook in batches, if need be. Remove and drain on paper. Drain off all but about 3 tablespoons of fat in pan. Return meat to pan, dark meat on bottom, white meat on top. Sprinkle with chopped sage. Reduce heat to medium low, cover, and cook about 12 minutes for breasts (then remove them), about 25 minutes for legs. Keep chicken warm on hot platter while you add wine and stock to pan; stir well, scraping up stuck bits. Reduce liquid until one-half original volume. Pour this sauce over chicken and serve. Add salt and pepper to taste and garnish with sage flowers.

2 cups water

2 medium heads of garlic

2 ounces fatback (salt pork, side
    meat, whatever you call it)

2 tablespoons unsalted butter

1 3-pound chicken, cut into pieces

2 tablespoons cider vinegar

2 tablespoons dry Sherry

4 thyme sprigs or ¼ teaspoon dried

1 bay leaf, crumbled

Salt and freshly ground black pepper

½ cup chicken stock

1 tablespoon Creole or Dijon mustard

Heat 2 cups water and boil garlic 15 minutes. Rinse under cold water. Slip the skins off and keep the garlic. Heat more water to boiling; blanch salt pork about 30 seconds. Drain and dry. Put butter and salt pork in heavy skillet. Cook about 10 minutes over medium flame or until meat is golden. Remove with slotted spoon. Brown chicken in fat. Cook in batches to avoid crowding, about 7 minutes for each side. Remove chicken from pan. Pour off all but thin coating of fat. Put chicken back, white meat on top. Add half of vinegar and Sherry. Put in garlic, salt pork, thyme, bay leaf, and a pinch of salt and freshly ground black pepper. Cover and cook until chicken is done. Put chicken and garlic on hot platter. Reduce liquid in pan by one-half. Stir in remaining wine, vinegar, chicken stock, and mustard. Heat to boiling; taste for seasoning. Pour sauce over chicken when ready to serve. Serve with Yellow Rice (recipe follows).

YELLOW RICE

2 tablespoons unsalted butter

2 ½ cups rice

Salt

1 heaping tablespoon turmeric powder

Dash of mace

5 cups warm water

Put butter in pot; add rice. Turn in melted butter until each grain is transparent-looking. Add salt to taste, turmeric powder, mace, and warm water. Cook covered, stirring once, until rice has absorbed liquid and you hear "creak" as first grains stick. Turn off fire at once; cover pot with towel. Each grain will be separate-cooked in this fashion. Oh yes, don't wash rice. No reason to pour off the nutrients. Bon appétit!

PRIMA DONNA CHICKEN

1 roasting chicken of	A little grated lemon peel
5 to 6 pounds	10 peppercorns
2 quarts water	Salt to taste
1 onion	10 ounces shelled pecan meats
1 carrot	2 ½ cups fresh white bread crumbs
1 stalk celery	1 cup light cream
1 bay leaf	A splash of dry Sherry or white
A few parsley sprigs	vermouth

Wash chicken and dry it off. Put it in a big pot with water, onion, carrot, celery, bay leaf, parsley, lemon peel, peppercorns, and salt. Bring water to boil over high heat; lower heat, cover, and simmer gently 1 ½ hours or until chicken is tender. While chicken is cooking, prepare the sauce. Grind the pecans in blender or food mill and put them in a bowl with the crumbs. When chicken has cooked, add enough broth to the nut-crumb mixture to make a thick sauce. Stir in cream; taste for salt. Stir in Sherry or vermouth; heat well. You can add whatever seasoning you like: a tiny glop of Tabasco or a few marjoram leaves or some chopped chives or a pinch of powdered ginger, etc. Use your imagination. Take chicken from pot and with sharp knife cut into portions. Place on warmed platter and pour a little sauce over it. Put rest of sauce in heated sauceboat or bowl. Serve at once.

CHICKEN WITH MADEIRA

1 nice broiler or fryer, about	½ cup water
3 to 3 ½ pounds	10 small red potatoes, scrubbed,
½ lemon	unpeeled
Salt and freshly ground	6 garlic toes, peeled
black pepper	Celery seeds
¾ cup Madeira wine	½ stick butter

You'll need a pan that goes in the oven as well as on the stovetop. Preheat oven to 400 degrees. Put aside giblets, body fat, and neck of chicken to make a broth later, or scald for cats. Rinse chicken and dry thoroughly. Rub inside and out with lemon half, then with salt and pepper. Prepare for roasting: tie legs together, etc. Place breast side up in ungreased pan. Pour ¼ cup Madeira over chicken. Add about ½ cup water. Place potatoes and garlic neatly around bird. Roast 1 hour, basting every quarter hour, or until juices run clear from thickest part. Place bird on heated platter surrounded by potatoes and garlic. Spoon off fat from roasting pan, then stir in remaining wine. Stir over high heat 1 to 2 minutes until some of the liquid has boiled away. Remove from heat and stir in celery seeds and butter until sauce is thickened. Place in gravy boat.

Some like to mash the garlic into the potatoes. Cooked in this fashion, the garlic is delicious IF it is fairly fresh. Smell it when you buy it. This serves 4 dainty eaters between soup and salad courses. Mild onions, roasted or boiled, are good alongside; so are peeled, cubed turnip roots with butter and nutmeg.

SPRING CHICKEN

1 whole fresh chicken	Dry white wine
Carrots	Salt and freshly ground black pepper
Onions	Butter
Turnips	Rice or barley (about ½ cup, depending
Parsnips	on the amount of liquid)
Grated lemon peel	Chopped parsley or chives

One of the very best spring dishes is a chicken boiled with carrots, onions, turnips, and parsnips (all whole) with a bit of grated lemon peel, dry white wine, and salt and freshly ground black pepper. Decide how many vegetables you want, add to pot with chicken and seasonings, cover all with water, and splash with wine. Bring to boil, then simmer until chicken is tender.

Preheat oven to 400 degrees. Remove bird and vegetables from broth and put in baking dish. Butter well and leave in oven while you cook some rice or barley in the broth. Check broth for seasoning, sprinkle with chopped parsley or chives, and serve. Turn bird and roots until golden brown, then slice vegetables and serve with chicken as course following soup. Welcome spring! Think lofty thoughts!

BARBADOS CHICKEN

Here's a delightful Caribbean dish.

2 to 3 small chickens	3 green peppers
½ stick unsalted butter	Freshly ground black pepper
Ham or bacon fat	Tabasco
2 sweet onions, such as Vidalia	Salt
1 pineapple or large can pineapple slices, drained	2 cups dry white wine

Cut chickens into serving portions. Melt a nice hunk of unsalted butter in your heavy skillet, along with a little ham or bacon fat. Brown the chicken pieces nicely, then place in a lidded pot with sweet onions peeled and cut in half, pineapple slices, green peppers cut in strips, a generous sprinkle of freshly ground black pepper, a dash of Tabasco, salt to taste, and dry white wine. Simmer, covered, over low to medium flame, until chicken is tender. Add more wine if necessary. Arrange chicken on platter; garnish with vegetables.

On the side, serve boiled Yellow Rice (page 103) and a cucumber salad flavored with lime juice, virgin olive oil, salt, and pepper.

MARK AND CLAIR'S CHICKEN

1 hot pepper, Scotch bonnet or jalapeno, seeded and finely chopped	Good quantity (your taste) freshly ground black pepper
4 tablespoons honey	6 boneless, skinless chicken breasts
	Unsalted butter, bacon fat, or white pork fat

Preheat oven to 450 degrees. Chop hot pepper very fine; mix with honey and black pepper. Rub this mix over chicken breasts after you've rubbed them very lightly with unsalted butter, bacon fat, or white pork fat. Roast in oven about 15 minutes.

Serve with boiled rice and Citrus Chutney (recipe follows).

" . . . But then, Mme. Pample-mousse, La Mandarine and Master Kumquat have their characteristics, too . . . ," Walter sketch. Courtesy of Eugene Walter estate.

CITRUS CHUTNEY

3 to 4 oranges, cuts into sixths

3 pink grapefruits, cut into spears

2 small tart apples, coarsely chopped

½ cup chopped golden raisins

2 to 3 cloves, crushed

A few coriander seeds, crushed

4 to 5 kumquats, seeded, finely
chopped, if you can get them
(dried or preserved syrup kumquats
are available from Asian groceries;
a bit of chopped candied ginger and
1 teaspoon grated lemon peel could
substitute for the kumquats)

¼ cup dark rum

Put all ingredients except rum in heavy pan and cook over low heat until thickened and the whole house smells good. Stir in the rum. Cool before serving.

CHICKEN WITH TARRAGON

1 3-pound chicken, cut into serving
pieces

Salt and freshly ground black pepper

5 tablespoons unsalted butter

3 tablespoons finely chopped shallots

2 tablespoons finely chopped tarragon

½ cup dry white wine

1½ cups heavy cream

3 tablespoons flour

1 tablespoon Calvados or applejack

Sprinkle chicken pieces with salt and pepper. Melt 3 tablespoons butter over high heat and put in chicken, skin-side down. Cook until golden brown, then turn. Sprinkle with all the shallots and half the tarragon. Cover; cook on low heat for 15 minutes. Remove cover, sprinkle chicken with wine, recover, and cook 15 minutes longer. Remove chicken to hot dish and keep covered while preparing sauce.

Add 1 cup of cream to skillet; stir well. In a separate pan, melt the remaining 2 tablespoons butter and blend in the flour, then add the butter-flour mixture, a little at a time, to simmering cream. Add just enough to make the desired consistency. Cook 5 minutes, then stir in the Calvados or applejack and add remaining cream. Put chicken back into skillet, spooning sauce over meat. Sprinkle with remaining tarragon and serve at once on a hot platter.

Unsalted butter and olive oil for
    greasing pan and birds
8 quail, trussed with white cotton string
Salt
10 fresh green grapes to each quail

1 cup Madeira
1 bay leaf
Freshly ground black pepper
1 cup beef or chicken stock
2 tablespoons unsalted butter

Preheat oven to 450 degrees. Mix together enough butter and oil to grease roasting pan and lightly grease the birds. Sprinkle with a hint of salt. Cook 20 minutes in oven. Place birds on heated deep serving dish; arrange grapes around them.

Pour off grease from roasting pan and pour in Madeira, bay leaf, salt, and pepper; cook till reduced by about half, then put in stock and bring to boil. Remove from fire; add butter and, when that is melted, pour over birds. Heated French bread to sop up sauce, naturally.

Baby turnips or baby carrots or both are good alongside, as is cooked celery coarsely chopped, then boiled or sautéed. Sprinkle all with minced chives, parsley, and inner celery leaves. Serves 4.

DUCK BREASTS WITH GREEN PEPPERCORNS

Green peppercorns aren't in every grocery store in America, but most cities have somewhere a gourmet spice shelf where they sit. Or any of the fancy food catalogs list them. They are completely delightful and have many uses ordinary peppercorns do not. For instance, noodles dressed with cream and a good handful of green peppercorns are a showstopper. Any fish dish benefits from them.

4 duck breasts
2 tablespoons unsalted butter
2 tablespoons minced shallots
    or chives
2 tablespoons green peppercorns
1 cup cognac

1 cup dry white wine
2 cups duck broth or beef stock
1 cup heavy cream
Salt
Hint of grated lemon peel

Sauté duck breasts until pink, remove from pan, pour off fat, and keep warm. Add butter to pan, then add shallots and peppercorns. When all is heated, pour in cognac and set aflame. Simmer to reduce sauce. Add wine; simmer again. Put in broth or stock, cook until reduced by two-thirds, and then add cream. Taste for seasoning; salt as needed, stingily. Heat sauce and pour over duck. Top with grated lemon peel.

For side dish: apple slices sautéed in butter, or celery puree, or peeled, diced, boiled baby turnip roots with butter, sprinkled with nutmeg.

BRAISED DUCK

2 tablespoons chopped bacon	Some chopped sage
2 tablespoons unsalted butter	Salt and freshly ground black pepper
1 large onion, chopped	Dash of powdered mace
2 carrots, chopped	2 cups duck broth or beef stock
1 white turnip, chopped	1 5-pound dressed duck
Grated peel of 1 orange	½ cup red wine
1 large bay leaf	1 piece fried bread per person
Several pinches of savory leaves	Sliced orange and parsley
(more fresh than if dried)	for garnish

Preheat oven to 350 degrees. Fry bacon with unsalted butter in heavy pan; sauté vegetables. Add grated orange peel, bay leaf, savory, sage, salt, pepper, and mace. Just cover all this with stock. Place trussed or skewered duck on this bed of vegetables, cover tightly, and simmer or bake in oven for 1 ½ hours. Add wine; cook for another 30 minutes. Cut duck into serving pieces. Skim fat off stock; thicken if you wish.

Serve duck on fried bread with sauce poured over. Garnish with orange slices and parsley. Some cooks recommend piercing the duck all over and hanging a couple of hours for fat to drip off before it is cooked. I think it is better to cook the bird in its fat, then skim it off. Fried grits is even, for some, better than the fried bread in this recipe.

Well, it's hunting season, and the turkey-trackers are already getting impatient. The Gulf States have always had a plentitude of the birds and a taste for their flesh. There was such a traffic jam of turkeys on our coast that the French settlers called one of their first villages Coq d'Inde ("Indian Cock"). The name was transliterated by the English into "Coden." The bird was a major staple of our diet in our early days here, whether for wandering hunters and trappers or for settled households.

The turkey originated in Mexico but has been widespread in the southern states since, probably, prehistory. The Spanish found it tasty as prepared by the Aztecs and introduced it into Spain. Of course, the bird that Cortez's men ate came from generations of domesticated fowl. It was probably wild birds that were introduced into France.

Charles Estienne wrote in 1564: "The flesh is delicate, but tasteless and hard to digest. That is why it has to be highly spiced, heavily larded, and seasoned. These birds eat as much as mules."

Well, those wild American turkeys were big; European mules were smaller then. A mature wild turkey cock easily reaches sixty pounds. For years, poulterers have bred for smaller birds.

All wild turkeys are a little tough, cocks more than hens, and the cocks often have scar tissue in the breast meat from spur wounds sustained in the usual macho battles. Experienced wild turkey cooks in the Deep South often use a hypodermic needle filled with vegetable oil, or oil with a little light dry wine, either red or white, to inject the breasts and thighs before cooking. An early English visitor reported watching Indians in mid-Alabama larding the birds heavily with bear grease, then coating them with crushed pecan meats before roasting a long time over very hot embers of a campfire.

The turkey has long been a kind of symbol of the day of Thanksgiving. The Pilgrims celebrated what in England was called Harvest Home, in France La Fête de la Vendange — a kind of sigh-of-relief party when the crops were harvested and stored, the meats curing, the potables brewing, common to all countries and cultures since the late cave dwellers started growing wild grasses. But the records exist in Massachusetts: They had four big turkeys for that first Thanksgiving and a very great deal of ale, which came as ballast on the Mayflower. That was 1621. George Washington proclaimed the first national Thanksgiving on November 26, 1789. Lincoln followed up in 1863, choosing the last Thursday of November.

Only in 1939 was the event duly entered into the list of official holidays, under Roosevelt. But confusion about the differences of dates chosen by different states made Congress pass a resolution in 1941 setting the fourth Thursday of November once and for all our official national holiday.

All right, the bird is official for Thanksgiving. But one of the more interesting developments in our culinary history is how the bird has gradually taken over our Christmas table as well. Early English settlers yearned for the traditional English Christmas dinner of roast beef or roast goose or both. The French have always served an assorted profusion of birds, beef, mutton, etc. Venison and suckling pig everywhere. In Italy, those famous eels at dinner after Midnight Mass on Christmas Eve; roast lamb or goat in Sicily and Greece. Thousands, not hundreds, of provincial variations.

If we can believe menus, family records, and newspaper accounts, the Old South did serve turkey, but it was "everyday" and not a "special" dish for Christmas. Roast haunch of venison appears in the sources as a Christmas dish; guinea hen occurs more often than not. But a great roast beef and a great baked ham as twin attractions are mentioned often.

Personally, I'd like a return to turkey for Thanksgiving and something else at Christmas. Or ham, guinea hens, or ducks for Thanksgiving and turkey for Christmas. My idea of a New Age Christmas or Thanksgiving dinner would be baked ham WITHOUT pineapple and cloves, corned beef, and a French liver pâté accompanied by a raisin pie, onion chutney, plain boiled white hominy, plain boiled wild rice, a huge salad bowl of watercress and inner celery leaves dressed with horseradish and buttermilk, and ginger ice cream for dessert. Finish with real cognac. Stretcher service by prearrangement.

Many people find turkey boring, less interesting, than good ham or roast beef. Why? Perhaps because the bird has not been properly treated.

If the turkey has been frozen, it must be thoroughly thawed, I say again, thoroughly thawed and, a third time, thoroughly thawed before being dealt with. We all know too well those beautiful, browned turkeys that make the saliva flow by their appearance but turn out to be flavorless cardboard and too pink around the joints.

Twenty-four hours for every five pounds of bird is about right to defrost a turkey. Soak a dishtowel in wine, drape the bird, and place in a pan in the refrigerator to thaw. Then scald the bird, dry it well, rub well with lemon halves and then with frayed garlic, and then slather it well with unsalted butter or bacon grease and sprinkle with finely chopped rosemary, thyme, sage, what you wish, and freshly ground black pepper. DO NOT SALT!

Every experienced cook has his or her own lore about oven heat, how long to cook, and I shall not presume to advise on these matters, since stoves differ, differences between gas and electric are enormous, etc., and all good cooks are temperamental.

But this is how I do it, and people who've been cool toward turkey in the past have enjoyed the bird:

Preheat the oven to 450 degrees. After preparing the bird as above, place it on its side in a roasting pan and tent with aluminum foil. After twenty minutes, baste and, using oven mitts, turn the bird on its other side. After twenty minutes more, turn breast side down, baste well, and cook twenty minutes longer. Then turn breast side up and place strips of lean bacon or fat cut from a ham over the breast and fasten with toothpicks. It takes about three and a half to three and three-quarters hours for a ten- to twelve-pound turkey, three and three-quarters to four hours for a bird of fourteen to eighteen pounds.

Heat should be lowered slightly in the last hour, and the bird should be basted constantly. You'll change your mind about the dryness and dullness of most turkey if you prepare it in this fashion.

Now I'll have certain cooks shouting, "Heresy!" Most really great cooks do not put any stuffing in the bird IF they plan to utilize the remains in the next days for the great stews, gumbos, salads, etc., that are based on the carcass. IF your family is going to finish off the bird the first day, by all means stuff. But, Oh, Heavens, scraping out the nasty bits of stuffing if you want to use the carcass is a problem. If, as many great southern cooks, you include bell pepper, sweet or hot, in your stuffing, you'll find it ferments the next day and ruins everything.

No, I say, make two or even three grand stuffings and cook then in casseroles or baking tins. You might boil up neck and giblets with a bit of onion, naturally, then chop them fine; moisten stale bread with the broth; and add salt, freshly grated black pepper, a little grated lemon peel, a few white raisins (currants) soaked in very dry Sherry or in bourbon whiskey, and a beaten egg for binding; and that's Very Good.

I assume you will put carrots, celery stalks, whole onions studded with a few cloves, and maybe some unpeeled turnip roots into the cavity of the bird in place of stuffing. Save them for next day's grand turkey soup, of course.

Here's another dressing: Fry bacon crisp; brown onions and mushrooms. When bacon is cooked, add to crumbled cornbread soaked in broth or in tomato juice; season as you will. Add a beaten egg and salt and pepper, then bake.

Or use equal parts of stale bread soaked in broth and white hominy or uncreamed corn kernels, combined with a lot of sliced cooked Conecuh County sausage, a dash of cream, and a beaten egg, with lots of fresh sage and black pepper.

Or mix cooked grits with chopped boiled celery and green onions with some of their juice, grated rat-trap cheese (sharp American Cheddar), salt, freshly ground black pepper, thyme, and savory.

Or boil some new potatoes, but don't let them get mushy. Peel them, chop them coarsely, and then chop the peels fine along with a toe or so of garlic. Add chopped inner celery leaves, freshly ground black pepper, a dash of paprika, and a half cup of cream beaten with an egg, then bake in buttered dish.

Everybody knows what to do with the leftover turkey and the carcass. Leftover stuffing? Take some smaller eggplants. Moisten the stuffing with broth and mix with chopped eggplant flesh (raw or parboiled) and grated onion. Stuff eggplant halves, top with grated cheese or buttered crumbs, and bake.

So you see . . . there is a way to get to those souls who've had it with the usual turkey dinner. I know an audacious lady in Demopolis who roasts her turkey the day before Christmas and on Christmas evening enchants her relations and friends with turkey gumbo, creamed turkey stew, salad of white meat, salad of dark meat, and a cold pâté made of giblets. But then Demopolis starts with *D* . . . just like Different.

If you scrape up all the pan drippings and add a little more wine, some mild onions cooked until golden, and freshly ground black pepper and salt to taste (almost none), then reduce this, you'll have a far better gravy than any with flour added, believe me.

THE DAY AFTER THANKSGIVING: COLD TURKEY PÂTÉ

Not all southern tables feature turkey hash or turkey gumbo on the day after Thanksgiving. The following, a kind of cold molded pâté, is mighty fine with small hot biscuits or flat yellow cornmeal hearth bread.

This cold pâté, following a first course of hot borscht or potato soup, makes a nice lunch the day after Thanksgiving.

½ cup finely chopped walnuts

½ cup finely chopped pecans

3 ounces rat-trap cheese, cut into small cubes

½ pound turkey meat (dark preferable), cut into thumbnail-size bits

2 strips lean, crisp-fried bacon, chopped very fine

⅓ cup finely chopped green onions or chives

¾ cup mayonnaise

Freshly ground black pepper

As you like: 2 fresh sage leaves, chopped; fresh marjoram; dash of celery seeds

Minced peel of ½ lemon

1½ teaspoons Dijon or Creole mustard

1½ tablespoons dry Sherry

Pinch of salt

Be sure everything is chopped fine. Mix well. If you need more mayonnaise, add it. Taste for salt. Spoon mixture into bowl, crock, or pan of your choice, which has been lightly oiled with olive oil. Chill at least 8 hours or overnight. Turn out on serving dish, surround with olives, gherkins, deviled or devilish eggs, watercress, or parsley. Raw carrot sticks are nice; so are cherry tomatoes cut in half and topped with caper juice and chopped capers.

TURKEY CASINO

This is a famous day-after-Thanksgiving or day-after-Christmas dish that lots of folks like much better than the big, dreary carcass on the holiday table.

½ cup chopped onion

½ cup chopped green pepper

2 tablespoons unsalted butter

¼ cup flour

1 cup milk

1 cup chicken broth

2½ tablespoons dry Sherry or Rhine wine

1 2-ounce can mushrooms, drained and sliced, about ⅓ cup

2 cups leftover turkey or chicken, diced

¼ cup pimientos, diced

2 hard-boiled eggs, sliced

Plenty of hot cooked rice

Cook onions and green pepper in butter till tender. Blend in flour. Add milk, broth, and wine. Cook till thick, stirring constantly. Add mushrooms, turkey or chicken, and pimientos. Season to taste. Heat thoroughly. Fold in sliced eggs. Serve over fluffy rice. Serves 4 to 6.

That's the basic combination. The dish can be made with leftover ham, roast pork, roast beef, etc. Some add black olives; some like a few chopped capers or a handful of dried tarragon leaves. Any version is good over thin spaghetti or boiled barley. Invent! Improvise! Have fun! Why not have Golden Rice? Boil up your rice with a generous tablespoon or so of turmeric (curcuma), the mild-flavored powder that colors food a nice golden yellow.

Fish, Shellfish, and Sauces

Steamed Fish Fillets with Three Sauces • Not Quite Tartar Sauce •
Olive Sauce • Celery Sauce • Radish Sauce • Fish with Rhubarb Sauce •
Asparagus Sauce • Tuna Casserole • Tuna Timbales • Quick Fish, Greek
Style • Trout à la Coden • Fish River Meurette • Seafood Marinade •
Pascagoula Marinade • Chef Bertrand's Scallop Tart • Dr. Willoughby's
Crab Kebabs • Sauce for Crab Balls or Baked Crabs • Crab Rarebit •
Mme. Robert's Lobster in Sauce • Mixed Garden Grill • Friday Crust with
Dill Sauce • Carib Shrimp • Pensacola Shrimp • Pickled Shrimp • Dip for
Boiled Shrimp • French-Fried Shrimp • The Huger Sisters' Famous Shrimp
Dish • Curried Shrimp with Lemon Rice • Shrimp Américaine • Fried
Oysters • Beer Batter • Oysters Casino • Oysters Tetrazzini • Oysters
Leontyne • Oysters Roffignac • Oysters Rockefeller • Baked Oysters •
Corn Oysters • Oysters in Champagne

Who & Where Is Sauce Tartare?

Nothing is more engrossing and amusing than tracing recipes from century to century, country to country. The manner in which dishes make their way around the world, changing names and ingredients, is just as fascinating as the voyages of languages or folk tales. We on the Gulf Coast, especially, can feel some of the immense mysteries of these processes, what with our French, Spanish, English, African, and Indian meetings and minglings spiced with Greek, Jewish, and Bavarian elements.

The other night I ate dinner in a well-known restaurant: pleasant ambience, smooth service, fresh seafood nicely prepared, fresh salad, a light dessert. But what was that grayish mush served me alongside the fish? A loathsome, sweetish mush that had the audacity to call itself Sauce Tartare! It wasn't! It never was! It isn't! The incident started me thinking of the variants of the sauce I've eaten in southern homes and in eateries around the world.

I went to the bookshelves and pulled out the *Larousse Gastronomique*. It was nothing if not laconic and rather surprised me. Under Sauce Tartare, I read: "Mayonnaise made with hard-boiled egg yolks and with chopped chives added." And left it at that.

The stalwart Mrs. Beeton (in *Mrs. Beeton's Book of Household Management*, first edition) gives the following: "One half pint of Mayonnaise, 1 tablespoon chopped gherkins or capers, a teaspoon of very finely chopped shallot (this may be omitted). Stir the gherkin (or capers) and onion lightly into the mayonnaise and use as required. Time. 25 minutes altogether." Quantity: about half a pint.

Backtracking a bit, I consulted the esteemed Jules Gouffé's *Le Livre de Cuisine* (1867). For him, Sauce Tartare begins with a one-egg mayonnaise into which the following ingredients are mixed: one teaspoon of powdered English mustard; two tablespoons finely chopped shallots; two tablespoons finely chopped cornichons; a little chopped chervil and tarragon and a little watercress or rocket; and one teaspoon of pepper vinegar or else a pinch of cayenne pepper.

Upon reading Gouffé, I was reminded of a memorable dinner in Paris. An English publisher invited me to the famous restaurant Le Grand Vefour, and after dinner, since he was a publisher of cookbooks, he insisted on our visiting the kitchen and meeting the cooks, as temperamental as any opera troupe. A few days later, I spotted one of the sous-chefs at the Les Halles market. I greeted him and asked about the tartare I'd particularly enjoyed.

"No two cooks make tartare alike," he smiled. "We have some violent disagreements. Most of the younger chefs are like me; they want some kren [horseradish] in the sauce, the older ones want mustard. Everybody agrees on cornichons and capers, a little onion juice or chives or shallots, lemon of course. But everybody makes it differently." I murmured, "Vive la France!" under my breath. Consistency is one of the virtues of the great restaurants, but Sauce Tartare is obviously a safety valve for individual talent.

In the summer of 1952, I dined at a waterfront café-restaurant at Collioure on the Côte Vermeille (that stretch of French Mediterranean coast that runs north and south just above Spain and becomes Azur when it bends eastward toward Nice). I had a wonderful salad of cold sliced chicken and watercress served with a sauce designated as tartare, which was a fresh mayonnaise made with lemon and orange juice, capers, minced onion, tarragon, and grated lemon AND orange peel. Delightful!

Later, at a seafood restaurant in Marseille, in the old Port section, I complimented the ample, smiling lady in black who had served me, referring to the broiled fresh fish with a little pressed glass of sauce alongside. "Your Sauce Tartare was especially good," I said. She made a mock-theatrical frown and tossed her head. "That's what they call it in Paris. We've been serving it since before Jesus Christ and we've always called it Sauce Rémoulade."

Remembering that Marseille had been a Phoenician and later Hellenic port before the Christian epoch, I realized that she was neither blasphemous nor frivolous. But I pondered. Indeed, both tartare and rémoulade exist around the Gulf of Mexico, but the difference is that often, not always, the rémoulade has either tomato or annatto waste in it. Or ketchup. Or finely chopped, very ripe tomatoes.

Never relinquishing my quest for Sauce Tartare, I ate at a quayside eatery on the island of Skopelas in the northern Sporades islands of Greece a wonderful version made of the good Greek yogurt (thicker and creamier) to which had been added lemon juice, chopped parsley, chopped pickles, a very few chopped wild thyme leaves, and a dash of horse mint! Alongside fresh fish roasted over coals, this was a real treat.

But the story doesn't end there! In Denmark, there is a Sauce Tartare consisting of mayonnaise to which is added chopped gherkins, sweet onion, parsley, lots of dill, chopped baby shrimp, lots of lemon, and . . . a dash of aquavit! Talk about good.

I have, in my archives, a battered Mobile law office envelope from sometime in the 1920s, on the back of which is penciled in a big unsteady hand: "TAR. — use grapefruit j. in the mayon., be sure the cornichs. are real — some of their juice — don't forget watercr. and celery leaves — 2 drops of Tabasco essential."

The "real" cornichons means imported French, of course, with their highly original sweet-tart liquid, rather than American gherkins, which have their own attractions.

Now allow me a parenthesis. In the Deep South, there is a form of humor totally misapprehended by outsiders. It is an intentional deformation of words or phrases, the solemn (comic) pretense that one has heard quite other than what has actually been said. It's a highly sophisticated African jokiness, of East African origins, and still going strong in the South.

For instance, in this tradition, words are turned backwards ("peckerwood" instead of "woodpecker") or totally transformed ("whiskbroom" becomes "wishbomb"), but the best example is the metamorphosis of "cush patties" into "hush puppies." "Cush" is an African word for cornmeal mush. Rather solid dumplings of cush deep-fried alongside fish fillets have always been served with catfish, bream, etc. The only reason I go into this is to explain certain sauces handed down, by oral tradition, which are known as "tatty sauce," "tarry sauce," or "roomy lard sauce."

And so it goes. If I live long enough to complete my researches, I'll write a thick volume called the "Kama Tartara" or the "Rémoulade Sutra" to set out all the traditions and possibilities. And I'll never forget the sweet little old southern lady who explained that no matter what version of these sauces you are preparing, one must sprinkle a few grains of salt in the mixing bowl and rub it with a toe of "fresh, frayed [not fermented] garlic," as she explained, adding that if the sauce were to be successful and memorable, one must have a "nostalgia of garlic." But there should not be a "presence of garlic" in any sauce having the slightest pretention of being either tartare or rémoulade.

STEAMED FISH FILLETS WITH THREE SAUCES

4 striped bass or 6 to 8 bream
(pronounced "brim" in the South)

2 cups water

1 cup dry white wine

2 to 3 small leeks

2 to 3 carrots

2 to 3 celery stalks

Good handful parsley and whatever
of these you can find: tarragon,
chives, chervil

Salt and freshly ground black or
white pepper

Spinach or lettuce leaves to wrap
fish fillets

½ cup heavy cream

¼ stick unsalted butter

Dijon or Creole mustard

Make a stock of fish heads and bones in water, wine, leeks, carrots, celery, and bit of parsley, chopped coarsely. Boil for 25 minutes. Meanwhile, chop tarragon and some parsley together. Strain the stock and put in bottom part of steamer. Season the fillets with a little salt, freshly ground black or white pepper, and the chopped herbs. Wrap each fillet neatly in spinach or lettuce leaves; butter the steamer basket and place wrapped fish in it. Bring liquid to a boil; put basket of fish on top, cover tightly, and steam about 7 to 8 minutes.

For the sauces, take half of fish broth and boil, reducing to about 5 tablespoons. Mix in saucepan with ½ cup heavy cream and 2 tablespoons butter. Place over low flame and whisk so it doesn't boil or burn.

Sauce One: Add 2 tablespoons chopped fresh herbs to half of sauce.

Sauce Two: Add 1½ teaspoons Dijon or Creole mustard to other half.

Sauce Three, known as Not Quite Tartar Sauce (recipe follows).

NOT QUITE TARTAR SAUCE

1 cup yogurt

1 teaspoon minced garlic

2 tablespoons minced mild red onion

1½ tablespoons minced capers

1 cornichon (gherkin), minced

1 tablespoon lemon juice

1 tablespoon best gin

Good dash of fresh or dried dill

Put yogurt in bowl; mix in all else. Chill.

This Not Quite Tartar Sauce has many variations. Sometimes one chops kosher dill pickle fine to add, or celery hearts with the leaves, or a bit of grated lemon peel. For a summer luncheon, nothing is better than tomato aspic or jelled consommé with a hint of lemon juice, for first course, and for second, one of these:

- Small new potatoes, well-scrubbed, boiled in their skins, cut in half, and placed in middle of dinner plate with a generous glop of sauce on top with lettuce leaves, stoned black olives, and radishes around.
- Boiled egg whites filled with boiled yolks mixed with Underwood Deviled Ham and a glop of cream, served on a plate with celery sticks and a generous glop of sauce.
- Plain boiled shrimp done in water with bay leaves, 2 to 3 juniper berries, and lemon slices piled on chilled romaine lettuce leaves, topped with a big glop of sauce.
- Cold boiled chicken cut in ribbons and mixed with sauce, plain sliced ripe tomatoes alongside.

OLIVE SAUCE

This was often served to accompany fish, veal, or chicken.

1 cup coarsely chopped sweet California black olives	Pinch of dried dill
1 lemon, juiced	Good pinch of celery seeds
8 to 10 capers, chopped	1 teaspoon best olive oil
	To your taste: a few chopped chives

Drain olives and sprinkle with some of the lemon juice. Mix all ingredients well and chill.

Note: A "secret ingredient" that can be, and often is, added to this sauce and to the following two fresh sauces consists of a splash of gin, vodka, or aquavit.

CELERY SAUCE

Celery Sauce and Radish Sauce (recipe follows) are forgotten garnishes for seafood dishes.

1 ½ cups chopped celery hearts (the inner small stalks with all their young yellow leaves)	½ cup chopped chives or shallots
	Dash of lemon juice
	Dash of Tabasco
¾ cup sour cream or yogurt	Salt and freshly ground pepper

Toss celery into boiling salted water for 3 minutes. Mix with other ingredients, season with salt and pepper, and chill.

RADISH SAUCE

1 ½ cups fresh young radishes, sliced thin	2 tablespoons chopped kosher dill pickles
1 teaspoon grated lemon peel	Dash of mild paprika
¾ cup mayonnaise	Salt and freshly ground pepper to taste

Toss radish slices and lemon peel into boiling salted water for 3 to 4 minutes. Drain well. Mix with other ingredients; chill.

FISH WITH RHUBARB SAUCE

2 cups rhubarb, cut in small pieces

½ cup tomato sauce

3 tablespoons virgin olive oil

2 teaspoons sugar

½ cup water

Splash of sweet white port

Salt

1 pound any firm-fleshed fish,
    salmon for instance

Wash rhubarb well. Peel off tough skin, if such there is. Cook everything except the fish about 10 minutes over medium heat. Reduce heat to simmer and continue cooking for 20 minutes. When rhubarb is done, add fish cut into small pieces and simmer until fish is just done. 4 servings.

ASPARAGUS SAUCE

Here's a "School of Monticello" creamy concoction that made its way from Virginia to Mobile. It's a sauce to serve with grilled or sautéed fish, in recent years much appreciated with catfish fillets.

1 ½ tablespoons unsalted butter

1 tablespoon best olive oil

2 tablespoons chopped green onion

½ cup dry white wine (Rhine seems
    preferable to most tastes)

1 cup chicken stock

Seasoning as you will: salt, freshly
    ground white pepper (black is
    second choice), dash of celery
    seeds, dash of dried dill

1 cup chopped cooked asparagus

2 ½ tablespoons cream

Paprika

Chopped parsley

Melt butter and oil in saucepan. Cook green onion, stirring, until just softened, less than a minute. Add wine, stock, flavorings, and asparagus. Bring to simmer. Add cream and cook 5 minutes, stirring occasionally. Whisk this well, taste for salt, and serve or blend thoroughly in food processor and reheat.

Serve alongside grilled, poached, or sautéed fish or over fish with a pinch of paprika and chopped parsley. Some like to garnish with 4 to 5 capers.

TUNA CASSEROLE

This is a well-known fishing camp dish, for when the fishermen don't catch enough or don't catch anything. Naturally, every fishing camp has dry vermouth for those martini cocktails when the sun goes down.

1 pound fettuccine noodles	1 tablespoon dry vermouth
1 can Mr. Campbell's cream of mushroom soup	Salt and freshly ground black pepper
	1 small packet potato chips
1 5-ounce can white tuna	Butter

Preheat oven to 350 degrees. Cook noodles in salted water till al dente: just right, not mushy. Mix noodles, soup, tuna, vermouth, salt, and pepper; put mixture into buttered casserole. Top with crushed chips and a few dabs of butter; cook in oven till it starts to bubble.

TUNA TIMBALES

Most of the new food snobs in the United States sniff and sneer at canned goods, but the South, remembering days before the refrigerator and the constant occurrence of unexpected guests, knows the value, indeed necessity, of a well-stocked store of canned goods. Personally, I'll never forget what I saw in the storeroom of a VERY fancy New York restaurant when I pretended to lose my way en route to the men's room. Opening a door in the corridor, I found shelf after shelf of quart tins of Mr. Campbell's various cream soups.

2 6 ½-ounce cans white chunk tuna	2 10 ½-ounce cans Mr. Campbell's cream of mushroom soup
4 tablespoons finely chopped onion	
4 tablespoons finely chopped green pepper	½ cup dry white wine
7 cups hot cooked rice	1 cup grated cheese, rat-trap, American Swiss, or Fontina,
Pinch of dried dill	as you think
Salt and freshly ground pepper (white, if possible)	Parsley
	Inner celery leaves
Dash of Tabasco or prepared horseradish	Mild paprika

Preheat oven to 350 degrees. Break the tuna into small pieces, then mix with onion, pepper, hot rice, and flavorings. Rinse out a mustard cup or individual ramekin and pack it full of the tuna mix. Unmold at once on baking sheet or shallow baking tin. Mix the mushroom soup and dry white wine and pour over the timbales. Sprinkle cheese over all.

Bake in oven for 30 minutes. Before taking to table, sprinkle with chopped parsley, chopped inner celery leaves, and mild paprika, or any combination of these three.

QUICK FISH, GREEK STYLE

4 ripe medium tomatoes	15 or more Greek olives, drained
2 tablespoons fresh marjoram or	2 bay leaves, torn in half
2 teaspoons dried	Salt and freshly ground black pepper
1 cup dry white wine	8 to 12 fish fillets

Chop tomatoes and marjoram (if fresh); put these with wine, olives (stoned and quartered), bay leaves, and seasonings in skillet. Heat well, then put in fish fillets. Cover and cook over medium heat 6 to 8 minutes, until fish loses its transparent look. Don't overcook! Serves 4.

Boiled pearl barley or rice is good alongside this, with sauce.

TROUT À LA CODEN

4 trout	½ cup dry white wine
3 anchovy fillets	Salt and freshly ground black pepper
Milk	2 tablespoons chopped parsley
1 cup sweet green olives	1 crushed garlic clove
1 tablespoon chopped capers or	Dash of savory (*sariette*) or thyme
green nasturtium seeds	1 lemon
½ cup olive oil	

Preheat oven to 375 degrees. Wash and prepare trout. Anchovies should soak in milk before using. Chop olives, capers, and anchovies. In the dish in which you will serve fish at table, heat olive oil, put in capers and anchovies, and sauté lightly, smashing the anchovies to bits with a wooden spoon. Add olives; simmer 1 minute. Arrange fish on top of all this and cook in oven for about half an hour, basting from time to time with wine. When wine has cooked away, salt and pepper fish. Mix parsley with garlic, and 5 minutes before fish is done, sprinkle over fish with the savory. After you take fish from oven, sprinkle lemon juice over all and serve as is, in baking dish, hot from oven.

Sautéed celery, done in butter, is good with this, and a salad of fresh cucumbers with dill.

FISH RIVER MEURETTE

3 pounds cleaned freshwater fish
   (trout, perch, whatever)
1 bottle dry rose wine (Meier's from
   Ohio is great)
3 carrots
1 big onion
2 leeks
3 cloves garlic

Thyme
Bay leaf
Nutmeg
Salt and freshly ground black pepper
¼ cup brandy
¼ cup unsalted butter
Sliced French or Italian bread

Cut the fish into thick slices and arrange in casserole. Put wine, carrots, onion, leeks, garlic, thyme, bay leaf, nutmeg, and salt and pepper together in a separate pan and bring to boil; lower heat and simmer for 15 minutes. Strain this court bouillon and pour over fish, adding good brandy. Cover casserole; cook the stew over very low heat for 30 minutes. Then mix in butter little by little.

Have slices of toasted French or Italian bread. Rub these warm slices with garlic. Arrange toast in serving dish and pour your *meurette* over them. A well-chilled rose wine goes well, or you might prefer very dry white.

SEAFOOD MARINADE

A welcome change from our usual tomato-y Creole barbecue sauces is this mixture for big shrimp, crayfish, and lobster, and it's great for salmon.

⅓ cup soy sauce

⅓ cup light oil, such as safflower

⅓ cup Sherry

1 tablespoon minced mild onion

¼ teaspoon ground ginger

Pinch of mace

Several pinches of dill

Combine all ingredients and marinate the seafood about half an hour at room temperature. Salmon takes 2 to 3 hours. Broil or grill. A whole salmon should be turned on the spit. Delicious.

PASCAGOULA MARINADE

Shrimp or scallops are marinated in this mixture at room temperature for an hour, or beef, chicken, or pork is marinated overnight in fridge. All are basted with this marinade as they are grilled.

½ cup Dijon or Creole mustard

⅓ cup best bourbon

Dash of soy sauce

½ cup firmly packed brown sugar

2 teaspoons Worcestershire sauce

⅓ cup minced scallions

Mix all well and marinate as indicated above.

CHEF BERTRAND'S SCALLOP TART

1½ pounds scallops, cut in half

3 tablespoons French dry white
    vermouth

3 tablespoons chopped parsley

¼ teaspoon dried thyme

½ teaspoon chopped shallots

Salt and freshly ground pepper to taste

Pinch of dried dill

Pastry for 1 single-crust 9-inch pie

4 lightly beaten eggs

1 cup heavy cream

Preheat oven to 450 degrees. Sprinkle scallops with vermouth, parsley, thyme, shallots, salt and pepper, and dill. Line pie pan with pastry and fill with scallop mixture. Whisk eggs and cream together and pour over scallops. Bake for 10 minutes; lower heat to 350 and bake 30 minutes more. Serves 6.

This can also be made with clams or any delicate white fish. A good accompaniment is a small portion of a salad made of chopped boiled egg, chopped inner celery stalks, and leaves of celery dressed with chopped capers and their juice, lemon juice, and best virgin olive oil. Or shredded romaine lettuce with capers, mild black olives, and chives, dressed in the same fashion, adding some grated lemon peel.

DR. WILLOUGHBY'S CRAB KEBABS

1 pound crab meat, picked over and
   shredded
1 teaspoon salt
1 teaspoon Dijon or Creole mustard
1 heaping teaspoon chopped chives

1 cup white bread crumbs
Splash of pale dry Sherry
Pinch of turmeric or mace
Sliced bacon

Preheat oven broiler. Mix crab meat, salt, mustard, chives, bread crumbs, Sherry, and turmeric (even a very slight hint of curry powder, if you're so inclined, but I do mean hint, not statement) or mace. Mix all well and form into little balls about walnut-size. Wrap a strip of bacon around each one; secure with toothpick. Broil the nubs for 15 to 20 minutes, turning once, to point that bacon is nicely browned. Serve with it either hollandaise sauce sexed up with finely chopped chives or Sauce for Crab Balls or Baked Crabs (recipe follows).

SAUCE FOR CRAB BALLS OR BAKED CRABS

1 cup plain yogurt
2 tablespoons Philadelphia
   Cream Cheese
8 capers, chopped
½ cup chopped inner heart
   celery leaves
Chopped parsley

Sprinkle of dill
1 tablespoon dry white wine or
   dry Sherry
Dash of Tabasco
Salt and freshly ground black pepper,
   to taste
Milk or cream

Mix yogurt, cream cheese, capers, celery leaves, parsley, dill, dry white wine or dry Sherry, Tabasco, and salt and freshly ground black pepper to taste. Thin with milk or cream if sauce is too stiff.

CRAB RAREBIT

2 tablespoons unsalted butter

½ tablespoon chopped onion

2 tablespoons chopped green pepper

2 tablespoons flour

1 teaspoon salt

⅛ teaspoon cayenne pepper

1 teaspoon Dijon mustard

1 cup tomato juice

1½ cups grated sharp cheese

1 well-beaten egg

½ cup cream

1 cup cooked, flaked crab meat

Pinch of mace, if you like; I do

Splash of Sherry

Melt butter; add onion and pepper and sauté until lightly browned. Mix flour, salt, and cayenne pepper; add to mixture. Stir, then add mustard and tomato juice. Simmer slowly, stirring constantly, until smooth and thickened. Add cheese; stir very well. Stir in egg. Simmer 3 minutes, stirring constantly. Remove from heat; add cream and crab meat. Mix well; heat through. Mix in mace and pale, dry Sherry. Heat a second longer, then serve at once over buttered toast. This is a grand main dish for a luncheon.

MME. ROBERT'S LOBSTER IN SAUCE

3 tablespoons unsalted butter

3 tablespoons flour

1¼ cups dry white wine
   (Sauterne or Rhine)

1¼ cups heavy cream

3 egg yolks

1 teaspoon each chopped parsley,
   chervil, and tarragon (if using dried,
   slightly less)

Salt and freshly ground black pepper

1 pound cooked lobster meat or
   crab meat

Unmolded rice ring

Parsley for garnish

Melt butter, then remove pan from fire, stir in flour well, and mix in wine, then cream. Cook this mixture over low flame, stirring constantly until smooth and slightly thickened, about 10 minutes. Stir in lightly beaten egg yolks to which a little of the sauce has been added to temper the eggs. Be CERTAIN sauce does not boil after yolks are added. Stir in seasoning, taste for salt, then gently stir in lobster; heat thoroughly. Serve in a rice ring with parsley for garnish. Dry white wine alongside.

MIXED GARDEN GRILL

Fish fillets, fresh or thawed	Basil
Lemon juice	Chives
White wine	Parsley
Tomatoes	Marjoram
Mild onions	Lovage
Zucchini	Inner celery leaves
Mushrooms	Capers
Bell peppers	Olive oil or unsalted butter
Cucumbers	Salt and freshly ground black
Dill	pepper

Get a charcoal fire going ahead of time so you have nice, burned-down coals. Use fresh or thawed fish fillets, cut into hunks, with a little lemon juice and/or white wine sprinkled over them. Cut tomatoes, mild onions, zucchini, mushrooms, bell peppers, and cucumbers (yes, cucumbers!) into wedges or chunks and sprinkle fresh herbs over them: dill, basil, chives, parsley, marjoram, lovage, and inner celery leaves plus a few chopped capers. Put a few drops of pure olive oil or dabs of unsalted butter over, plus a bit of salt and a little freshly ground black pepper. Put everything on a great big sheet of heavy aluminum foil and fold up to seal top and sides. Put over fire for a few minutes until fish is done. Easy! Good!

FRIDAY CRUST WITH DILL SAUCE

½ pound butter	1 tablespoon chopped capers
2 cups flour	4 hard-boiled eggs, chopped
½ teaspoon salt	1 teaspoon grated lemon peel
3 ⅔ cups plain yogurt	2 tablespoons dry white wine
1 big can (15 to 16 ounces)	Salt and freshly ground pepper
best pink salmon	1 lightly beaten egg
5 tablespoons dried dill	⅓ cup mayonnaise
1 tablespoon chopped parsley	1 tablespoon lemon juice
1 onion, minced	1 tablespoon dry vermouth
2 celery stalks, chopped	

Cut butter into flour and salt, little bits at a time. Add ½ cup yogurt and mix well. Divide dough into 2 parts, wrap, and refrigerate an hour.

Preheat oven to 425 degrees. Mix salmon, ⅔ cup yogurt, 2 tablespoons dill, parsley, onion, celery, capers, hard-boiled eggs, lemon peel, wine, salt, and pepper.

Roll out dough into 2 4 × 12-inch rectangles. Place 1 rectangle of dough on a cookie sheet and spread salmon mix over it evenly, then place other rectangle on top and press edges together. Brush with beaten egg and bake in oven for 10 minutes. Lower heat to 350 degrees and cook 30 to 40 minutes longer.

A highly interesting variation of this recipe would use fresh nasturtium flower buds or green nasturtium seeds in place of capers.

For the sauce, mix together 2 ½ cups plain yogurt, 3 tablespoons dried dill, mayonnaise, lemon juice, and dry vermouth. Chill. Slice the salmon crust and serve with sauce.

CARIB SHRIMP

45 small to medium shrimp or	Salt and freshly ground black pepper
30 big shrimp, head on	1 ½ tablespoons corn or peanut oil
2 cups fish stock	2 heads iceberg lettuce
2 to 3 green onions or 1 leek, white	Lemon
part only, finely chopped	8 tablespoons lumpfish caviar,
½ cup dry white wine	half red, half black if possible
2 tablespoons dry vermouth	Inner celery leaves
Dried dill	Parsley
1 cup heavy cream	

Clean the shrimp, saving heads, tails, and shells. In big pot, put fish stock, shells, onions or leek, wine, vermouth, and a dash of dried dill and bring to boil; cook 8 to 10 minutes. Strain well into small pot. Reduce by half, then add cream, salt, and freshly ground black pepper to taste. Cover and keep over low heat.

In another big pot, heat oil and cook hearts of lettuce, sliced thin, 5 to 6 minutes until tender; season with salt and pepper. Cook shrimp 1 to 2 minutes (3 for big shrimp) in boiling salted water, drain, and dribble with lemon juice if you like.

Divide the sauce among 4 plates, pile lettuce on top, and arrange shrimp around. Put caviar on lettuce in center, dribble with lemon juice, and sprinkle chopped celery leaves and chopped parsley over all. Fingers of pumpernickel bread very good with this.

PENSACOLA SHRIMP

1 ½ pounds medium-sized
    head-on shrimp
2 bay leaves
1 lemon peel
Dash of salt and freshly ground
    pepper
Dash of dried dill
2 ½ sticks unsalted butter
12 green onions, chopped

15 garlic toes, minced
2 cups best dry white wine
    (a Rhine wine is good)
6 tablespoons fresh lemon juice
Pinch of dry mustard
2 cups minced parsley and inner
    celery leaves
Lemon slices, quartered
1 28-ounce can hominy

Boil the shrimp about 4 to 5 minutes (according to size) in water with bay leaves, lemon peel, salt, pepper, and dried dill. The instant they start looking pink, remove from fire and add cold water to pan to prevent further cooking. Let shrimp cool in this water, then behead and peel.

Melt butter in heavy big skillet over medium to low heat. Add onion and garlic and sauté 3 minutes. Add white wine and simmer 15 minutes, then add lemon juice and mustard. Simmer over low another 15 minutes, then add half of parsley-celery leaf mixture. Stir till greens are wilted, then add shrimp and heat 5 minutes. Serve as you would a gumbo, in low bowls in which you've placed a scant cup of buttered white hominy with a lemon quarter on the side. Sprinkle rest of greens over the top and, if you feel, some crisp, crumbled bacon.

Note: Cooked this way, the garlic is barely noticeable. But you'll note afterward a great relief for sinus problems, cleansed nasal passages, general euphoria.

PICKLED SHRIMP

This is a wonderful hot weather luncheon dish, nice after jellied consommé and before cold lemon pie.

1 pound shrimp	Dried dill
1 cup white wine	Celery seeds
1 whole lemon, finely chopped,	¼ cup virgin olive oil
with juice	Romaine lettuce
Crushed garlic	Lemon juice
Chopped parsley	1 cup sour cream
Chopped capers	2 tablespoons horseradish
Chopped dill pickle (kosher's best)	Splash of gin
Chopped chives or shallots	Mild paprika
Pinch of salt	

Cook shrimp but don't overcook. Peel and put aside. Mix wine, lemon, garlic, parsley, capers, dill pickle, chives, salt, dried dill, and celery seeds together in a pot. Bring this marinade just to boiling point; simmer 5 minutes or so. Put in shrimp; simmer 1 minute. Take from heat and mix in olive oil. Put into jars with lids and chill a day or so, shaking jars now and then.

To serve: Tear up chilled romaine lettuce (don't cut!), arrange on plate with heap of shrimp on top, and sprinkle all with lemon juice. Mix together sour cream, prepared horseradish, and a good splash of best gin and put nice glop over shrimp and lettuce. Top with mild paprika.

Small hot biscuits or whole-wheat crackers good alongside.

DIP FOR BOILED SHRIMP

1 cup sour cream	Freshly ground white pepper
2 tablespoons prepared horseradish	Dash of dill (anything from a three-
2 tablespoons finely chopped bread	fingered pinch to a heaping
and butter pickles	teaspoon), as you like
1 heaping teaspoon chopped capers	½ teaspoon grated lemon peel
with 1 teaspoon caper juice	Dash of celery seeds (or 1 ½ tablespoons
(vinegar)	chopped inner celery leaves)
1 tablespoon ketchup	1 tablespoon dry vermouth
Pinch of salt	Parsley for garnish

Mix all well; serve in bowl with shrimp in a circle around. Garnish with parsley. Or, if you wish to alarm the bourgeoisie, with nasturtium flowers.

FRENCH-FRIED SHRIMP

½ cup flour

½ teaspoon or slightly more salt

Pinch of paprika

⅓ cup milk

1 tablespoon cooking oil

Pinch or so of dried tarragon

1 egg white

1 pound raw, headless shrimp,
     peeled and deveined

Oil for deep frying

Sift flour, salt, and paprika together. Add milk, oil, tarragon, and egg white; beat until smooth. Dip peeled shrimp in this batter; let excess drain off, then lower into deep cooking oil heated to 350 degrees. Fry about 3 minutes till golden brown. Drain on paper towels. Serve with the following sauce.

1 cup mayonnaise

1 cup ketchup

Juice of 1 lemon

1 tablespoon vermouth

Dash of Worcestershire sauce

Dash of Tabasco

Salt

Freshly ground pepper

A little prepared horseradish,
     if you wish

Mix all ingredients together thoroughly.

THE HUGER SISTERS' FAMOUS SHRIMP DISH

Most people overcook shrimp, even though the serious cooks and eaters have long ago complained, even shouted. Miss Ruth and Miss Meta Huger never tired of telling folks to whom they gave copies of their famous shrimp dish, "If you overcook the shrimp," they'd say, "you are offering your guests bits of pink and white rubber, not shrimp." Small shrimp can be dropped into flavored simmering broth and, the instant they turn pink, removed from the stove, splashed with a bit of cold water, and left to cool in the pan in which they were cooked. The jumbo shrimp are better cooked in their shells about 3 to 6 minutes before being peeled.

6 tablespoons unsalted butter

2 pounds cleaned and peeled
     small shrimp

½ cup chopped green onions

2 teaspoons chopped tarragon
     (estragon) or 1 teaspoon dried

½ cup dry Sherry

1½ cups heavy cream

1 tablespoon Dijon or Creole mustard

Melt 4 tablespoons butter and sauté shrimp 1 minute on each side. Remove shrimp from pan; add green onions and tarragon and stir 3 to 4 minutes until onions are soft. Remove from pan. Pour in Sherry and scrape up pan. Reduce Sherry to half. Add cream and cook at medium heat. Reduce cream to half; swirl in 2 tablespoons butter and mustard. Mix well. Pour this sauce into serving dish; place shrimp on top.

The Huger sisters liked to serve plain boiled barley or white hominy with this, chilled white Rhine wine to accompany. Mmmmmm.

CURRIED SHRIMP WITH LEMON RICE

For curried shrimp:

2 pounds shrimp	1 cup chopped onion
2 bay leaves	½ stick butter
1 cup young celery leaves	1 cup dry white wine
1 cup fresh dill	1 cup cream
¼ cup cracked peppercorns	1 scant tablespoon curry powder
2 tart green apples, unpeeled and chopped	Good dash of mace
	1 teaspoon confectioner's ginger
2 cups chopped celery	Celery seeds

For lemon rice:

Butter	1 tablespoon grated lemon peel
1 ½ cups rice	1 teaspoon powdered turmeric
2 ½ cups warm water	Salt
½ cup lemon juice	Dash of cayenne

Cover shrimp in a pot with water. Simmer with your usual boiled-shrimp flavorings, not forgetting the all-important torn bay leaves, young celery leaves, dill, and cracked peppercorns. Let shrimp cool in this water after cooking 7 to 12 minutes, depending on size. You judge! Separately cook apples, celery, and onion in butter till all are coated, then add dry white wine; let all simmer on low, stirring now and then. Meanwhile, peel shrimp and have ready, if you haven't done so. When vegetables are tender and mixture has cooked to a fairly thick consistency but not mushy, add cream, shrimp, another splash of the dry white wine, curry powder, mace, ginger, and a few celery seeds. Mix well; heat when about to serve. Let sit to "hatch" while preparing rice.

To prepare rice: Put a nice lump of butter in pot. Put in unwashed rice after you've picked it over. Stir until each grain is coated and shiny. Put in water, lemon juice, lemon peel, turmeric, a little salt, and cayenne pepper. Let cook, stirring well once or twice, until water is absorbed and you hear the first clicking sounds as the first grains stick to the bottom. Turn off heat at once and place towel over covered pot.

Heat shrimp before serving with the rice alongside and a salad of paper-thin cucumbers dressed with yogurt and dill, a dish of toasted peanuts, and a nice chutney or green tomato pickles. Very cold dry white wine or very cold beer goes well with this.

SHRIMP AMÉRICAINE

2 tablespoons unsalted butter	½ glass Madeira or dry Sherry
1 heaping tablespoon tomato paste	Salt
1 pound large shrimp, cooked and peeled	Dried dill
	Cayenne
Glass of dry white wine	Chopped parsley for garnish

Heat butter in a saucepan. Add tomato paste. Plunge shrimp into this, along with wine and Madeira or Sherry. Salt slightly. Season with dill and a dash of cayenne pepper. Cover; let cook 8 minutes. Add a small splash of the same dry white wine you used earlier or Champagne. Cook 5 minutes longer over low to moderate flame. Taste for salt. Sprinkle generously with chopped parsley. Serve hot with hot crusty bread and chilled white wine.

Oysters

If we consider the oyster, we must glance at the world of myth that has accumulated around the oyster since ancient Roman times. The oyster has long been considered both aphrodisiac and restorative. In ancient and medieval times, physicians prescribed oysters for childless couples, for jaded gentlemen, for wilting adolescents, and for consumptive or merely languid ladies. The clam and mussel, not too unlike the oyster in their chemical elements, have never had the reputation of the oyster or the wink-and-smile publicity that attends the bivalve. Rich in minerals and vitamins, too, those cousins, but oysters contain more phosphorous ("brain food") than any other source and have long since been determined as a great preventative of goiter and similar growths. Louis XI of France ordered his court advisers and secretaries to eat a specific quantity of oysters every day in order to be mentally alert.

Madame de Pompadour subscribed to the belief that oysters and watercress were the greatest aids to male potency and, when she wished to get a rise out of Louis XV, consulted long with her chef to invent dishes with new variations based on those ingredients. The *Almanach des Gourmets* (1803) states that oysters "are the usual opening to winter breakfasts." But the insistent long-held belief is that oysters augment the sexual prowess of human beings . . . and are the best cure for the "morning after," whether after amorous or potable excesses.

The old Greeks served them always for first course at banquets, the Romans brought British oysters to Italy packed in snow, and there was much debate over the relative merits of the imported oysters and the Italian varieties. The American Indians ate untold quantities. Dauphin Island, just south of Mobile, was the scene of an annual oyster feast at some kind of family reunion or meeting of related tribes. Only when airplanes flew over that island in the twentieth century was it possible to see that the empty shells, after these feasts, had been carefully heaped up to form a great serpent shape, almost a mile long, readable only from the air.

The nineteenth century in the United States saw a veritable craze for oysters, and those from the Gulf Coast were as famous as the Long Islands, Chincoteagues, and Bluepoints were later. Packed in barrels of ice, they went by train to Washington, Philadelphia, and New York. The Bon Secour oysters from Mobile Bay were much sought, but the greater numbers were consumed locally.

The size of some of those oysters, plucked from long-established reefs before the days of over-harvesting and pollution, seems phenomenal to us today. For decades now, no one has seen oysters six to eight inches long.

A journalist described the visit of William Makepeace Thackeray to New Orleans in 1852. He was served a dish of six huge oysters, whereupon "he first selected the smallest one . . . then bowed his head as if he were saying grace. Opening his mouth very wide, he struggled for a moment, after which all was over. I shall never forget the comic look of despair he cast upon the other five over-occupied shells. I asked him how he felt. 'Profoundly grateful,' he said, 'as if I had just swallowed a small baby.'"

In Mobile, 1980s.
Photo by John Ray;
courtesy of Eugene
Walter estate.

George Rector of Rector's, the famous Gay Nineties restaurant fre-
quented by Diamond Jim Brady, Lillian Russell, and other larger-than-life
personalities, wrote years later: "We use to have our oysters shipped up
to us from Baltimore and every second or third shipment would include a
barrel of extra large Lynnhavens with the words 'For Mister Brady' painted
on the side of it. Down in Maryland and even as far as the Gulf Coast,
seafood dealers knew about Diamond Jim and his prodigious appetite for
oysters and saved all the giant oysters for him."

Medical historians are still studying with interest an oft-described phe-
nomenon common to Mobile, New Orleans, Baltimore, Philadelphia, and
other oyster ports: a sudden "oyster hunger" in which an individual is sud-
denly possessed of a pressing need to down several dozen raw oysters, which
is perhaps best explained as a quite genuine and instinctive hunger for io-
dine, which seems to occur more frequently in port cities than elsewhere.
The great culinary writer Brillat-Savarin wrote, in the last century, that it
is unthinkable that any serious banquet begins with other than countless
oysters. Robert Courtine described a feast where Honoré de Balzac put

away 100 oysters "just for starters." Even given the fact that French oysters are smaller than American ones, 100 oysters is still 100 oysters!

The oyster has a life span of about twenty years and enjoys at least one sex change. They tend to be male when young and female the rest of their lives, the change occurring after four to six years, depending on the individual oyster.

The nineteenth and twentieth centuries, up until World War II, might be called the Era of the Oyster. The period after might be titled the Good-bye Oysters Era, since the pollution of coastal waters continues with breathless rapture on the part of the quick-buck chasers. Soon, the oyster will join the dinosaur and the dodo bird.

But Mobile was once Oyster Town for sure, with every restaurant serving them. Dozens of oyster bars downtown on Water, Dauphin, and Royal Streets served fresh-shucked raw oysters, fried oysters, oyster stew, and . . . the oyster loaf. These places had a definite male club atmosphere, with their pressed-tin ceilings, four-bladed slow-turning fans, chandeliers of frosted glass globes, and mirrored bars, which had zinc tops with a raised border. Under the bars were receptacles of ice and fresh oysters that were opened just as you ate them. Along the counters were cases of Tabasco, vinegar of several kinds, salt and pepper shakers, horseradish, dishes of lemon quarters, and bowls of oyster crackers. A common refrain was: "First dozen plain, second with lemon juice, third with horseradish sauce." Ketchup was not universal, and most ketchups in the bars were homemade forms now unknown: walnut ketchup, onion ketchup, tomato, yes, but not the mush known now. It was usual for men to eat a dozen or so raw oysters, leaning on the bar, then go to lunch in one of the then famous downtown restaurants.

Other than raw oysters, these oyster bars served oyster stew and . . . and . . . and the ubiquitous oyster loaf. Ah, the oyster loaf! In the French-colonized Gulf Coast regions, this loaf of lightly toasted bread filled with fried or sautéed oysters was known as La Mediatrice ("The Mediator"), since gentlemen who'd worked late in their offices or met with their lawyers or worked on a planning session for whichever mystic society (the secret Carnival committees) . . . or so they said . . . always took home one of these hot oyster loaves to placate wives waiting up for these errant husbands. In San Francisco, the oyster loaf was called The Squarer. Further north, it was simply "boxed oysters."

Fashions in "takeouts" or "bring-homes" have changed radically over the last century. The pizza has almost taken over in the last decade, with fried chicken in near-cement batter running second. The hamburger reigned briefly, as did the hot dog, especially the tasty Dew Drop Inn hot dogs with their bit of sauerkraut, bit of chili con carne, and, back then, always a little bouquet of small, chilled celery stalks. But for over a century, hereabouts, the oyster loaf was the favorite.

Mobile ladies seemed seldom to prepare oyster loaves for home consumption, but for picnics or church bazaars or lawn parties, they vied with each other in offering their individual variations on the oyster loaf. One remembers well the annual Convent of Mercy lawn party behind St. Joseph's with its deep buckets of charcoal and lard vats full of oil where bold cooks with heavy canvas aprons and rubber gloves were shaking the wire baskets of oysters in the bubbling cauldrons.

As in all things southern, there were decidedly opposed positions and rigid stances as to whether the oysters were fried (in later years, the fried school predominated) or simply "shaken," that is, sautéed in butter until they plumped up, before they were packed into the loaves with the bit of cream or flavorings and put into a hot oven about ten minutes before serving.

I don't know about you, but I have had it with those pizzas with ropey cheese, those soy and garlic takeouts that rumble in the tummy for years after. Let's go back to the oyster loaf while it's still, though barely, possible!

One of the earliest recipes we find is in Mrs. Elizabeth Raffald's *The [Experienced] English Housekeeper*, which was known in Gulf Coast kitchens either in its original 1769 edition or any subsequent reprinting. The "French rasp" she mentions is a small loaf of French bread. "Take small French rasps, or you make little round loaves, make a round hole in the top, scrape out all the crumbs, then put your oysters into a tossing pan, with the liquor and crumbs that came out of your rasps of loaves, and a good lump of butter, stew them together five or six minutes, then put in a spoonful of good cream, fill your rasps or loaves, lay the bit of crust carefully on again, set them in an oven to crisp. Three are good enough for a side dish."

The classic oyster loaf always consists of a small individual loaf of French bread lightly toasted, buttered, or thickly spread inside with mayonnaise (laced with horseradish), but many variations employed bits of crisp, crumbled bacon, chives, or capers. As many oysters as could fit were loaded into these hollowed loaves, the lid replaced. Often that splash of cream Mrs. Raffald recommended was smeared inside the loaf.

Flavored mayonnaise was once more common than now; some cooks liked a mayonnaise flavored with very finely chopped parboiled onion and some grated lemon peel with a dash of Tabasco, no more than a dash! Parsley or watercress always accompanied the oyster loaves; fried potatoes, never! Those French pickles known as cornichons, which are milder than their American cousins, the gherkins, were often at hand. O weep for the demise of that famous Solari's Delicatessen in New Orleans, which occasioned more cultural expeditions to that city than any concert or art exhibition.

FRIED OYSTERS

The traditional way to fry oysters is this: Open fresh oysters, catching all juices in a saucepan. Bring oysters and juice just to boiling point; let stand a couple of minutes, then drain thoroughly (save the juice for sauce or gumbo). Sprinkle oysters with lemon juice, then coat with Beer Batter (recipe follows). Heat oil to 375 degrees and fry oysters till golden; DON'T crowd them. Some, rather than employ the batter, like to dredge them in seasoned flour, then in an egg beaten with a dash of cold water, and then with bread crumbs or cracker meal, or even (as did the Huger family) with finely ground toasted pecans.

BEER BATTER

2 big eggs
½ cup flour
½ cup beer
½ teaspoon baking powder

½ teaspoon salt
Pinch of powdered mace
Additional flour for dredging,
    if needed

Whisk all ingredients together.

The secret ingredient in this batter and in many oyster recipes is the pinch, no more, of powdered mace. Flavoring for the batter differs from household to household: Some are faithful to dried dill or celery seeds; a famous cook of the 1920s used a bit of juice from Zatarain capers instead of lemon juice; or you could even use a few drops of mild vinegar from homemade dill pickles.

4 slices lean bacon	Dash of Worcestershire sauce
1 tablespoon unsalted butter	Dash of dried dill
1 small onion, minced	1 tablespoon dry Sherry
½ green bell pepper, minced	4 slices whole-wheat, French,
2 inner stalks of celery, minced	or Italian bread, toasted
Pinch of salt	24 medium oysters
Freshly ground pepper to taste	Fresh parsley or inner celery leaves
1 small sweet pimiento, minced	for garnish
1 teaspoon lemon juice	

Dice the bacon and place over low heat; fry slowly 3 to 5 minutes. Put aside. Melt butter in another pan over medium heat; add onion, bell pepper, celery, salt, and pepper. Sauté about 5 to 8 minutes or until vegetables are wilted; now combine with bacon and fat in skillet. Add pimiento, lemon juice, Worcestershire sauce, dill, and Sherry; mix well and cook a minute or so.

In a shallow baking dish, arrange 4 slices toasted whole-wheat, French, or Italian bread. Put 6 plump raw oysters on each; divide mixture over them. If you like, you can sprinkle blanched chopped almonds on top, or a bit of lime juice, or a sprinkle of mild paprika. Place about 3 inches under hot broiler and cook 4 to 5 minutes; serve AT ONCE! Garnish with parsley. Serves 4.

This dish might be the true memorial and monument to the great coloratura soprano Luisa Tetrazzini (born Florence, Italy, 1871; died Milan, 1940), since few remember her now, but this dish goes on forever. She made her debut in Meyerbeer's *L'Africaine* (1890) and triumphed for several seasons in San Francisco and at the Met in New York. Her older sister Eva was a Met star, too, but married early and retired. They came of a family that honored Good Eatin'.

3 ½ tablespoons butter

⅛ cup flour

1 cup milk

¼ cup grated Swiss or Gruyère
cheese

1 cup chopped parsley

1 can small mushrooms

1 pint oysters with juice

⅛ cup dry Sherry

Salt and freshly ground white
(or black) pepper

Good dash of Worcestershire sauce

2 ½ cups cooked vermicelli or
fettuccine (wide noodles)

Bread crumbs sautéed in butter

Slices of baked ham

Parsley sprigs for garnish

Preheat oven to 350 degrees. Melt butter in pan over low heat; add flour, little by little, and add milk and cheese. Stir in parsley, mushrooms, oysters with their juice, Sherry, and seasonings. Butter casserole and put in pasta. Place oyster mixture on top. Cover with bread crumbs. Bake for 20 minutes. Place slices of ham on plates; serve Oysters Tetrazzini over ham, garnished with parsley sprigs.

OYSTERS LEONTYNE

1 quart oysters with liquid

2 tablespoons unsalted butter

4 celery stalks, finely chopped

2 medium onions, finely chopped

2 thin slices lemon, finely minced

1 garlic toe, grated

1 bay leaf, torn in half

Pinch of thyme

Good splash of dry Sherry

2 cups bread crumbs, soaked in
oyster juice, then squeezed out

Tabasco

Salt

1 lightly beaten egg

Paprika

Drain oysters, pick over for bits of shell (most irritating to crunch down on!), and chop oysters fine. Melt butter in skillet and simmer celery and onions, but don't let them brown. Pale gold is enough. Add lemon, garlic, bay leaf, thyme, and Sherry. Squeeze out juice from crumbs and add to skillet. Simmer over very low heat, then add oysters, Tabasco, and salt. Simmer until oysters are cooked, a few minutes or so. Taste for seasonings. Stir in 1 lightly beaten egg. Simmer over low heat 2 minutes. Remove bay leaf. Now divide all this into 6 to 8 flat seashells, seashell-shaped dishes, or individual ramekins. Bake at 350 degrees about 20 minutes and serve immediately, topped with a sprinkling of paprika.

This is one of those Gulf Coast recipes of wildest variability. For dainty eaters, three oysters on the half shell are considered the thing for first course; for serious eaters, six oysters. If the dish is the main course, decide how many oysters and adjust amounts of ingredients for sauce accordingly. Properly, the oysters should be on the half shell, but they are served, as well, in individual ramekins, in foil muffin cups, or, if you wish, cupped in a green romaine leaf resting on a little base of boiled rice.

1 bunch scallions, minced

6 tablespoons unsalted
    butter

¼ cup flour

1 pint oyster liquid

2 garlic toes, minced

⅓ cup chopped mushrooms

½ cup dry white wine (or half wine,
    half Pernod or Greek ouzo)

1 cup raw shrimp, chopped

2 tablespoons lemon juice

Salt

A little freshly ground pepper
    (white preferable)

Pinch of dried dill

20 to 30 oysters, drained, with
    liquid reserved

Sauté the minced scallions in butter till soft but not browned. Add flour; stir till smooth. Add oyster juice, garlic, and mushrooms. Boil for 20 minutes, adding wine, shrimp, and lemon juice in last few minutes. Let simmer on low for 8 minutes. Taste for salt; add seasonings.

Arrange oysters on their half shells on a baking dish, covered with sauce, or in ramekins or cups, or placed a little apart in pie dishes. Place in 400 degree oven and bake until edges of oysters curl, 10 or 12 minutes.

Those on shells or in ramekins or whatever are next transferred to individual serving plates; those on baking sheet carefully scooped up and placed on leaf on rice. Heated French bread alongside for sopping.

This is usually made with anisette, but the best version of the dish employs the delightful Herbsaint made in New Orleans.

Plenty of rock salt	1 ½ cups chopped raw spinach
24 fresh oysters on the half shell	2 tablespoons Herbsaint
¾ cup unsalted butter	½ teaspoon celery seeds
3 tablespoons minced green onions	2 teaspoons lemon juice
3 tablespoons minced parsley	¼ teaspoon cayenne
½ cup bread crumbs	

Preheat oven to 450 degrees. Fill 6 pie plates with rock salt. Arrange oysters on half shells on salt. Heat ¼ cup butter in heavy skillet till it foams; add minced onion and cook slowly till soft. Stir in parsley, bread crumbs, spinach, Herbsaint, celery seeds, lemon juice, and cayenne. Add rest of butter; mix well. Spoon evenly over oysters. Bake 8 to 10 minutes. Serve in pans of salt as they come from oven.

BAKED OYSTERS

3 tablespoons unsalted butter	1 half-slice of bacon, minced
1 garlic toe, minced	1 teaspoon lemon juice
Dash of Tabasco	Good dash of freshly ground
1 to 2 (according to size) green	white pepper
onions, top and bottom, minced	Pinch of salt
2 tablespoons chopped parsley	1 tablespoon dry Sherry
1 tablespoon chopped capers	1 pint oysters

Preheat oven to 400 degrees. Combine all ingredients except the oysters. Simmer 10 minutes over low heat, stirring gently. Carefully drain the oysters. Make single layer in bottom of buttered shallow baking dish. Pour sauce evenly over mollusks; bake for 15 minutes. Serve oysters and sauce over hot, unbuttered toast with more toast on side. Or serve with Corn Oysters (recipe below).

Good alongside is plain boiled young mustard greens, or salad of French sorrel, dandelion, and baby romaine dressed with lemon, oil, salt, and pepper. Serves 4.

Corn oysters, served up in a folded napkin or clean cotton dishcloth, look like oysters. You'll find this recipe in some of the Episcopal parish cookbooks through the years under the name of Mock Mollusks (a High Episcopal form of humor!). When I first heard the name as a child, I somehow associated it with the names of Chicago gangsters of the Prohibition period, names very much in the news. The point is, these golden-brown goodies are very good with many of the dishes included here.

1 cup cooked or canned
    corn kernels
5 tablespoons milk
1 beaten egg
1 tablespoon melted, unsalted butter
½ cup flour
1 teaspoon baking powder
½ teaspoon salt
1 teaspoon sugar

A generous amount of freshly
    ground white pepper (black,
    if you don't have white, but this
    is one of those dishes where the
    difference between black and
    white pepper is noticeable)
About ¼ inch of fat in a skillet
    for frying

Mix corn, milk, egg, and butter. Sift together flour with baking powder, salt, and sugar. Now mix everything together except the fat. Meanwhile, fat has been heating in your skillet. Drop little spoonfuls of mixture into fat. Fry until golden brown, turning to brown on all sides. When you serve them, everybody will think they're oysters. Maybe that's why they are often served alongside creamed or baked oysters. Interesting variations: When you think it suitable, you can add dried dill, celery seeds, or chopped chives.

This was once a traditional midnight feast opener: New Year's Eve, during Carnival, birthdays, etc., in the old hotels and restaurants of the Gulf Coast.

16 scrubbed oyster shells

16 Bon Secour oysters (or any
   plump medium-sized ones),
   with their juice

2 cups dry Champagne

2 tablespoons minced green onions

1 cup heavy cream

8 tablespoons unsalted butter

2 tablespoons chopped chives
   for garnish

Preheat oven to 200 degrees or lowest setting. Place 16 half shells on 2 serving dishes in oven to warm. Strain oyster juice into small saucepan. Add half of Champagne and green onions. Heat to boiling over medium heat till reduced by half. Remove from heat and whisk in cream. Return to heat; boil about 5 minutes or reduced by about one-third. Whisk in butter, little by little, then cover to keep sauce warm. Heat rest of Champagne over medium heat till simmering. Add oysters all at once and cook for no more than 10 seconds. Remove shells from the oven and use a slotted spoon to place 1 oyster in each shell. Spoon sauce over oysters and garnish with chives. Serve immediately.

Vegetables

VEGETARIAN'S DELIGHT, OR CELERY SURPRISE

1 ½ cups short-grain white rice

Salt

3 tablespoons unsalted butter

1 tablespoon best olive oil

1 medium onion, minced

3 ½ cups coarsely chopped celery
  stalks (tender white parts,
  remove lower inch or so)

Minced parsley

1 scant teaspoon fennel seeds

½ cup dry white wine

Freshly ground black pepper

¾ cup chopped Fontina, Provolone,
  or Swiss cheese

½ cup grated Parmesan cheese

Boil 3 quarts water; toss in rice and a pinch of salt. Bring back to boil,
then simmer about 15 minutes, till rice is tender. Heat 2 tablespoons
butter and oil in big skillet. Sauté onion, celery, a good handful of parsley, and fennel seeds 3 to 5 minutes. Add wine; cook till wine is reduced
by half, about 3 minutes. Stir in remaining butter and season with salt
and pepper.

To serve: Drain rice, put in big bowl, stir in cheeses, add celery mixture, and toss to combine. Sprinkle top with more parsley; serve at once. If you're not vegetarian, you might want to serve this with tiny pork sausage patties or paper-thin small slices of ham or sprinkle crumbled, crisp bacon over all.

CELERY WITH MUSTARD SAUCE

2 bunches celery	1 ½ tablespoons flour
1 cup water	1 cup heavy cream
½ cup dry white wine	1 teaspoon Dijon or Creole mustard
3 tablespoons butter	1 teaspoon dry mustard
½ teaspoon salt	Lemon juice
¼ teaspoon sugar	3 tablespoons chopped celery leaves

Pick and clean celery, keeping aside the tender inner leaves and some of the younger leaves as well. Scrape the stalks to remove strings. Cut the stalks into convenient lengths, perhaps each bit 3 inches long. Toss into boiling, salted water for 1 minute, then drain. Transfer to another pot with 1 cup water, dry white wine, 1 ½ tablespoons butter, salt, and sugar and cook covered over low heat for 15 to 25 minutes. Celery should be tender but not mushy. Reserve cooking liquid.

In a small skillet, melt 1 ½ tablespoons butter; add flour and cook this roux over low heat, stirring for 2 minutes. Remove from heat and add the reserved cooking liquid and heavy cream mixed with either Dijon or Creole mustard and dry mustard.

Cook this sauce over low heat, whisking it till it's smooth and thick. Season with salt and lemon juice to taste, pour over celery, and sprinkle 3 tablespoons chopped celery leaves over all.

1 stick unsalted butter

1 ½ pounds fresh mushrooms,
   trimmed and cut in quarters
   or sixths if they're huge

A little freshly ground white pepper

½ cup ruby port

1 tablespoon brandy, if needed

4 French rolls

1 cup heavy cream

½ cup blue cheese

Heat about 4 tablespoons butter over medium heat; sauté mushrooms, stirring the while, till they are golden. Add pepper. Heat the port, set it on fire, and stir into mushrooms, turning skillet back and forth till flames subside. You should try your port first; if it doesn't burn easily, you might wish to add a tablespoon of heated brandy to the heated port, using slightly less port. Cut tops off rolls, hollow out, melt rest of butter, and pour over rolls. Broil till golden; fill with mushrooms. Place cream and blue cheese in a pan over low heat and stir until blended. Top mushrooms with blue cheese mixture.

In the northern reaches of Mississippi, near Corinth, I ate this dish with fried grits rather than rolls. Splendid! Nothing English about grits, of course, but the port and brandy are associated with those isles.

Cook up a batch of grits and put into pie plates about ¾-inch deep. Let harden in fridge overnight. Cut into wedges, flour well, and fry in butter with a little bacon fat. Split wedges lengthwise, pour mushrooms over, and serve hot.

TIPSY MUSHROOMS

2 medium onions, sliced thin

¾ cup water

½ cup vinegar

⅓ cup red Burgundy or any
    dry red

1 ½ teaspoons unsalted butter

1 teaspoon salt

½ teaspoon celery seeds

½ teaspoon mustard seeds

3 to 4 whole cloves

½ pound fresh mushrooms

¼ cup vegetable oil

Mix well the onions, water, vinegar, wine, butter, salt, and seasonings; bring to a boil and cook 5 minutes. Add mushrooms; simmer 5 minutes. Remove mushrooms with slotted spoon and place in bowl. Strain liquid, discarding onions. Add oil to mix and pour over mushrooms, mixing gently.

Serve hot over meatloaf, or cold with Melba toast as appetizer.

HOT MUSHROOM PIE

A nice luncheon starts with this pie, then follows up with three or four kinds of fresh vegetables and yellow cornbread, with some kind of sweet-and-sour pickle or chutney.

1 unbaked 9-inch pie shell

1 pound mushrooms

2 tablespoons unsalted butter

2 tablespoons olive oil

1 Vidalia or sweet purple onion

1 tablespoon flour

1 pint cream

2 beaten eggs

2 tablespoons dry Sherry

Pinch of celery seeds

Pinch of powdered mace

Salt and freshly ground black pepper

Preheat oven to 450 degrees. Prick the bottom of the pie shell and bake about 15 minutes, just long enough to set the crust without browning it. Clean and slice mushrooms. Sauté in butter and oil with finely chopped onion until onion becomes transparent. Stir in flour and go on cooking about 2 minutes. Combine cream, eggs, Sherry, and flavorings, then pour this mixture over the mushrooms and cool.

Reduce oven to 425 degrees. Pour filling mixture into pastry shell and bake until brown, about 25 minutes. Serves 6. Salad of French endive good alongside.

NEW POTATOES IN WATERCRESS SAUCE

12 small new potatoes in their skins

4 tablespoons unsalted butter

3 tablespoons flour

1 cup cream

1 cup milk

Splash of dry white wine

Salt and freshly ground pepper

2 ½ tablespoons Creole or Dijon
mustard

Celery seeds

1 cup chopped watercress,
with extra for garnish

Cook potatoes in their skins. Make a sauce with butter, flour, cream, milk, and wine. Cook in double boiler, stirring the while, till it's like heavy cream. If it's cooked too thick, add a little more cream. Season with salt, freshly ground black pepper, mustard, a few celery seeds, and chopped watercress.

Now make the decision of your life: Should you peel or not peel the potatoes??? I say don't peel, in order to relish that earthy, nutty, vitamin-rich goodness of the potato skins. It's up to you!

Heat potatoes and sauce together and serve very hot. Sprinkle dish with the finely chopped watercress. If you don't have watercress, finely mince green onions or chives with inner celery leaves.

YORKSHIRE POTATOES

1 pound red potatoes

½ cup chopped onion

½ cup chopped celery

Unsalted butter

3 tablespoons Dijon or Creole mustard

Splash of beer

Salt

¼ cup chopped green onions

¼ cup chopped parsley

Wash and peel potatoes and cut into round, not-too-thin slices; rinse in fresh water. Put in clean water with a little chopped onion and celery and cook until fork will pierce, but not soft. Drain. Discard onion and celery.

Melt a big glop of unsalted butter in shallow pan and simmer potatoes a few minutes, then add mustard and a splash of beer to make a sauce. Salt to taste. If too much liquid, simmer a bit to reduce.

In saucepan, sauté chopped green onions and parsley in a little butter. Place potatoes and sauce in serving dish; pour green onions and parsley over all.

2 pounds potatoes
1 good splash of dry white wine
Butter
6 hard-boiled eggs, chopped
1 cup chopped fresh chives or
    baby green onions

½ cup mayonnaise, thinned with
    a little lemon juice
1 ½ teaspoons curry powder
½ teaspoon celery seeds
Ripe tomatoes
Chopped parsley or inner celery leaves

Boil potatoes and peel while hot. Set aside peels. Chop potatoes into cubes; while potatoes are still warm, splash a little dry white wine over them. Fry chopped potato peels in butter, until brown and crisped. Mix potatoes with chopped egg and chives and dress with mayonnaise mixed with curry powder and celery seeds.

Put potato salad in a nice rounded mound on serving platter and surround with little heaps of fried peels alternating with sliced tomatoes, all sprinkled with a little chopped parsley or chopped inner celery leaves.

CODEN POTATO SALAD

If you're serving boiled or baked ham, this potato salad, originating in a hotel or boarding house in Coden of the 1890s, is a certain success.

6 large potatoes
¼ cup chopped scallions
2 tablespoons minced parsley
¾ cup dry white wine
2 tablespoons white wine vinegar
½ cup best olive oil

2 pimientos, chopped
½ cup almonds, blanched, halved,
    and toasted
A small glop of Dijon or Creole mustard
Celery seeds
Salt and freshly ground black pepper

Boil, peel, and slice potatoes. While they are still warm, mix them with scallions, parsley, white wine mixed with white wine vinegar, olive oil, pimientos, and almonds. Add mustard, a few celery seeds, and salt and freshly ground black pepper to taste.

This may be served warm or chilled. Some people like a little finely chopped dill pickle added to the dish. Others want it to share a serving platter with VERY HOT deviled eggs (Tabasco AND chili powder!).

1 tablespoon grated orange peel

3 to 4 oranges

¼ cup tightly packed brown sugar

½ cup good brandy

¼ cup light cream

Pinch of salt

¼ cup melted unsalted butter

4 cups cooked sweet potatoes, mashed

Preheat oven to 350 degrees. Grate zest from oranges, then peel. Slice 1 peeled orange into thin half-slices; cut up rest of oranges into very small pieces. You want 2 heaping cups drained orange flesh. Sprinkle slices with brown sugar and set aside. Heat together grated peel, brandy, cream, salt, and butter, then beat this mix into sweet potatoes till well blended. Stir in sweetened, drained orange pieces. Spoon mix into well-oiled casserole; top with slices.

Sprinkle a bit more brown sugar over, if desired. Baroque types sprinkle finely chopped candied (crystallized) ginger over top. Bake, uncovered, for 35 to 50 minutes. This can be prepared well in advance and cooked at the last minute.

SWEET TATER PONE

There was an elderly couple near Valdosta whose idea of breakfast was these pones with cold, fresh buttermilk, then very hot black coffee with a glop of the best cognac in it. This is called High Style. There are hundreds of versions of this pone, most calling for rose water or orange blossom water.

1 ½ sticks unsalted butter

¾ cup packed brown sugar

2 cups cooked, mashed sweet potato

2 tablespoons sweet Sherry

Good slug of nutmeg

Good slug of cinnamon

1 teaspoon powdered ginger, or a little more if you like

2 tablespoons chopped candied ginger

Splash of rose water, if available (careful: not cosmetic rose water but culinary rose water)

1 cup dark molasses

2 cups milk

2 tablespoons orange marmalade

Preheat oven to 325 degrees. Butter 2-quart round baking dish. Cream butter and sugar together till smooth, then add sweet potato, flavorings, rose water, molasses, and milk. Mix very well; add marmalade. Put mix into baking dish and bake about 1 ½ hours, until tater is complete mush, sticky and moist. Slice and serve with whipped cream with a little bit of grated orange peel in it.

BAKED BABY LIMAS

1 pound dried baby limas	1 tablespoon dry mustard
¾ cup unsalted butter	1 tablespoon molasses
3 teaspoons salt	2 tablespoons dry Sherry
¾ cup light brown sugar	1 cup sour cream

Soak beans overnight in cold water. No, don't do the hurry-up boil-then-let-sit technique. Drain, wash in cold water, and drain again. Cover with fresh cold water and cook until tender, about 30 to 40 minutes. Drain again, rinse under hot water, and place in medium casserole. Dab butter on top, add 1 teaspoon salt, and mix.

Preheat oven to 350 degrees. Now mix sugar, mustard, and the rest of the salt together; sprinkle over beans. Stir in molasses and Sherry. Last, pour on sour cream and mix well. Bake about an hour. Very good! Serves 6 greedy-guts or 8 polite guests.

ASIAN CABBAGE

1 pound green outer leaves of cabbage (buy 2 cabbages if need be; save the inner leaves for the Polish dish in the following recipe)	Peel of 1 lemon, grated
	Splash of Worcestershire sauce
	Dash of Tabasco
	Pinch of powdered ginger
1 red bell pepper	6 tablespoons vegetable oil
2 garlic toes	Salt
1 mild purple onion	Splash of dry white wine

Wash cabbage leaves, stack, and cut crosswise into thin ribbons. THIN. Clean pepper; cut coarsely. Grate garlic. Peel onion and chop coarsely.

Make a paste in your food processor of pepper, garlic, onion, lemon peel, and seasonings, adding a splash of water. Put a wok or sautoir over high heat, add oil, and stir paste in this for 5 minutes. Then toss in cabbage, add a pinch of salt, and stir, stir, stir about half a minute. Cover, lower heat, and cook 10 to 12 minutes until cabbage is just done.

Check halfway to see how it's doing and add a splash of dry white wine. This is good with chicken fingers or catfish fingers.

POLISH CABBAGE

¼ cup unsalted butter	1 cup dry white wine
1 cup chopped mild onion	10 to 12 juniper berries, cracked
4 cups shredded white inner cabbage leaves	Salt and freshly ground pepper to taste
1 cup sauerkraut	Pinch of sugar

Melt butter in big pot. Sauté onion till golden; add shredded cabbage and cook over medium heat, stirring, until wilted. Add all else and cook on low about 25 minutes, adding a little more wine or some water if need be.

The ideal accompaniment for this cabbage dish is the fat from a pork roast, cut into thin ribbons and baked on a cookie sheet until crisp and golden brown. Or small ground lean pork patties flavored with sage.

Ice-cold beer or dry white wine with any of these cabbage dishes.

SUNDAY SUPPER ONION PIE

Okay, you have the wreckage of a baked ham, roast beef, or pork. So prepare your favorite flaky pastry for a deep pie pan — not a casserole, not a shallow pie pan, but a deep pie pan. Bake it; chill it.

Then, make your onion pie filling. There are dozens of recipes. And, just like the 2,000 green tomato pie recipes are about evenly divided between sweet versions and savory ones, same's true of onions. Many eighteenth- and early-nineteenth-century green apple pie recipes were simply northern apple pie recipes with, in the apple-less South, green tomatoes substituted for Eve's preference. This is very good.

2 medium Vidalia or sweet
   purple onions

Sugar

Salt

1 can Mr. Campbell's cream of
   potato soup

1 beaten egg

White pepper (or black if you
   don't have white)

Chopped leftover meat

1 pie crust, baked in a deep
   pie pan

1 small can baby green peas

Tarragon

Preheat oven to 350 degrees. Cut onions coarsely and drop into boiling water with a dash of sugar and a dash of salt. Turn heat down to simmer; let cook about a minute, maybe half a minute more. Onion bits should be pierceable but not mushy. Drain onions; add Mr. Campbell's soup well mixed with beaten egg. Season with pepper. Add lots of chopped meat. On the bottom of your crust, spread peas, well drained and well washed, flavored with tarragon, salt, and freshly ground pepper, then pour the onion mixture into crust. Bake until pie "takes," that is, the knife comes out clean.

Serve pie hot with sliced ham and green butter beans alongside or with cold chicken salad and dill pickles or with sliced head cheese and a salad of celery hearts and string beans flavored with lemon, oil, capers, and grated lemon peel.

A filling of coarsely chopped chicken or turkey with the onion in the creamy sauce is delicious, BUT be sure to add a little splash of dry Sherry or Madeira. You can use Sauterne or Rhine wine, too, but be sure to add a few drops of Tabasco in this case.

If you don't have a cold-biscuit-and-ham fan, crumble the biscuits left over from midday, moisten with a little melted butter and milk or buttermilk, flavor with chopped fresh sage, and make this the crust of your onion pie.

Or crumble your leftover French bread, ditto.

Another crust for an onion pie: crumbled cornbread with some crumbled, crisp bacon and a few mustard seeds.

"Miss Cabbage, deceased from overboiling, mourned
by vegetable friends fearful of a similar fate," Walter
sketch. Courtesy of Eugene Walter estate.

This, hot, is traditional with baked pork, ham, or any game dish. A Sunday night supper of cold ham and chicken salad, with buttered barley as the only hot dish with these onions cold, is just what the doctor ordered. Madeira is far and away the best wine for the dish, but rutabaga wine or Beaujolais with a hint of grated orange peel in it can be employed. During Prohibition, one of the Mobile banks had a cellar full of Madeira, a supply laid down when Prohibition was imminent or later smuggled from Cuba and Barbados, strictly for use by the bank officials. The social glass, oh, yes, but for dishes such as this and for children with colds as well.

2 pounds little white onions	1 ½ cups dark honey, or molasses
1 ½ teaspoons unsalted butter	if you prefer
1 teaspoon corn oil	Salt to taste
1 cup Madeira	Mace

Toss onions into big pot of boiling water for 5 minutes. Drain and put into cold water a minute or so. Drain and peel. Put butter and oil into enameled or stainless metal frying pan, add onions, and turn a few minutes over medium heat till onions take on a golden color, then add Madeira and honey (or molasses) and a mere hint of salt. Cover and cook about 15 minutes over moderate flame till onions are pierceable but not mushy.

Now take off lid, lower heat, and cook about 15 minutes, spooning sauce over onions till sauce is reduced and onions are golden brown. Keep close watch during last minutes of cooking. Taste; maybe add a few grains of salt and a little powdered mace.

This can be made a day ahead and reheated when needed in a double boiler or covered Pyrex in oven. This is about right for 4 people.

For Christmas breakfast, try country pork sausage, baked apples, hot biscuits, and these onions. Oh, my!

Note: Ginger fiends like to chop up a bit of candied ginger in this dish.

10 to 12 medium-sized onions, preferably the purple ones

3 tablespoons unsalted butter

¾ cup milk

¼ cup dry Sherry

Good pinch of salt and freshly ground pepper

Freshly grated nutmeg

Few drops of Tabasco, no more

4 eggs

Preheat oven to 350 degrees. Peel and chop onions. Melt butter in big skillet and fry onions very SLOWLY until they start to turn golden. Remove from heat; drain off fat. Bring onions, milk, Sherry, and flavorings to a simmer. Let sit a minute or so while you beat eggs just enough to mingle yolks and whites. Put all in buttered 2-quart baking dish, after mixing well. Set dish in pan of hot water; bake for 45 minutes or so until knife comes out clean. Serves 6.

This is perfect for first course at supper, followed by cold sliced ham, potato salad, and ripe olives.

FRENCH ONIONS

2 pounds small white onions

3 ripe tomatoes

1 ¼ cups dry white wine

⅔ cup olive oil

⅓ cup white raisins (currants)

Crushed coriander seeds

Bit of grated orange or lemon peel

½ garlic toe, minced

Pinch of sugar

Salt and freshly ground black pepper to taste

Peel the onions and put them in a pan that will hold them in one layer. Seed and chop small the 3 ripe tomatoes, cover the onions with them, and then pour the wine and the oil over. Add raisins and seasonings. Cover; bring to boil. Turn down heat and simmer about 20 minutes or until onions are done. Put into serving bowl; let cool at room temperature. Salt and freshly ground pepper to be added according to individual taste. A table without a good pepper mill is a family without a spiritual leader.

King Garlic & Queen Onion

"King Garlic and Queen Onion," Walter sketch. Courtesy of Eugene Walter estate.

SPY'S BROCCOLI

2 pounds broccoli

1 onion, sliced

3 ounces sharp Provolone cheese, sliced

Olive oil

3 tablespoons (a scant cup) black olives, pitted and quartered

8 anchovy fillets

Salt to taste

¼ cup red wine

Chopped parsley or inner celery leaves for garnish

Wash the broccoli and separate into florets. If the stems are thick, split them after peeling them and discarding leaves. Slice the onion and cheese paper-thin.

Place 2 tablespoons best quality olive oil in a terra cotta casserole and make a layer of onions, olives, anchovy fillets, and cheese. Cover these with a layer of broccoli and sprinkle with oil and salt. Alternate ingredients in layers, ending with broccoli.

Sprinkle with more oil and the red wine. Cover the casserole and cook over fairly low flame for about 1 ½ hours. The wine should have evaporated completely by the time cooking is complete. Top with parsley.

FOUR-STAR STUFFED PEPPERS

4 large red or green peppers

1 ½ cups cooked short-length macaroni

1 cup diced sharp cheese

1 cup diced fresh ripe tomatoes

½ cup Triscuit cracker crumbs

1 small onion, minced

½ teaspoon sugar

Scant ½ cup dry white wine

Salt and freshly ground black pepper

Dash of paprika

Dash of cayenne

Preheat oven to 350 degrees. Remove insides from peppers by hollowing out from stem end. Cover with boiling water and boil 5 minutes. Drain. Mix remaining ingredients and stuff peppers.

Pack peppers tightly in baking pan. Pour boiling water ½ inch deep around them. Bake for 30 minutes.

Carrots

We take so many foods for granted. Carrots, for instance. Carrots are just there, have always been there, are tolerated because of a long-held supposition (superstition) that they are "good for you." Well, they are. Those primitive cave dwellers had figured that out. The root is native to Afghanistan and figures in medicinal and culinary texts going way back when. It was one of the earliest cultivated root foods. Early on, the carrot had traveled from India to China and was cultivated in Gaul (France) at least 1,000 years before Christ. The ancient Greeks and the Romans preferred the beet, the only vegetable with a higher sugar content than the carrot.

In twelfth-century England, people were cultivating wild carrots in their gardens and preferred them to the garden varieties. That plant we know as Queen Anne's lace, common all over America, is nothing more or less than the wild carrot garden types "gone native." The name (Queen Anne reigned in England from 1702 to 1714) would indicate that it is a garden escapee from late-seventeenth-century or early-eighteenth-century New England gardens.

In India and Afghanistan, the carrot is the basis for delicious desserts that often include honey and ginger, favorites of the Punjabis in particular. In England, the country people make a carrot wine that has its devotees as well as those who scorn it sneeringly. Most carrots offered for human consumption are the golden yellow types in dozens of shapes, while the varieties with white, red, yellow, or purple roots are usually fed to livestock.

One of the best carrot tales is related by Dr. Burton Roueche in one of his *New Yorker* medicinal/detective stories. It seems a lady was admitted to the hospital for tests after her skin and hair had taken on a pronounced yellowish tint; some form of galloping jaundice seemed evident. But dozens of the most elaborate, last-word, precise examinations were conducted and proved the lady in excellent health. Specialists consulted and shook their heads. It was a trained nurse who figured out the problem. She visited the lady at home and discovered that she, out of a fixed idea of the healthful value of carrots, ate three bunches a day and had begun to glow with golden good health. A walking phial of natural vegetable dye.

Cooks of the Old South always included carrots in their kitchen gardens. Thomas Jefferson, a pioneer in studying what grew best with what, instructed his gardeners to plant carrots as companions to onion and garlic but no other root vegetable, ever. Carrots and tomatoes help each other thrive, too.

I'll pause right here in midstream and explain that I have always liked carrots. Most children go through a hate-spinach, hate-carrots, hate-anything-unexpected-like-broccoli-or-artichokes period. I never did. My grandfather had a wonderful kitchen garden behind the house at the corner of Bayou and Conti. He grew a deeply golden form of carrot, a kind of Bavarian offshoot of the famous Nantes carrot. My reward for helping in the garden was a brace of carrots to take to a huge rabbit in a cage, belonging to Mrs. Allen across the street. The rabbit gazed unblinkingly at me with the kind of "forewarned" look one sees on registrars for school, the draft, or credit cards. But he grabbed the carrot and munched happily. I soon followed suit.

But then my grandmother always had a carrot dish alongside pork chops or spareribs or roasted pork. Small, fat carrots, halved lengthwise, cooked with small whole mild onions, slivered kumquat peels, chopped candied ginger, a slug of molasses, a pinch of mace, salt, and freshly ground black pepper. Fresh country butter added at table. If this is one's introduction to the carrot, you can see that the "good for you" public relations for the carrot was never heard. One only heard "Yum!" and "Mmmmm"s of various pitch, duration, and profundity. Vitamin A was never mentioned at that table. But plates were certainly licked clean. The message learned, I suppose, was "Vive la carotte!" and no nonsense about it.

There are literally hundreds of forms of carrot. Serious eaters and serious gardeners would do well to study the seed catalogs.

CARROTS MARSALA

12 medium carrots	½ cup unsalted butter
Salt	½ cup dry Marsala wine

Wash and scrape carrots; slice in thin disks. Sprinkle with a little salt and fry in bubbling butter for a couple of minutes. Sprinkle with Marsala, cover pan, reduce heat to medium, and continue cooking for 8 minutes or so until carrots are tender. Serve hot.

KENTUCKY COLONEL TOMATO SAUCE

1 tablespoon olive oil	2 tablespoons bourbon whiskey
1 medium-sized onion, chopped	1 tablespoon fresh lemon juice
3 garlic toes, minced	1 teaspoon grated lemon peel
1 28-ounce can tomato puree	⅛ teaspoon cayenne
1 14- to 16-ounce can whole	Salt to taste
tomatoes	Generous amount freshly ground
1 14-ounce can crushed tomatoes	black pepper
¼ cup tomato paste	1 to 2 cracked corianders,
¼ cup chopped fresh basil	if you like

Heat oil over medium heat in big pan. Sauté onion and garlic till onion softens, about 6 minutes. Add all else; bring to boil. Turn down heat and simmer until reduced to about 4 cups, breaking up big hunks of tomato with wooden spoon, stirring now and then. The cooking process takes about 50 minutes. This can be prepared 1 to 2 days in advance, covered, and put in fridge. This sauce serves for a huge gallimaufry of dishes.

Delicious over pasta, pearl barley, wedges of fried grits, and baked whole onions with slivers of ham and on pizza with sausage, etc.

LEMON BUTTER

This is good on asparagus or artichokes, boiled beet greens, boiled baby shrimp, or a bed of watercress.

1 ½ tablespoons unsalted butter

3 tablespoons minced shallot

¾ cup dry white wine

2 tablespoons lemon juice

Pinch of salt

Good dash of freshly ground white pepper (black if you don't have white, but you ought to have it)

3 tablespoons heavy cream

Melt butter in heavy saucepan, medium heat. Sauté shallots about 4 minutes. Add wine and lemon juice; bring just to a boil. Add salt and pepper and boil till liquid is somewhat reduced, about 6 to 7 minutes. Mix in cream.

FRIENDLY SALAD DRESSING

I hope you have a garden and that you have a little raised bed or a few big pots full of French sorrel, rocket, dandelion, mâche lettuce, or even leaves of baby radishes. In our supermarkets, we are too often offered little of truly fresh salad greens, and nothing is more boring or dull than the iceberg lettuce foisted on us all year long only because it survives long travel and long rests in cold storage. Romaine and red-leaved and curly leaved lettuces are fussier, and usually you can tell their state at a glance. Iceberg always looks right, even when it's been far too long away from mother and has lost that indefinable tang of garden-fresh. Here are two dressings from Asian households in the South. They're both delightful, with any kind of greens.

¾ cup mayonnaise

1 cup sour cream

¼ pound crumbled blue cheese

1 tablespoon fresh lemon juice

½ teaspoon celery seeds

2 teaspoons minced mild onion

1 garlic toe, minced

Salt and freshly ground black pepper to taste

1 ½ tablespoons best cognac

Combine mayonnaise, sour cream, and blue cheese, then add all else, cognac last. Whisk until well blended. Chill, covering for 24 hours, but let dressing return to room temperature before serving.

GINGER SALAD DRESSING

1 cup virgin olive oil

2 ½ teaspoons peeled and minced
    ginger root

Innermost 2 to 3 heart stalks of
    celery bunch, chopped

¼ cup lightly toasted sesame seeds
    (in Charleston say "benne")

Freshly ground white pepper to taste

Small glop of ketchup or tomato relish

Dash of Worcestershire sauce

A few capers, chopped

Juice of half a lemon

Good splash of white vermouth

Mix all well.

SPINACH SALAD FLAMBÉ

1 pound fresh spinach

3 to 4 hard-boiled eggs

½ cup shredded Mozzarella

Dash of salt

½ teaspoon freshly and coarsely
    ground black pepper

½ cup strained bacon drippings

¼ cup best tarragon vinegar

2 tablespoons lemon juice

¼ teaspoon Worcestershire sauce

½ cup cognac

6 strips bacon, fried crisp and
    busted up

Into a large bowl, tear spinach. Add sliced eggs, cheese, salt, and pepper. Heat bacon fat, vinegar, lemon juice, and Worcestershire sauce in small saucepan.

Warm brandy, ignite, and slowly pour into dressing. When cognac ceases to flame, add dressing to salad and toss well. Dressing should be warm enough to slightly wilt spinach. Add crumbled bacon and serve.

"The Spinach Lady with Her Parsley Dog," Walter sketch. Courtesy of Eugene Walter estate.

Rice, Pasta, Soufflés, and Sandwiches

Rice • Palermo Pasta • Individual Cheese Custards •
Miss Minnie J. Cox's Soufflé • English Monkey • Whoopsadaisy
Toast • Po'-Boy Sandwich • Rich Boy Sandwich

RICE

Rice, the preferred accompaniment to many southern dishes, seems easy to cook. But remembering how much gum, goo, and glop had been served to me under the name of "rice" in various parts of the world, I decided to find out how to cook the white, puffy, every-grain-separate rice that is so good with gumbo or chicken gravy or any other southern dish.

My instructress was the famous, cool Marie Honorine Julac, a kitchen-proud female if ever there was one. (No store-bought mayonnaise or pickles for her; she makes her own or doesn't serve them. When she cooks, she washes bowls and pots as she goes along, so that when the food is on the fire, there is no trace of its manufacture in the kitchen.) She is known as "Hon," diminutive both of "Honey" and of her own name.

"Hon," I inquired, "do you really have to wash the rice that much?"

"Watch me," she said. She put the rice in a big bowl and picked through for gravel or dark grains. Then she filled the bowl with cold water and rubbed the rice between her fingers. She dumped out that water and repeated the process twice more. The water was milky with starch. Next, she placed the rice in a colander and let cold water run through it while she rubbed it again. She kept this up until the water ran clear.

"I am perfectly aware," she explained almost impatiently, "that a certain amount of food value goes right down the drain, but the point is, this rice is going to be the ideal accompaniment to my chicken gravy. My gravy does

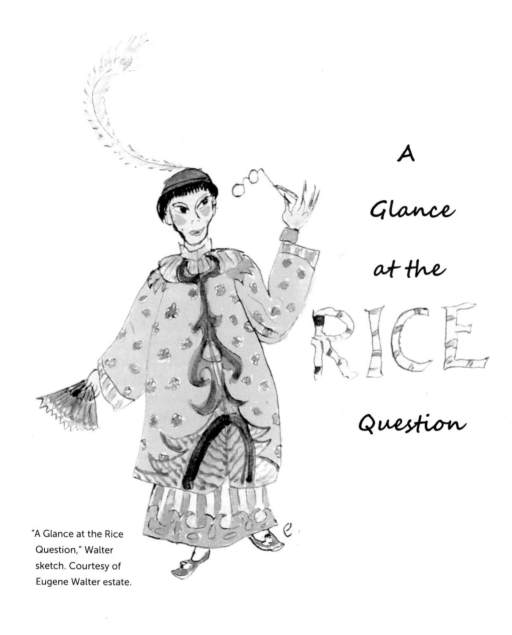

A
Glance
at the
RICE
Question

"A Glance at the Rice Question," Walter sketch. Courtesy of Eugene Walter estate.

a star turn . . . think of it this way: like the pas de deux of the Prince and the Swan Queen when they first meet by the old, wrinkled lake. We are breathless watching her float and turn, but he's there holding her up . . . and he has to be damned good at it, but unobtrusive. Well, my rice is the Prince and my gravy is the Swan Queen. Got it?"

"Sure," I said, watching her carefully measure two quarts of water for each cup of rice. She added a scant tablespoon of salt. When the water was boiling noisily, she began to drop the rice in, slowly, so that the water never stopped boiling. She added a teaspoon of butter "to keep the mess from boiling over" and stirred it up just once with a wooden spoon. After 4 to 5 minutes, she began to spoon out a few grains and feel them. About ten minutes later (it varies according to type of rice and circumstances), when the grains felt soft between her fingers, she poured the rice into the colander and washed it under the cold water. She melted salt to taste (very little since her gravy would be flavored) in warm water and poured it over the rice. She put the colander over a pot of hot water and steamed the rice in the oven for five minutes. The result was dry, light, fluffy.

When I tested it, I admitted she had done the trick, but she only looked mysteriously triumphant and said, "I won't show you how I make the gravy but I'll tell you the flavoring. After the chicken is fried, I pour off all the fat. I put one tablespoon of brandy in the skillet and scrape up the good scrunch from the bottom. Then I add light cream . . ." — here she looked about wild-eyed as if ascertaining whether her kitchen were bugged and lowered her voice confidentially — "and I stir in a pinch, just a little-bitta pinch, of fresh curry powder, not old yellow dust but fresh curry powder, just a pinch, so you can't taste curry but you somehow feel the gravy is sexy somehow. Understand?"

"Oh, I do!" I replied, swallowing.

She went on in her sibylline style, pointed her spoon at me, and said, "However . . . !"

"Ah?"

"However, if I am going to use the rice as a dish unto itself, or add bits of ham or chicken to it, I don't wash one damn grain!"

"But you said — "

"Oh, no!" she went on. "I melt a tablespoon of butter in a deep pan. I pour in the rice and stir it up until the grains all look transparent a little. Then I put in precisely twice as much water as there is rice; you have to measure accurately. Sometimes I use bouillon or a nice broth instead of water. I put in a little salt and maybe a bay leaf. I stir it all up, put on the lid, and turn up the heat. When the liquid boils up, I stir just once more and take out the bay leaf, then I turn down the fire and let the rice cook until the water is absorbed and the bottom of the rice goes 'creak, creak!' meaning it is about to stick if you let it. Then I turn off the fire, clap the lid on tight, wrap a dishcloth about it, and let it stay put until time to serve it. It can stay like that twenty to thirty minutes, but if it must wait longer, leave it in an open oven with very low heat. It must sit for at least ten minutes, though. To make golden rice, you cook it just like this but add a tablespoon of turmeric to the liquid."

"I see," I said, impressed.

"The point is, everybody has his own way with rice, but these are the two extremes: either you wash, wash, wash, or you don't wash at all."

"Now, if I want . . . "

But again she charged.

"There is also natural, or unpolished, rice. So good, has a nutty flavor, perfect with turkey or duck, game or roasts. I put a nut of butter in a deep pan. I pick the rice over carefully and put it into the melted butter until the grains look somewhat transparent. Then I add lots and lots of water and a little salt. When it boils, I turn it down a little and cook about twenty minutes, or, that is, until the grains bite well when I try them. Then drain the rice in a colander and wash it under the tap, and return it to the pot with butter, a pinch of salt, and some freshly ground black pepper. Turn fire up high, stir rice about, add a splash of hot water, and put on a lid. After a minute, when the water has steamed away, turn off the fire and close tightly and leave under a dishtowel until ready to serve."

"But you said . . . "

"It's a woman's prerogative, and a cook's, to change her mind."

"What about wild rice?"

She blazed up and waved her wooden spoon.

"Ha! Wild rice is neither wild nor a rice! It's a perfectly divine cultivated American swamp grass, and the directions are on the package!"

First years in Rome, 1950s. Courtesy of Eugene Walter estate.

2 lemons

1 pound spaghetti or little-string
   spaghetti

¼ cup best brandy

1 cup heavy cream

Salt and freshly ground black pepper

¾ cup freshly grated Parmesan cheese,
   genuine Italian if you can find it

Peel lemons — just thin, outer peel. Mince fine. Cut all inner peel and pith from lemons and cut flesh into small dice, removing all seeds. Cook spaghetti according to directions on packet, in plenty of boiling, salted water. While it's cooking, heat brandy, cream, and lemon flesh over low heat, bringing just to a boil. Simmer, uncovered, 8 to 10 minutes till reduced a little. Drain spaghetti, put in big heated bowl, and add sauce and salt and pepper to taste; toss well. Add cheese; toss some more. Serve at once on heated plates; sprinkle with minced lemon peel.

Some add a few chopped capers to this and a pinch of nutmeg; others add smashed green peppercorns, omitting the ground black pepper, of course.

1 cup bread crumbs

1 cup evaporated milk

¾ cup water

¼ cup dry Sherry

3 well-beaten eggs

¼ teaspoon salt

½ teaspoon mustard powder

Dash of cayenne (or 3 drops of Tabasco)

1½ tablespoons melted unsalted butter

1¼ cups grated American rat-trap
   cheese (orange-colored Wisconsin,
   New York State, whichever you like)

Good handful minced chives or green
   onions

Preheat oven to 325 degrees. Soak bread crumbs in liquids 5 minutes or so; add all else and stir till blended. Turn into 6 large buttered custard cups. Set in warm water and bake for 60 to 70 minutes or till knife comes out clean. Serves 6.

MISS MINNIE J. COX'S SOUFFLÉ

1 tablespoon quick-cooking tapioca

1 teaspoon salt

1 cup milk

Splash of English gin

1 cup grated American rat-trap cheese

3 well-beaten egg yolks

Good glop of Worcestershire sauce

3 stiffly beaten egg whites

Preheat oven to 350 degrees. Combine tapioca, salt, milk, and gin; cook in double boiler 10 to 12 minutes, stirring the while. Add cheese; cook till cheese melts. Add a few drops of hot mix to egg yolks, then a little more, then stir eggs into mix. Add Worcestershire. Cool a few minutes, then add egg whites. Bake in ungreased casserole about 1 hour and 15 minutes. Good served with tomato chutney. Serves 4 greedy-guts or 6 polite eaters.

ENGLISH MONKEY

The name of this dish always elicited giggles from Mobilian Mrs. D. J. Hartzog's dinner guests. Until a few years ago, it was a popular luncheon dish, served with a salad of lima beans and chives dressed with dill and sour cream and sliced avocados with lemon juice.

1 cup stale bread crumbs

1 cup milk

1 tablespoon unsalted butter

½ cup soft mild cheese, cut in
   little pieces

1 slightly beaten egg

Salt to taste

Touch of cayenne

1 teaspoon dry Sherry

Soak crumbs about 15 minutes in milk. Melt butter and add cheese; when it's melted, add soaked crumbs, egg, seasonings, and Sherry. Mix well and cook 3 to 4 minutes. Serve over toast, crackers, biscuits, or grits, plain or fried.

This is a mad dish from the 1920s. It is for breakfast or lunch after a late night.

2 tablespoons unsalted butter	Dash of mace
½ pound grated Cheddar cheese	Salt and freshly ground white pepper
¼ cup dry Champagne	Toast

In your chafing dish, melt butter over hot water, then add grated Cheddar cheese. As it melts, gradually add Champagne. Put in a dash of mace, a pinch of salt, and a hint of freshly ground white pepper; serve immediately over warm toast. Chilled Champagne, of course, with it.

PO'-BOY SANDWICH

New Orleans invented the name and makes splendid greedy-guts sandwiches of this genre. BUT, the South being the South, personal variations exist on no matter what theme you might care to mention. Two delightful sisters of Biloxi (I speak of the 1930s, mid-Depression) known as Miss Alice and Miss Boojums invented this highly successful effect to serve for a passel of unexpected relatives arrived from Tennessee.

2 long, thin French bread loaves	Creole mustard
Unsalted butter	Blackberry wine—port
Vermouth	Cucumber, thinly sliced
Freshly ground black pepper	Salt
Onion, grated	Paprika
Deviled ham, Underwood brand preferred	Dried dill

Slice French loaves lengthwise into 2 sections. Remove most of soft white (for the birds). Spread the bread with unsalted butter highly flavored with dry vermouth, black pepper, and a bit of grated onion. Next layer: deviled ham with a drop of Creole mustard and a few drops of blackberry wine (port). On top: parboiled cucumber slices, salted and dusted with mild paprika and dried dill. All arranged on baking sheet and put under grill a few minutes. Alongside: heavy, dark homemade beer. Think about this!

2 long French loaves

Unsalted butter

Chopped chives or shallots

Dried dill

Salt and freshly ground pepper

Fresh basil or inner celery leaves

Canned luncheon meat or chopped ham, capers, and sour cream

Tomatoes, green or slightly yellowing

Olive oil or mayonnaise

Capers or pickled green peppercorns

You'll want rather thin French loaves. Cut into convenient lengths, 9 inches for males, 5 inches for ladies' bridge club. Paper towels a-plenty for all. Slice pieces lengthwise. Pull out most of soft center; save to feed birds. Spread bread thickly with unsalted butter into which you've mixed chopped chives or shallots, dried dill, salt, and freshly ground black pepper.

Put a layer of fresh basil leaves or inner celery leaves on this, then a thick slice of your favorite CANNED luncheon meat, or, if you subscribe to the new snobbism toward old-fashioned canned goods from those pre-refrigerator days in the South, you can use a spread made of chopped ham, capers, and sour cream.

Next layer is paper-thin slices of green or slightly yellowing tomatoes with a smear of best olive oil or mayonnaise over them. Then a nice scattering of capers or pickled green peppercorns, as you prefer.

Place these heaped bread sections on baking sheet and put into 375-degree oven until the house smells good. Serve a MUG of cheap Champagne alongside each pair of these delights.

Some like to do these without the luncheon meat or ham spread, as above, only with raw oysters sprinkled with lemon juice and a little horseradish as top layer, in this case cooked under broiler. But always paper towels and cheap Champagne. Some things are simply indicated.

Desserts

PUDDINGS AND MOUSSES

Gulf Coast Bread Pudding • Monkey Pudding • Porcupine
Pudding • Meringue Pudding • Chocolate Crumb Pudding • English
Summer Pudding • Summer Pudding (Government St., circa 1900) •
Apricot Puff • Lime Lick-the-Plate • Baron Rothschild's Mousse •
Mrs. Luce's Bavarian Cream • Georgia Belle Mousse • Peach Mousse •
Carolina Custard • Rum-Bum • Two-Faced Mousse • Orange Whiskey
Cream • Candied Orange Peel Cream • October Parfaits •
Champagne Jelly • Barbados Shake

CAKES

Tipsy Cake • Bishop's Cake • Conti Street Cake • French Tea
Cake • Dixie Orange Cake • Family Reunion Cake • Upside-Down Cake •
Hello, Columbus! or Pineapple Right-Side-Up Cake • Aunt Jack's White
Fruit Cake • Sizzle Cake • Yesterday's Pound Cake • Plaquemine Pecan
Cake • Demopolis Caramel Cake • Plantation Skillet Cake • Jenny Lind
Rice Cakes • Lacey-Edge Cakes • Ginger Pancakes

PIES, TARTS, AND COBBLERS

Bourbon Pecan Pie • Traditional Mince Meat Pie • Tallulah
Pie • Brandy Alexander Pie • Pear Pie • Cider Raisin Pie • Orange
Custard Pie • Charleston Orange Fluff Pie • Prohibition Pie • Tennessee
Pie • Demopolis Raisin Pie • Sunday Pie • Creole Pie • Coffee Break
Pie • Carolina Berry Tart • Valdosta Tart • Mrs. Hans Curjel's Pear
Tart • Peach Cobbler • Lafayette Cobbler

COOKIES

Bourbon Balls • Bette Davis Cookies • Eggnog Cookies •
Brittany Shortbread • Lebkuchen (German Cookies) • Rum Balls •
Boobaloos • Rum Bunnies • Lafayette Crunch

SHERBETS AND ICE CREAMS

Applejack Ice • Arkansas Sherbet • Applesauce Sherbet • Cantaloupe
Sherbet • Marquise au Champagne • Grenadine Sherbet • Jade
Sherbet • Midsummer Sherbet Dream • Simonette's Sherbet • Bellini
Sherbet • Buttermilk Sherbet with Ginger Sauce • Melanie's Revenge:
Watermelon Sherbet with White Rum • Southern Belle Sherbet •
Southern Belle Ice Cream • Italian Sundae • San Francisco Sundae

FRUIT DESSERTS

Point Clear Banana Fritters • Orange Parfait/Orange Sog • Spiced
Oranges • Bananas Flambé • Peaches Flambé • Baked Peaches • Baked
Peaches with Liqueur Topping • Peach Gratiné • Roasted Peaches •
Poached Pears • Pears in Wine • Tipsy Parson • Apple Meringue •
Pineapple Fritters • Prune Soufflé • Rhubarb Conserve • Rhubarb-Pear
Compote • Strawberry Crumbly • Strawberries Romanoff • Kentucky
Compote • Hasty Crunch • Jam Muffins

DESSERT SAUCES

Hard Sauce for Fruitcakes and Puddings • Strawberry Sauce •
Mango Sauce • Bourbon Sauce • Whiskey Cream

Yankees have an idea that southerners indulge in gargantuan repasts, piles
and piles of everything dripping with bacon fat, butter, cream, all that.
And so they do, but not every day, and the secret is that these feasts are
orchestrated. They'd say balanced, I reckon. The rich rich rich dishes are
for feasts, which is not the same as daily meals. The rich rich rich desserts
are another story. They usually follow a luncheon of fresh greens cooked
with fatback and cornbread or corn muffins, with side dishes of pickled
beets, bread and butter pickles, and relishes and chutneys. If pork chops
or meatloaf or fried chicken or fish is the main course, the dessert would
more likely be big slices of watermelon or Persian melon or strawberries.
I can remember lunching at a household in New Orleans in a summer in
the 1930s where a soup of mixed greens was the main dish, followed by a

few slices of exquisite cold ham and THEN the reason for the gathering: not one but two big persimmon pies with brandy-flavored whipped cream, one-fourth of a pie for each person.

Puddings & Mousses

GULF COAST BREAD PUDDING

3 cups milk

½ cup bourbon

1 cup seedless raisins

Pinch of salt

6 tablespoons sugar

2 teaspoons grated lemon peel

4 teaspoons grated orange peel

1 ½ tablespoons melted unsalted butter

3 slightly beaten egg yolks

3 cups stale bread cut into ½-inch cubes

For meringue:

3 egg whites

6 tablespoons sugar

Grated cloves, nutmeg, cinnamon, as you like

Preheat oven to 325 degrees. Heat milk and bourbon together and pour over raisins. Let stand about 10 minutes. Add a pinch of salt, 6 tablespoons sugar, grated peels, butter, and egg yolks. Mix well, then add the bread cubes. Pour into greased 2-quart baking dish and bake for an hour.

While dish is baking, beat egg whites on high in your mixer until soft peaks. Continue beating, slowly adding sugar until meringue is stiff. Remove dish from oven and pile your meringue on top of pudding, sprinkling with spice of your choice. Return to oven and bake 15 minutes longer, until meringue is golden brown. Serve warm. For 6 hungries, 8 polite.

In the words of Celestine Eustis, 1904: "Take about half a loaf of stale bread. Let it soak in nice milk (as much as you would for a bread pudding) several hours. Add a little cream to it. Put in three heaping spoonfuls of brown sugar, two heaping spoonfuls of powdered cinnamon, a few stoned raisins, a splash of rum. Cook in the oven with a slow fire until it looks like an old monkey. Serve with a stiff sugar and butter sauce, flavored with a little wine."

In all those old recipes, stale bread just means yesterday's or day-before-yesterday's bread, which has dried a little. "Stale" has become a sniffy term in our modern cooks' usage.

PORCUPINE PUDDING

From Miss Banks of South Carolina, 1904: "Take six good apples. Peel and core them. Make a little syrup with sugar and water. Let your apples cook in that syrup, roasting them. When the apples are soft, take them out, put them in a flat dish. Let your syrup thicken a bit, pour it over the apples, and let them get cool. Beat the whites of two or three eggs stiff. Put it over the apples, shaping it in the form of a pudding. Stick in it all over blanched almonds. Let it brown in the oven."

Miss Banks doesn't mention spirits, but in a copy of the recipe sent to a friend in Mobile, a margin notation says: "Rum or brandy."

MERINGUE PUDDING

This comes from Savannah, about 1906: "One pint of stale bread crumbs, one quart of milk, nearly one teacupful of sugar, three eggs, leaving aside the white of one of them for the meringue. Season the pudding with the grated peel of one lemon.

"Mix all together and bake until you can put the handle of a teaspoon in and it comes out clean. Then cover the pudding with some nice fig preserves flavored with orange liqueur. Make your meringue of the one white of egg and teacupful of sugar. Spread it on top of the preserves, and put in the stove until it is lightly browned. Double the recipe if more is wanted."

CHOCOLATE CRUMB PUDDING

¼ cup unsalted butter

¾ cup firmly packed brown sugar

2 cups scalded milk

2 cups cold milk

2 beaten eggs

2 cups soft bread crumbs

2 teaspoons dark rum

Pinch of cinnamon

½ of 7-ounce packet of semisweet
   chocolate

Preheat oven to 350 degrees. Melt butter, add sugar, and stir until melted. Add to scalded milk, stirring till dissolved. Add cold milk, then slowly add to eggs. Add crumbs, rum, cinnamon, and coarsely chopped chocolate. Pour into 1 ½-quart casserole that you place in a pan of warm water. Bake for 1 ½ hours or until silver knife stuck in center comes out clean. Serve warm, with or without cream.

ENGLISH SUMMER PUDDING

The British Isles make up the Magical Kingdom of Puddings. They have literally hundreds. The following is positively feebleminded, it's so simple. But oh, is it good!

8 to 10 slices of real white bread,
   crust removed (Pepperidge Farm
   is best, if you don't have homemade;
   but none of that gooey, spongy
   stuff, please)

½ cup sugar

Splash of white rum

5 cups assorted berries: raspberries,
   blackberries, mulberries, strawberries, blueberries, sliced
   strawberries, as you please

Chilled heavy cream, ice cream,
   or frozen yogurt alongside

Line a 1-quart bowl with sliced bread, cutting it to fit. Combine sugar, rum, and fruit in saucepan and heat just until sugar is dissolved and the berry juice has started to run, roughly 4 to 5 minutes. Pour the fruit and juice into bread-lined bowl. Top with a layer of bread and cover loosely with plastic wrap. Place on plate and put a plate that fits just right on top of the pudding to weigh it down. Then put weight on top of all. Keep in fridge overnight.

When ready to serve, take off weight, plate, and plastic and run a knife around edge of pudding to loosen it. Turn out on chilled plate.

Whipped heavy cream with finely chopped candied ginger in it is very good with this, but there are hundreds of sauces, creams, etc., which you might prefer to choose from to accompany this delicious pudding.

SUMMER PUDDING (GOVERNMENT ST., CIRCA 1900)

¼ pound candied cherries	2 eggs
2 slices candied pineapple	1 pint cream
½ cup Sherry	Fresh chilled peach halves
1 cup milk	soaked in brandy
1 cup sugar	Candied ginger
2 tablespoons flour	

Cut cherries and pineapple into small pieces; soak in Sherry a few hours. Scald milk in double boiler. Stir together sugar and flour. Add eggs; beat until light and creamy. Add to scalded milk; cook until foam disappears and the custard is creamy. Let cool; stir in cream and fruit. Let stand in icebox several hours.

Serve with chilled brandied peach halves with chopped ginger in cavities where peach stones were removed.

APRICOT PUFF

Many of the now-lost southern desserts, in the days before refrigerators, depended on dried peaches, apricots, prunes, currants, and raisins. The following is so luscious that it never abated, even for a day.

1 cup dried apricots	½ cup dark honey
2 cups water	3 tablespoons lemon juice
3 tablespoons best brandy	4 egg whites

Cover apricots with the water and slowly bring to a boil; simmer on low heat about 15 minutes. Strain. Put apricots, 4 tablespoons of their cooking juice, and the brandy, honey, and lemon juice in a big bowl and either by food processor or elbow grease whisk them well together. Let cool in a big bowl, then beat in the whites, which have been whipped until stiff. Chill.

This was often served, in times past, with sweetened cottage cheese, but lately it has been coupled with frozen yogurt.

⅓ cup light rum

1 envelope Mrs. Knox unflavored
    gelatin

2 limes, juiced

1 tablespoon lemon juice

1 tablespoon grated lime peel

3 big eggs, room temperature,
    separated

½ cup sugar

Pinch of salt

¼ cup heavy cream

Put rum in heavy pan, sprinkle gelatin over, and let sit 1 to 2 minutes. Stir in lime juice, lemon juice, lime peel, egg yolks, and ¼ cup sugar. Cook this mixture over low heat, stirring constantly, until it begins to thicken. Remove from fire, put pot in big bowl of ice cubes and water, and let it cool, stirring now and then, until it has a syrupy texture, but don't let it set.

In a bowl, beat egg whites with a pinch of salt till they hold peaks, then beat in remaining sugar, a little at a time; go on till they hold stiff peaks. Stir about ⅓ of the egg whites into lime mixture, then carefully but completely fold in remaining whites.

In another dish, beat the cream till it peaks; fold into lime mixture. Spoon this mousse into dessert glasses and cover loosely with plastic. Chill from 1½ to 24 hours.

Garnish with twists of lime or a few rose petals. Serves 6. Thin almond cookies alongside. But anise wafers are good, too, in this case.

Variation: Instead of lime, use candied ginger soaked in best bourbon, orange juice instead of lemon, and white wine instead of rum.

BARON ROTHSCHILD'S MOUSSE

¾ cup chopped candied fruit
    (pineapple, apricot, orange peel,
    etc., and ginger, please no cherries)

2 tablespoons brandy

32-ounce carton vanilla-flavored
    yogurt (or plain yogurt and
    1 teaspoon vanilla extract)

¼ cup sugar

2 tablespoons cornstarch

Pinch of allspice

2 lightly beaten eggs

Put the fruit to soak in the brandy. At least 6 hours before, drain the yogurt. Preheat oven to 375 degrees. In a good-sized bowl, mix the yogurt, sugar, cornstarch, allspice, and fruit. Stir in the eggs, pour all into a buttered 8-inch pie pan, and smooth off the top. Bake about half an hour or until knife comes clean from center. Cool a bit, then put into fridge until well chilled.

When serving, garnish with candied rose petals, violets, or mint leaves. Very cold Champagne alongside.

MRS. LUCE'S BAVARIAN CREAM

1 cup finely chopped candied fruit
  (no cherries, ginger yes)
½ cup best cognac
⅓ cup finely chopped toasted
  almonds or macaroon crumbs
1 cup sugar
1 envelope Mrs. Knox unflavored
  gelatin

¾ cup milk
4 big eggs, separated
2 tablespoons light molasses
Good dash of powdered mace
Pinch of powdered allspice
Hint of salt
1 cup whipping cream

Soak fruit in cognac an hour. Oil a 7-cup mold and sprinkle with nuts or crumbs. Mix ½ cup sugar and gelatin in top of double boiler, add milk, and let stand 5 minutes. Beat yolks lightly and add to milk, set over boiling water, and cook, stirring constantly, till slightly thickened, about 5 minutes. Cool. Stir in fruit, cognac, molasses, and spices. Cool until mixture begins to thicken.

Beat egg whites with a pinch of salt to soft peaks. Add remaining sugar; beat until a soft meringue. Beat cream to soft peaks. Fold meringue and cream into gelatin mix. Chill in prepared mold till firm. To serve, place mold briefly in hot water bath; unmold onto chilled plate and garnish with fresh or candied fruit or flowers. (No cherries!)

This dessert is, of course, always accompanied by very cold dry Champagne.

1 ½ cups dried peaches	3 big eggs, room temperature, separated
1 ½ cups water	½ cup sugar plus 3 ½ tablespoons sugar
½ cup peach liqueur (not peach brandy)	2 cups cold whipping cream
1 tablespoon Mrs. Knox unflavored gelatin	Pinch of cream of tartar
	Mint sprigs or small flowers for garnish

Let peaches and water soak in saucepan about half an hour, then bring to boil, turn down heat, and let simmer roughly 20 minutes or until peaches are very soft. While this is going on, put half of the peach liqueur in a bowl, pour the gelatin over it, and set aside to soften. In top of double boiler, beat egg yolks, ½ cup sugar, and the rest of the liqueur until a nice light color. Then put over simmering water and stir till thick enough to coat the back of a spoon, about 2 minutes. Don't boil. Add gelatin to hot peach mix and whisk until very smooth. Cool to room temperature, stirring now and then so that mixture doesn't set. Add custard to peach mix and whisk, whisk, whisk. Whip cream and add ⅓ to peach mix. Gently fold in remaining cream in two rounds.

Using clean, dry beaters, beat egg whites and cream of tartar in another bowl till frothy. Gradually add remaining sugar and beat till smooth, shiny, and almost stiff. Put ⅓ of whites into peach mix. In 2 batches, fold in remaining whites. Cover bowl with plastic and refrigerate overnight, or at least 6 hours.

If you have an old-fashioned pastry bag with a big star tip, you can pipe the mousse into glasses. No matter what, garnish with mint sprigs or fresh viola (Johnny-jump-up) flowers or violets.

PEACH MOUSSE

2 teaspoons dark rum	3 tablespoons sugar
1 teaspoon vanilla extract	3 egg yolks
Good dash of powdered mace	¾ cup whipping cream
1 ¼ teaspoons Mrs. Knox unflavored gelatin	½ cup confectioner's sugar
1 pound ripe peaches, peeled and pitted	½ teaspoon grated lemon peel
	Mint sprigs for garnish

Combine rum, vanilla, and mace in small bowl. Pour gelatin over and let soften at least 10 minutes. Puree peaches, mechanically or by elbow grease. Pour peaches into heavy saucepan. Add sugar and bring to simmer, stirring to melt sugar. Simmer 10 minutes or so on low. Whisk yolks separately, then add simmering puree to yolks, whisking like mad. Now add gelatin mix and stir over medium heat about 2 to 3 minutes. Put in big bowl and refrigerate until cold, about 40 minutes, stirring now and then. Now whip cream with confectioner's sugar until peaks form, whisk in lemon peel, and fold cream mix into peach mix about ⅓ at a time. Cover and refrigerate.

This is good on Persian melon "boats": quarter slices of the very cold melon. Or serve in cookie "boats." Mix up your favorite cookie dough. Butter the underside of your muffin tin and mold cookie dough to it to make cups. Garnish with mint.

CAROLINA CUSTARD

This is a southern version of the classic crème caramel. If you don't have Grand Marnier, use any of the famous orange liqueurs; avoid the nasty, cheap ones.

¼ cup water

2 cups plus 2 tablespoons sugar

2 ⅔ cups milk

5 teaspoons grated orange peel

2 teaspoons grated lemon peel

½ teaspoon powdered ginger

½ teaspoon powdered cinnamon

7 big eggs

2 ½ tablespoons Grand Marnier

Preheat oven to 350 degrees. Put ¼ cup water in medium saucepan and add 1 cup and 2 tablespoons sugar. Cook over low until sugar melts. Turn up heat and boil without stirring till syrup is dark brown. Divide evenly among 8 custard cups the syrup and any sugar crystals that formed.

Bring milk and flavorings to simmer in heavy saucepan. Turn off heat, cover, and let sit about 10 minutes. Whisk eggs well, stir in remaining sugar, then gradually whisk in hot milk. Strain into another bowl. Add liqueur. Ladle into the caramel-lined cups and put in baking pan with hot water halfway up sides of custard dishes. Bake until custards don't move when shaken, about 45 minutes. Remove from baking pan and cool about an hour. Cover and chill overnight. When ready to serve, take sharp little knife and go around edges of custards and place each one on chilled plate.

1 ½ tablespoons Mrs. Knox
   unflavored gelatin
2 tablespoons cold water
6 tablespoons boiling water
1 cup sugar
⅓ cup rum

4 tablespoons best bourbon
2 egg whites
1 pint cream
½ cup finely chopped candied
   orange peel

Soften gelatin in cold water. After 5 minutes, put into boiling water. Add sugar, rum, and bourbon, stirring until sugar melts. Strain. When mixture begins to thicken, beat until frothy. Beat egg whites well. Add to mixture. Beat cream, gradually adding all of it. Beat all until light. Put in mold and chill. Serve with whipped cream and sprinkled with candied orange peel. Serves 6.

This dessert consists of alternate layers of caramel mousse and chocolate mousse in tall, clear glasses. This makes about 8 servings.

For caramel mousse:

¾ cup whipping cream
¼ cup light brown sugar,
   packed tight
½ cup white sugar
5 tablespoons water

3 tablespoons unsalted butter
1 ¼ cups chilled whipping cream
1 teaspoon vanilla extract
Pinch of mace

For chocolate mousse:

5 ounces chopped semisweet
   chocolate
1 ½ cups chilled whipping cream
½ cup confectioner's sugar

3 tablespoons unsweetened
   cocoa powder
1 ½ tablespoons dark rum
1 teaspoon vanilla extract

For caramel mousse: In heavy pan, heat cream to lukewarm; remove from heat. In another heavy pan, mix brown sugar and white sugar with water over medium heat till sugar melts. Turn up heat and boil till sugar turns deep golden brown, swooshing pan now and then and scraping down sides with wooden spoon or paddle, about 8 minutes. Add warm cream and cook on low heat till mix is smooth, stirring all the while. Mix in butter. Pour caramel into bowl. Cover and chill at least 2 hours. Then beat chilled cream, vanilla, and mace to soft peaks in big bowl. Fold in caramel. Cover and refrigerate.

For chocolate mousse: Melt the chocolate in a big bowl over pan of simmering water. Stir till smooth. Let cool down, stirring occasionally. With electric beater, if you have one, beat in another bowl the chilled whipping cream with confectioner's sugar, cocoa, rum, and vanilla till peaks form. Whisk ¾ cup of whipped cream mixture thoroughly into melted chocolate. Fold remaining cream mix into chocolate.
Spoon chocolate mousse into bottoms of glasses, then put in a layer of caramel, then chocolate, then caramel, until you've used all. Cover and refrigerate at least 4 to 5 hours.

Some like whipped cream flavored with a bit of powdered cinnamon on top, others a bit of finely chopped candied ginger. Others, the baroque ones, like candied violets.

ORANGE WHISKEY CREAM

1 packet orange-flavored gelatin
  (Jell-O)
1½ cups boiling water
2 teaspoons Mrs. Knox unflavored
  gelatin

2 tablespoons best bourbon
2 cups heavy cream
5 tablespoons thick orange
  marmalade

Mix the Jell-O with boiling water. Pour 1 cup of this into a bowl and stir well as you add the unflavored gelatin. Chill to a shaky goo, but don't let it get firm. Add the bourbon to the remaining Jell-O and cool to room temperature. Whip the cream, but not to stiffness. Add the marmalade, mix in well, and stir into the 1 cup of half-set Jell-O. Now pour half of this mixture into a dish and hurry into freezer. When it's set, carefully pour on the ½ cup of whiskey-flavored jelly. Again, hurry into freezer until set, then pour on the rest of the cream and set in fridge.

CANDIED ORANGE PEEL CREAM

2 cups milk (not low-fat or nonfat)

2 cups whipping cream

1 tablespoon plus 1 teaspoon
    candied orange peel

8 egg yolks

⅔ cup sugar

2 tablespoons Grand Marnier or other
    good quality orange liqueur

Bring milk, cream, and 1 tablespoon peel to simmer in heavy medium pan. Remove from heat and let steep an hour. Then return pan to heat. In a separate pan, whisk yolks and sugar to blend. Gradually whisk in some of the hot milk mix to temper the eggs and sugar. Return all to saucepan; stir over medium heat till custard thickens and leaves path on back of spoon when finger is drawn across, about 5 minutes. DON'T BOIL. Strain custard into bowl. Refrigerate overnight or at least 4 hours. Mince 1 teaspoon peel and add. Stir in liqueur. Put into ice cream machine and follow manufacturer's directions. Freeze in covered container. Can be prepared 4 days in advance.

OCTOBER PARFAITS

2 cups grapes, halved and seeded

5 tablespoons best French brandy

¼ cup sugar

2 tablespoons cornstarch

⅛ teaspoon salt

1 beaten egg

2 cups milk

Freshly ground nutmeg to taste

Tiny pinch of allspice

Combine grapes and 4 tablespoons brandy; marinate in fridge at least 1 hour. Mix sugar, cornstarch, and salt in saucepan; add egg and milk. Cook over medium heat until thick and smooth, about 5 minutes. Take from heat; stir in remaining brandy. Put in fridge to cool.

In chilled parfait glasses, put ½ cup grapes in each glass, then top with ½ cup pudding. Sprinkle nutmeg and allspice on top.

Some put an inch of crushed graham crackers, or any sugar wafer dampened with orange liqueur, packed solid into bottom of parfait glasses before putting glasses in fridge. This serves 4.

Traditional for engagement parties, wedding breakfasts, christening fetes, and the 100th birthday celebration of those who drink wine with their food. Longevity is in the wine bottle.

1 envelope Mrs. Knox unflavored
   gelatin
¼ cup cold water
½ cup sugar
½ cup strained fresh orange juice

1 ½ cups Champagne or other
   sparkling white wine or elderberry
   flower Champagne
1 tablespoon crème de cassis or a
   raspberry or blackberry liqueur,
   as you like

Mix gelatin and water in a large pan on the stove. Turn the heat to high and boil for about a minute, stirring, stirring, stirring. Lower the heat to medium and add sugar, orange juice, and Champagne. Keep the heat just below boiling and stir until sugar dissolves. Remove from heat and stir in liqueur. Skim off foam with metal spoon. Pour into hot, sterilized half-pint jars. Seal immediately with hot paraffin or canning lids.

If Champagne is brut (dry), you might wish to add a little more sugar; if it is sweet, you might wish to go scant on sugar.

Ladyfingers are traditional with this. Serve either in dessert dishes or in Champagne glasses. This recipe makes 3 portions; multiply measurements to your need.

2 cups coarsely chopped fresh
   pineapple
1 cup vanilla ice cream
1 cup chilled pineapple juice

1 cup white rum
3 to 4 pieces candied ginger,
   minced
Mint sprigs for garnish

Blend first 5 ingredients well. Pour into tall, chilled glasses. Decorate with mint sprigs.

Cakes

TIPSY CAKE

Tipsy Cake has so many different family recipes that it would take the Good Housekeeping Institute a half-century to try them all. Not only that, other versions of the same go under the name of Trifle. Many "pre-Victoria" dishes that came from England to the South are very different from versions in current English cookbooks.

Tipsy Cake or Trifle may be a yellow cake flavored with lemon peel and juice, with a big opening in the middle filled with custard. The sauce is a creamy sauce flavored with bourbon and molasses. Or yellow cupcakes cut in half and spread with blackberry jam, then covered with custard and a bourbon and honey or molasses sauce.

Yet another sweet going by the name of Tipsy Cake is a yellow pound cake iced with an icing made of brown sugar, cream, and bourbon. This very same icing is sometimes served as topping for frozen yogurt.

All cooks are unanimous in using only fine bourbon in cookery, not the inferior labels. They feel the same about wine in cookery. Always the best.

BISHOP'S CAKE

½ cup butter

1 cup sugar

3 well-beaten eggs

1 ½ cups unbleached flour

1 ½ teaspoons baking powder

¼ teaspoon salt

¼ pound semisweet chocolate

3 cups mixed candied citron, ginger, and dates soaked in brandy or bourbon

Preheat oven to 325 degrees. Cream butter and sugar, then beat in eggs. Sift dry ingredients together. Chop chocolate into pea-size bits; add with fruits to flour mix. Fold in egg mixture. Line bottom of 5 ½ × 9 ½-inch greased loaf pan with wax paper. Pour in the dough; bake 1 ½ hours. Serve sliced like fruitcake with slightly sweetened yogurt, sour cream, or unsweetened whipped cream.

There are several versions of this cake. Some cooks prefer candied ginger or candied orange peel to the raisins; some like a mixture of all three.

2 cups flour	1 teaspoon freshly ground nutmeg
2 teaspoons baking powder	Pinch of powdered mace
½ cup unsalted butter, softened	½ cup best bourbon whiskey
1 cup sugar	1 cup chopped raisins
4 eggs	2 cups coarsely chopped pecans
½ teaspoon salt	

Preheat oven to 325 degrees. Mix flour and baking powder in a big bowl. Set aside. In another bowl, cream butter and sugar till fluffy; beat in eggs one at a time. Add salt, nutmeg, and mace. Add flour mixture alternately with slops of whiskey, saving aside ¼ of flour mix. Blend well after each addition.

Combine fruit and nuts, toss with reserved flour, and then fold into batter. Grease generously and lightly flour an 8 × 8-inch baking pan. Pour in batter and bake about 1 hour, till cake is firm to the touch. Cool in pan, then cut into squares. Makes about 9 servings.

Buttermilk sherbet flavored with any orange liqueur is good with this.

You'll want a 4 ½ × 8 ½-inch loaf pan, for this is sliced and served plain or with unsalted butter.

5 tablespoons cognac	¾ cup cake flour
1 ½ cups raisins	1 teaspoon baking powder
¾ cup softened unsalted butter	Pinch of salt
1 ¼ cups confectioner's sugar	¾ cup mixed chopped candied
2 eggs	orange and lemon peel, candied
⅓ cup milk	ginger, citron if available, pineapple
1 ½ cups all-purpose flour	if you like

Pour cognac over raisins and refrigerate 4 to 6 hours, occasionally giving a stir. Preheat oven to 375 degrees. Beat butter and sugar till fluffy. Beat in eggs one at a time, beating extra after each egg. Stir in milk. Sift the two flours, baking powder, and salt onto sheet of wax paper. Add dry mix to raisin mix and candied fruits to butter mix. Combine all and stir enough to mix all those elements, but don't overstir. Pour into buttered, floured loaf pan and level top. Bake 25 minutes, reduce heat to 325 degrees, and bake 25 minutes longer until cake is golden brown and wooden pick inserted comes out clean.

DIXIE ORANGE CAKE

¼ cup orange liqueur

1 cup raisins

2 cups unbleached flour

¼ teaspoon salt

1 teaspoon soda

Peel and pulp of 1 juiced orange

1 cup chopped pecans

½ cup shortening

1 cup sugar

2 eggs

⅔ cup buttermilk

½ cup sugar dissolved in ¾ cup orange juice and ¼ cup orange liqueur

Preheat oven to 350 degrees. Pour orange liqueur over raisins and let soak. Sift together flour, salt, and soda. Grind up orange peel and pulp, raisins soaked in orange liqueur, and nuts. Cream shortening and sugar; add eggs. Stir in ground nuts, raisins, and orange. Add dry ingredients alternately with milk. Pour batter into well-greased tube or loaf pan; bake about 40 minutes or until done. Remove cake from oven. Pour well-mixed ½ cup of sugar, orange juice, and orange liqueur over hot cake and let cool in pan. Buttermilk sherbet is good with this. So is very cold Champagne.

If you can't get orange liqueur, simply chop an orange (peel, seeds, juice, all) with some cloves, a bit of grated lemon peel, and a dash of honey or brown sugar and soak in 1 ½ cups of best bourbon in a glass jar for 24 hours. Strain and use.

For cake:

1 cup vegetable oil

¾ cup molasses

¼ cup warm water

4 eggs

2 cups unbleached flour

2 teaspoons baking soda

1 teaspoon salt

Heaping teaspoon cinnamon

1 teaspoon ginger

½ teaspoon grated nutmeg

2 teaspoons vanilla extract

1 cup cooked wild rice soaked in
    ¼ cup bourbon

1 cup chopped dates soaked in
    ¼ cup bourbon

3 cups finely grated carrots

For icing:

2 8-ounce packages cream cheese

¼ cup molasses

¼ cup bourbon

1 cup heavy cream, whipped with
    light touch of allspice

Preheat oven to 350 degrees. Combine oil, molasses, and water, then add eggs and beat till blended. Combine dry elements and sift together. Add to mixture and beat. Add vanilla, rice, dates, and carrots. Mix.

Divide this batter evenly among 3 greased and floured 8-inch layer cake pans. Bake for 35 minutes till cake tests done. Let stand on racks 5 minutes or so, then turn out.

For icing: Beat cream cheese till smooth, adding molasses and bourbon gradually. When well blended, beat in whipped cream. Spread between layers and over top and sides of cake. If you can find candied kumquats, sliver them and arrange on top.

UPSIDE-DOWN CAKE

This oldest local version comes from Kate Middleton. On occasion made with peaches, apricots, or plums.

1 tablespoon butter

1 cup brown sugar

Sliced pineapple, enough slices
    to lie in 1 layer on the bottom
    of the pan

Pecan pieces for the holes and
    between slices

2 egg yolks

1 cup sugar

1 tablespoon hot water

1 cup flour

1 ¾ teaspoons baking powder

Pinch of salt

3 egg whites

2 teaspoons vinegar

White rum

Take a large iron frying pan and melt butter and brown sugar. Put in as many slices of pineapple as will lie flat in the bottom of the pan, and in between slices and in holes of pineapple put nuts.

Preheat oven to 350 degrees. For the batter: Beat the yolks until they are thick and light yellow. Add sugar slowly and keep beating. Next add water and flour, which has been sifted with other dry ingredients. Add the whites of eggs beaten stiff, then the vinegar. Pour batter over the pineapple and bake about 35 minutes. Remove from oven, sprinkle with a little white rum, and immediately invert onto serving platter.

HELLO, COLUMBUS! OR PINEAPPLE RIGHT-SIDE-UP CAKE

The titles of this dessert are both examples of southern jokiness. Christopher and his crew drooled when they tasted the pineapple on Guadalupe in 1493, then introduced it to Europe and the world: It was already being cultivated in China in 1594 and was a greenhouse pet in Europe soon after.

Pineapple upside-down cake has long been a southern favorite. Versions appear in Gulf Coast family recipe books as early as the 1870s. The pineapple is usually placed on the bottom of the cake, which is cooked in a heavy iron skillet and turned over when served. In this version, the pineapple is placed on top before the cake goes into the oven.

1 8-ounce can unsweetened sliced pineapple with its juice	¼ cup milk
2 tablespoons dark rum	3 tablespoons melted unsalted butter
1 ½ cups flour	1 beaten egg
½ cup sugar	Pinch of mace
2 teaspoons baking powder	Pinch of nutmeg
Good pinch of salt	¼ cup firmly packed brown sugar

Preheat oven to 350 degrees. Drain pineapple, saving about half of the juice, into which you pour half of the rum. Put pineapple and juice aside. Mix flour, sugar, baking powder, and salt and stir well. Combine juice, milk, melted butter, egg, and spices; add to dry ingredients. Add rest of rum and mix all very well. Don't beat the dickens out of the stuff; just be sure the dry ingredients are moistened. Put batter into greased baking pan. Top with pineapple, sprinkle with brown sugar, and bake for a generous 30 minutes or until blade or pick comes out clean. Cool before serving.

If you wish to be showy, you can serve with melon balls. For baroque tastes, whipped cream flavored with Cointreau or Triple Sec is always served alongside.

AUNT JACK'S WHITE FRUIT CAKE

A manuscript sheet stuck into an old copy of the *Boston Cooking-School Cook Book* is labeled Aunt Jack's White Fruit Cake — Good!!! Three cheers for the good lady, long since eating sunbeams in heaven, whoever she might have been.

It used to be, in the Mobile of an earlier and less hurried time, that early November brought about a making of lists, a digging in kitchen cabinets or pantries for round cake and loaf pans, the cracking of nuts, and all the hectic exploits of the Fruitcake Cult. Fruitcakes, sampled at Thanksgiving and brought out for callers and visitors throughout December, always have been serious business.

Back when, tables were set up in the bigger grocery stores, where on a white muslin cloth sat boxes (each edged with a frill of colored wax paper) of candied orange and lemon peel, pineapple, apricots, candied currants, muscat raisins, cherries, and the translucent pale-green strips of a melon known as "citron." Fruitcake Cult members fell into camps: those who did or did not include crystallized ginger (found at George's Candy Shop down on Dauphin Street), and those who included insanely red cherries for color and those who loathed them. Such candied fruits, covered on those tables with a pink, cerise, or yellow length of tarleton — that same glazed cotton net that serves for ballet skirts — resembled a wild, baroque display of costume jewelry. The grocery clerks used wooden spears and forceps to fill little white paper bags with these fruitcake jewels.

Every cult cook had a private recipe for fruitcake, ranging from a white fruitcake, really white with currants, white cherries (haven't seen them for centuries), blanched almonds, and a great deal of grated coconut, to a black fruitcake, with molasses and rum-soaked prunes. The usual cake was ocher or brown. Dark cakes always took dark rum or bourbon; white port or even cognac diluted with scuppernong wine went into paler cakes. The normal procedure was to douse the cakes after they'd "settled" for a day or so, wrapped in wax paper, reposing in tin boxes in a pantry.

Most people had a bootlegger connection during the dry, unhappy years of Prohibition. For fine cognac, ladies had to get a prescription from their doctors on the grounds of nausea, anemia, or melancholia. They'd sally over to Van Antwerp's pharmacy at the corner of Dauphin and Royal.

That merry soul Dr. Gaines would cock his eye at my grandmother when she turned up at his office in fruitcake season.

"Are you having low spirits?" he'd inquire.

"Oh, yes, Doctor!" she'd exclaim. "Barely an inch left in the brandy bottle." He'd chuckle and scribble the prescription.

Looking back, this seems to me another proof that art and civilization triumph in even the darkest time.

1 pound white raisins	1 cup milk
1 pound chopped candied	7 egg whites
pineapple	1 pound grated coconut
¼ pound chopped citron	3 cups flour
1 pound slivered almonds	2 teaspoons baking powder
1 wine glass good brandy	⅛ teaspoon salt
1 wine glass good port	Pinch of powdered ginger and
1 cup butter	powdered mace
1 ½ cups sugar	

Preheat oven to 250 degrees. Put everybody to work chopping fruit and nuts. Put fruit, save coconut, to soak in brandy and port. Cream butter. Add sugar gradually; beat, beat, beat; then add milk, egg whites, the fruit in brandy and port, coconut, and flour sifted with baking powder, salt, and spices. Bake 3 hours. This improves with age: It should be kept at least a week before eating and should have a "benediction" of best bourbon every day.

SIZZLE CAKE

Here's a delightful almost-forgotten cake from the environs of Demopolis.

1 ¼ cups dark raisins

1 ¼ cups golden raisins

¾ cup chopped candied ginger

1 cup chopped pitted prunes

½ cup mixed chopped candied
  orange and lemon peel

1 ½ cups dark rum

1 cup unsalted butter

1 ⅔ cups packed dark brown sugar

2 cups all-purpose flour

2 teaspoons baking powder

½ teaspoon ground cloves

1 teaspoon powdered cinnamon

Dash of powdered mace

6 eggs

4 tablespoons molasses

Put all the fruits in a bowl and pour about ¾ cup of rum over them; let soak, covered, for 24 hours, giving an occasional stir. Preheat oven to 300 degrees. Line a 10-inch round loose-bottomed cake pan with buttered parchment paper. In a big bowl, cream butter and sugar until fluffy. In another bowl, sift together flour, baking powder, and spices, then gradually add flour mix to butter-sugar mix, adding eggs one at a time and beating well after each egg is added. Stir in molasses, then fold all into mixed fruits and mix well until completely combined. Spoon mixture into cake pan; bake in center of oven for 2 to 2 ½ hours or until a skewer inserted into center comes out clean.

Remove cake from pan; prick all over with fork. Pour remaining rum over cake, and when it stops sizzling, cover and let cool in pan. After slices are cut, keep remaining cake in rum-soaked cloth. Some like to cover this cake with a layer of marzipan and icing; I think it's better without.

YESTERDAY'S POUND CAKE

Tear up the pound cake; soak in white rum. Add some heavy cream and rather a lot of powdered cinnamon; pack into loaf pan. Chill well. Serve as pudding with fresh strawberries and a splash of orange liqueur, or plain with crème de cacao poured over.

PLAQUEMINE PECAN CAKE

7 egg yolks

1 ½ cups sugar

2 teaspoons dark rum

1 teaspoon vanilla

2 cups finely ground pecans

½ cup plus 2 tablespoons
  all-purpose flour

1 teaspoon baking powder

¼ teaspoon salt

⅓ cup melted unsalted butter

7 egg whites at room temperature

⅛ teaspoon cream of tartar

¼ cup unsalted butter

2 tablespoons heavy cream

¼ cup chopped pecans

Preheat oven to 350 degrees. Grease and flour bottom only of 9-inch springform pan. Beat yolks and ¼ cup of the sugar in big mixing bowl till thick and pale yellow, then beat in rum and vanilla. Combine ground nuts, ½ cup of the flour, baking powder, and salt. Stir into egg mix, then stir in melted butter. Beat egg whites and cream of tartar till foamy, then gradually beat in ¼ cup of the sugar; beat until peaks form. Fold into yolk mix, then pour batter into the prepared pan. Bake till center springs back when tapped, about 40 minutes. Cool on wire rack.

Preheat broiler. Now mix remaining sugar and flour in small pan; add ¼ cup butter and cream. Heat to boil; go on boiling as you stir constantly for 1 minute. Remove from heat and stir in pecans.

Now turn out cake into an ovenproof baking pan. Spread nut mix on top, then broil 4 inches from heat until topping bubbles, about 1 minute. If you like, garnish with pecan halves. Let cool to room temperature before serving.

Some like to add a pinch of powdered cloves or cinnamon or both to the topping. More often than not, vanilla ice cream is served with this cake.

Amid a hectic comparison of handed-down fruitcake recipes I heard lately, a very old lady turned to me and said wistfully, "Dudn't anybody make caramel cake anymore?" My grandmother's caramel cake! A wave of sudden nostalgia hit me; for an instant I could smell it cooking, sending forth a perfume that cheered the world for a block in every direction.

For cake:

2 ¼ cups sugar

¾ cup boiling water

3 cups flour

1 teaspoon baking powder

½ teaspoon baking soda

¼ teaspoon salt

⅓ cup unsalted butter

2 eggs, separated

1 cup cold water

1 teaspoon vanilla extract or 1 tablespoon Grenadine syrup or any orange liqueur, as you prefer

For icing:

2 cups sugar

2 tablespoons unsalted butter

¼ cup burnt sugar syrup

½ cup sweetened condensed milk

¾ teaspoon vanilla extract

Preheat oven to 375 degrees. First, make the syrup. In skillet over medium heat, melt ¾ cup sugar, stirring constantly until quite dark. Add boiling water; stir till sugar is dissolved. Set aside to cool.

Sift flour once; add baking powder, baking soda, and salt, then sift three times. Cream butter thoroughly, then gradually add remaining sugar. Go on creaming till light and fluffy. Add well-beaten egg yolks. Add flour mixture and water alternately, a little at a time. Beat till smooth. Add vanilla, Grenadine, or liqueur, then ¾ cup of syrup, and blend well. Fold in beaten egg whites. Put batter in two buttered and floured 9-inch round layer cake pans. Bake for 25 to 30 minutes or until knife comes out clean. Let layers cool before icing.

For icing: Mix everything in saucepan except vanilla, and let boil until soft ball forms in cold water. Cool, add vanilla, beat until creamy, then spread on cake.

TO WASH IT DOWN: Champagne, elderflower sparkling wine, or any white Rhine wine goes well with caramel cake.

SEND IN THE POSSE. Can't you see the "eat light" people gasping at this recipe? The anti-cholesterol cult would send a posse! But certainly the climate of our region requires lush sweets on occasion.

This is known in different localities as Paris Breakfast, Plantation Puff, and Wind Pudding. In the far West, its name is Dutch Baby.

This delightful "cake" is really a kind of popover or puff-up. The batter is poured into a hot skillet, then baked in the oven until risen and turned a golden brown. Highly popular in Charleston early on, it made its way to the Gulf Coast in the 1840s and 1850s. It is served with all manner of toppings: warm applesauce and a dash of brown sugar, or honey, or maple syrup with a splash of fresh orange, lemon, or tangerine juice. Best of all is a generous glop of any berry jam thinned with the best bourbon, cognac, or rum. Usually made in an iron skillet, but any Pyrex or oven ceramic vessel will do the job.

¼ cup unsalted butter

3 eggs

¾ cup milk

1 tablespoon fresh orange juice

1 tablespoon orange liqueur

¾ cup all-purpose flour

Pinch of freshly grated nutmeg
  (or mace or allspice, as you like)

Confectioner's sugar

Put butter in a heavy skillet not more than 3 inches deep. Set in preheated oven at 425 degrees. In a big bowl, beat eggs until light yellow; add milk, orange juice, liqueur, flour, and nutmeg and beat until smooth. Tilt skillet and swirl butter around to coat sides as well as bottom. Pour in batter, return skillet to oven, and bake until golden and puffed up, about 25 minutes. Dust with sugar and serve immediately.

Many like to offer a bowl of sour cream as well as a sweet sauce or relish alongside these cakes. Ice-cold Champagne good alongside, too, for special occasions.

JENNY LIND RICE CAKES

Rice cakes have been served in the South ever since Thomas Jefferson popularized rice and rice dishes. Plain white rice is perfect alongside dozens of stews, casseroles, gumbos, and mixed dishes of all kinds, where there is a luscious gravy or sauce. So there is always some plain boiled white rice left over to employ in hundreds of southern cakes, puddings, and all those side dishes for breakfast and luncheon. This version of the rice pancake is from New Orleans; Jenny Lind is said to have enjoyed it and ate a pile, according to legend.

4 egg yolks	2 teaspoons baking powder
1 ½ cups milk	2 tablespoons sugar
¼ cup melted unsalted butter	Pinch of salt
1 teaspoon vanilla or almond extract, as you wish	Good pinch of powdered cinnamon (or allspice or mace, as you think)
2 teaspoons best brandy	½ cup coarsely chopped pecans
1 cup all-purpose flour	1 cup cooked, cold rice

Beat eggs till light yellow, then beat in milk, butter, vanilla, brandy, flour, baking powder, sugar, salt, cinnamon, pecans, and rice, in that order. Beat well after each addition. On a preheated griddle or in a pan, pour about ½ cup batter for each cake. Bake till bubbles form on top and the undersides are lightly browned, about 1 minute. Turn cakes over; lightly brown other side. This makes about 15 pancakes.

Serve with heated syrup or with honey, heated and thinned with brandy, or whatever sauce you like. These go like wildfire; better ask a cousin to stay at the stove making more.

LACEY-EDGE CAKES

These are said to have originated in Holland, but they've been known in the South since time was. This batter is very thin; it dribbles and drools on the griddle, forming lacey edges, which are very important when serving the pancakes since the little edges catch and hold the syrup or jam sauce as it is poured.

2 eggs	1 teaspoon sugar
2 cups milk	½ teaspoon salt
1 cup fine cornmeal	6 tablespoons melted unsalted butter

Beat eggs with a rounded whisk till light in color, then whisk in milk, cornmeal, sugar, salt, and butter. On a preheated griddle or pan, drop 3 tablespoons batter for each cake. When they are firm and light brown underneath, flip over and brown lightly on other side, ½ minute to 1 minute a side, roughly. This makes about a dozen cakes.

Serve with honey heated with white rum, or any tart jam thinned with white port and heated, or regular old blackstrap molasses heated with brandy.

Important: Beat up the batter well before cooking each cake. It tends to thicken (that cornmeal!); add a little milk if necessary. And be sure your griddle or pan is really HOT to begin with.

GINGER PANCAKES

This is a dish for holiday breakfasts.

1 ½ cups milk	Pinch of salt
¾ cup oats, either the quick-cooking or the regular rolled	¼ teaspoon baking soda
	1 beaten egg
1 cup flour	3 beaten egg whites
1 ½ teaspoons baking powder	2 tablespoons cooking oil
½ teaspoon powdered ginger	1 ½ tablespoons molasses
Dash of cinnamon	½ teaspoon dark rum

Heat milk over low heat till just hot, stirring. Stir in oats, take pan off stove, and let stand 5 minutes. Mix flour, baking powder, spices, and a good pinch of salt. Now add everything else and stir well. Have your lightly greased skillet hot and ready. Pour into skillet a scant ¼ cup of batter and fry till edges look dry and surface bubbles; turn and cook other side. This makes about 12 to 14 pancakes. Fetch those fig preserves from the pantry.

This batter can be prepared in advance and kept in fridge up to 24 hours.

BOURBON PECAN PIE

Master chef Scott Wilson, author of the delightful cookbook *Dining under the Magnolia*, for just under a decade owned and cooked at the Magnolia Inn at Grove Hill, Alabama, which was located in a handsome yellow pine overseer's house amidst rolling pastures and groves that had belonged to his family for almost 200 years. People from all over the United States found their way to this establishment, not least for such desserts as this.

For crust:

2 ¼ cups all-purpose flour

½ teaspoon salt

¼ cup cold unsalted butter,
   cut into bits

½ cup cold vegetable shortening,
   cut into bits

¼ cup iced water

Mix well the flour and salt; add the butter and shortening. Blend with two knives until mixture looks like coarse meal. Add the iced water, tossing mixture with fork. Add more water if necessary to form a soft, but not sticky, dough. Shape the dough into a ball. Divide in halves to make 2 crusts. This makes 2 9-inch crusts for lidless pies. Dough may be chilled in plastic wrap for up to 2 days or frozen in plastic for up to 1 month.

For filling:

½ cup unsalted butter

2 tablespoons flour

3 cups Alaga syrup (cane syrup)

1 cup sugar

2 beaten eggs

⅓ cup best bourbon

1 cup coarsely chopped pecans

Preheat oven to 350 degrees. Melt butter, add flour, and stir until smooth. Add syrup and sugar. Boil 3 minutes, let cool, and then add eggs, bourbon, and pecans, blending all well. Pour into pans lined with unbaked crust. Bake for 35 to 40 minutes. This makes 2 pies.

For crust:

²/₃ cup plus 2 tablespoons chilled
    vegetable shortening

2 cups flour

1 teaspoon salt

4 to 6 tablespoons ice water

When you're ready to make mince pie, make your dough by cutting vegetable shortening into flour and salt until mixture looks like small peas. Sprinkle in water 1 tablespoon at a time. Stir with fork until all flour is moist. Add more water, 1 teaspoon at a time, as needed so that dough almost cleans side of bowl. Flour surface to roll out dough. Sprinkle your rolling pin with flour. Form dough into 2 balls, flatten them with floured hands, and then roll them out to make 2 pie crusts.

For filling:

1 beef tongue

2 pounds beef suet

1 dozen apples

2 pounds raisins

1 pound citron

2 pounds sugar

1 teaspoon salt

1 ½ teaspoons powdered mace

1 ½ teaspoons cinnamon

1 teaspoon powdered nutmeg

Good pinch of powdered ginger

Chopped orange and lemon peel
    to taste

1 quart cream Sherry

1 pint best bourbon

Cover tongue with boiling water and simmer gently until tender. Set aside to cool in water. Shred suet; chop fine. Pare, core, and chop apples. Stone raisins. Chop citron. When tongue is completely cool, peel off and discard the skin and chop the meat fine. Mix everything together well. Pack into a stone jar. Pour Sherry and bourbon over, cover tightly, and store in a cool place. This will keep all winter.

When ready to bake, preheat oven to 450 degrees. Line pie plate with dough, scoop out enough mince to fill, and put on top crust, taking care to prick out a design or simply make air holes so steam can escape. Bake about 30 minutes.

This is very good and is ideal for a winter luncheon of, say, soup, salad, cheese, and pie. If served as dessert for dinner, many like a dip of vanilla ice cream on top.

TALLULAH PIE

1 unbaked 9-inch pie shell

⅓ cup best bourbon

4 ounces semisweet chocolate

½ cup light brown sugar

4 eggs

½ cup Karo Light corn syrup

1 tablespoon blackstrap molasses

Good pinch of salt

2 cups pecan halves

Prepare pie crust. Set bourbon on fire, let it flame a second or so, then extinguish and set aside to cool. Preheat oven to 425 degrees. Melt chocolate in top of double boiler over simmering water, then pour into mixing bowl. Beat with sugar until fluffy. Beat in the eggs, one at a time, then add, always beating, the syrup, bourbon, molasses, and salt. Now fold in pecans. Mix well. Pour batter into pie shell. Bake 10 minutes, then lower temperature to 325 and bake 30 minutes or until pie is set.

BRANDY ALEXANDER PIE

s'UTHUN YUM-YUM: In 1933, just before Christmas, the ill-advised 18th Amendment was repealed, and little by little, some of the glorious old Gulf Coast dishes requiring brandy, various liqueurs, all that, slowly took center stage in the dessert world.

Now they're back, and here is a recipe, excuse me, *recette*, from the Thibault family in south Louisiana.

3 cups mini-marshmallows

½ cup milk

1 standard Hershey bar

¼ cup dark crème de cacao

3 tablespoons cognac or Armagnac

2 cups heavy cream

1 baked 8-inch pie shell

Heat marshmallows and milk over low heat till marshmallows melt. Add ¾ of chocolate bar to this; save the rest. Stir to blend, then put mix in fridge till slightly thickened. Blend in crème de cacao and cognac. In chilled bowl, beat cream till stiff. Fold in marshmallow mix. Pour into baked pie crust. Grate remaining chocolate on top. Chill completely before serving.

Since most of the pears in the markets are brickbats and even a session in the sun won't make them edible as fruit, many old recipes for dealing with such have been dug up. This pie is delicious.

Pastry for 1 double-crust
   9-inch pie
½ cup sugar
3 tablespoons unbleached flour
Pinch of salt
Pinch of powdered cinnamon,
   allspice, and cloves

1 teaspoon grated lemon peel
5 cups peeled, sliced pears,
   sprinkled with a few drops of
   any orange liqueur (Grand Marnier,
   Triple Sec, etc.)
1 tablespoon unsalted butter
1 tablespoon lemon juice

Preheat oven to 450 degrees. Line pie plate with pastry and set aside. Combine sugar, flour, salt, spices, and peel. Mix well. Place pear slices in your pie plate in layers, alternating with sugar-flour mix. Dot with butter and sprinkle with juice. Arrange top crust and seal edges; cut slots in top. Bake for 10 minutes; reduce heat to 350 and continue baking 35 to 40 minutes till pears are tender. Serve with whipped cream or vanilla ice cream.

CIDER RAISIN PIE

Pastry for 1 double-crust 9-inch
   deep-dish pie
1 ½ cups water
15 ounces dark raisins
3 ½ cups apple cider
¾ cup sugar
1 cup chunky applesauce

Pinch of salt
Good dash of powdered cinnamon
Pinch of allspice
¼ cup Triple Sec or Grand Marnier
3 tablespoons unsalted butter
3 tablespoons cornstarch

Preheat oven to 425 degrees. Line pie plate with pastry and set aside. Combine 1 cup water with raisins, apple cider, sugar, applesauce, salt, spices, orange cordial, and butter in saucepan. Heat to boil. Mix cornstarch with remaining water, stir into mixture, and cook till thick, stirring. Let cool a bit. Pour into crust, cover with top, flute edges, and make vents in top. Bake for 15 minutes, then turn down to 350; bake 35 minutes more. Cool completely before serving.

1 ½ cups fresh orange juice

1 cup skim milk

4 big egg yolks

½ cup sugar, plus extra for
   sprinkling

3 tablespoons cornstarch

1 envelope Mrs. Knox unflavored gelatin

Pie crust of graham crackers,
   already baked

2 oranges, peeled, sectioned, with
   white pith removed, sliced thin

Kirsch, gin, or brandy

In thick pan combine juice, milk, yolks, sugar, cornstarch, and gelatin until well blended. Cook over medium heat, stirring till mixture is smooth and just beginning to simmer. Remove from fire, cool a bit, and then pour into crust. Chill at least an hour or until very firm. Sprinkle orange slices with kirsch, gin, or brandy; sprinkle with sugar and chill. Spread slices over pie before serving.

CHARLESTON ORANGE FLUFF PIE

For crust:

2 tablespoons sugar

2 tablespoons unsalted butter,
   melted

1 tablespoon dark rum

1 cup or a little more of smashed
   graham crackers

Preheat oven to 350 degrees. Mix sugar, melted butter, rum, and graham cracker crumbs well together. Put aside 1 tablespoon of this mix; press rest into 9-inch pie plate. Bake for 10 minutes; put aside to cool.

For filling:

½ cup sugar

2 eggs, separated

2 teaspoons cornstarch

1 teaspoon grated orange peel

½ cup unsweetened orange juice

1 envelope Mrs. Knox unflavored
   gelatin

¼ cup cold water

¼ cup light rum

½ cup whole-berry cranberry
   sauce

1 teaspoon vanilla extract

Pinch of cinnamon

Pinch of allspice

Orange slices for garnish, soaked in
   an orange liqueur if possible

Combine ¼ cup sugar, egg yolks, and cornstarch in top of double boiler; stir well. Add orange peel and juice; stir well. Cook 10 minutes over simmering water until thickened, stirring constantly. Soak gelatin in cold water; let stand a minute or so.

Add gelatin to yolk mix, stirring till gelatin has dissolved. Add rum, cranberry sauce, and vanilla to gelatin mix. Pour into a big chilled bowl, cover, and put into fridge till it has the consistency of a syrup. Beat reserved egg whites (at room temperature) until foamy. Add rest of sugar, a little at a time, beating till peaks form. Gently stir about ¼ of the egg white mixture into gelatin mix, then carefully fold in remaining egg white mixture. Spoon this into crumb crust; sprinkle reserved crumb mix along with cinnamon and allspice around edge of filling. Chill at least 8 hours. Garnish with orange slices. Serves 6.

PROHIBITION PIE

4 tablespoons flour

¾ cup sugar

½ cup water

1 ¼ cups grape juice

¼ cup whatever wine you have
hidden in closet: port, blackberry,
elderberry, scuppernong

1 baked 9-inch pie shell

For meringue:

3 egg whites

6 tablespoons sugar

Make a paste with flour, sugar, and water. Bring juice and wine just to boiling point; add paste, stirring constantly, till it's smooth and clear. Cool, then put into baked pie shell.

To make meringue, beat egg whites on high in your mixer until soft peaks. Continue beating, slowly adding sugar until meringue is stiff.

Cover pie with meringue and brown under broiler. Some prefer to put marshmallows, sliced horizontally, on top. Chill a few hours in refrigerator.

If you're serving this to temperance workers, you refer to this as Welch Pie, that is, Welch's Grape Juice.

¼ cup raisins

¼ cup best brandy

Pastry for 1 double-crust 9-inch pie

5 to 7 Granny Smith or other tart
    green apples

½ cup sugar plus 1 tablespoon

¼ cup firmly packed brown sugar

2 tablespoons all-purpose flour

Good dash of powdered cinnamon

Pinch of powdered allspice

Pinch of cloves

Few grains of salt

1 tablespoon unsalted butter

Put raisins and brandy in covered jar and let sit in fridge overnight.

Preheat oven to 400 degrees. Line pie plate with half of pastry, then set aside. Peel and core apples and slice thin. Combine sugar, brown sugar, flour, spices, and salt; stir to remove lumps. Drain raisins; save liquid. Add apples and raisins to sugar and spice mix, spoon into pie shell, and dot with butter. Put on the top crust, sealing and crimping the edges. Cut slits to let steam escape. Sprinkle 1 tablespoon sugar on top of pie; bake for 50 minutes or until golden brown. Sprinkle some of brandy-raisin liquid on top before serving.

DEMOPOLIS RAISIN PIE

Back before refrigeration, there was a time in late winter that might be called Raisin Pie Time. Fruits were scarce, and the baskets of yams were running low. Oh, there were those shining jars of figs and pears and peaches preserved at home, but somehow the raisin pie was what diners enjoyed in mid-January. There are as many raisin pie recipes in the South as there are fruitcake recipes, and that is something staggering to consider. The following was scrawled in a shaky Spencerian hand on a bit of lined tablet paper. At the bottom was written later in pencil "Marie-Yvonne," but at the top, the recipe was titled "Vonne's Raisin Pie." Most raisin pies are made of the common dark raisins; the ones made of white raisins usually had a bit of candied ginger or candied orange peel chopped into them.

During hard times, this pie, without embellishments or spices, no cream, served as accompaniment to venison, squirrel, rabbit, duck, etc. I'd love to see it replace the woefully overdone cranberry at holiday tables; it's grand with turkey or indeed any meat.

1 ½ cups raisins	Pinch of allspice
½ cup molasses	1 ½ tablespoons dark rum
1 cup water	Squeeze of lemon juice
¾ cup sugar	2 teaspoons unsalted butter
2 tablespoons cornstarch	Pastry for 1 double-crust
Pinch of salt	9-inch pie
Pinch of nutmeg	Whipped cream

Preheat oven to 425 degrees. Stir raisins, molasses, and water together in a saucepan. Sift in sugar, cornstarch, salt, and spices. Mix well. Cook over moderate heat until it begins to bubble, then cook about 2 minutes longer, stirring well. Remove from fire and stir in rum, juice, and butter. Pour into pastry-lined pie plate. Don't worry if filling seems rather liquid. Put on the top crust, flute edges, and cut slits. Bake for 10 minutes, turn down to 375 degrees, and bake about 30 minutes more or until crust is golden. Serve hot with whipped cream. If you prefer ice cream, be sure it's real ice cream, not some watery anti-cholesterol horror.

Note: The recipe calls for the usual pie crust, but crusts made of mashed graham crackers or even mashed ginger snaps are interesting alternatives. If you use the graham cracker crust, add a bit of powdered cinnamon to the crust.

SUNDAY PIE

This can be made with sweet potatoes (cooked and mashed), yams (cooked and mashed), pumpkin (cooked and mashed), peaches (mashed), nectarines (mashed), pears (mashed), or ripe bananas (mashed). All should be peeled, cored, whatever, naturally.

1 9-inch pie crust, bottom only	1 ½ cups sweet potatoes, fruit,
½ cup dark brown sugar, packed	whichever you choose
hard into measuring cup	2 eggs
½ teaspoon salt	¾ cup milk
1 teaspoon powdered cinnamon	2 tablespoons unsalted butter,
1 teaspoon powdered allspice	melted
1 teaspoon powdered nutmeg	⅓ cup best bourbon
Pinch of ginger or mace, as you will	Sweetened whipped cream

Preheat oven to 400 degrees. Prepare crust and set aside. Mix well sugar, salt, and spices. Stir in potatoes or fruit. Add eggs. Beat well. Add milk, butter, and bourbon. Pour into pie crust and bake 25 to 35 minutes or until pie tests done. Let cool, then chill. Serve with whipped cream.

Variations are infinite, as you like. A little grated orange peel is good in the sweet potatoes, a bit of grated crystallized ginger in the peaches, nectarines, and pears. A bit of finely chopped pineapple and a splash of pineapple syrup sexes up the banana version.

CREOLE PIE

1 cup whipping cream
²⁄₃ cup sweetened condensed milk
Generous ½ cup very strong black
    New Orleans coffee
½ teaspoon vanilla extract
2 small white chocolate bars, crumbled

Splash of good brandy
1 pie crust made of crushed ginger
    snaps
Handful of candied orange peel
    for garnish

Mix cream, milk, coffee, and vanilla slowly over low heat, until very thick. Continue stirring; add candy and brandy. Let cool, then pour into pie shell. Garnish with minced candied orange peel. Chill in refrigerator before serving.

COFFEE BREAK PIE

1 cup cold milk
1 package (4-serving size) Jell-O
    vanilla instant pudding
1 tablespoon instant Maxwell House
    coffee
2 cups Cool Whip topping, thawed

3 tablespoons Jim Beam bourbon
    whiskey
1 9-inch prepared graham cracker
    pie crust
Dash of powdered cloves or allspice,
    as you wish

Pour milk into mixing bowl. Add pudding mix and coffee. Beat a couple of minutes with wire whisk. Gently stir in 1 ½ cups of topping and the whiskey. Spoon into prepared crust. Freeze 2 hours or until firm. Half an hour before serving, remove from freezer and place in fridge to soften. Top with remaining topping and cloves or allspice. After serving, return any remaining to fridge. Serves 6 to 8.

For crust:

2 cups smashed cookie, graham
    cracker, or zwieback crumbs

¼ cup sugar

2 tablespoons unsalted butter

Pinch of powdered cinnamon

Pinch of powdered allspice

Mix all very well and press into bottom and sides of a 9-inch pie pan. Chill, covered, while preparing filling.

For filling:

⅔ cup orange juice

⅓ cup best bourbon

¼ cup sugar

1½ teaspoons grated orange peel

1 envelope Mrs. Knox unflavored
    gelatin

1 cup heavy cream

½ cup milk

4 cups berries (blackberries,
    mulberries, or black currants),
    washed and cleaned

Put orange juice, bourbon, sugar, and orange peel in a saucepan and stir over heat until sugar is dissolved. Sprinkle gelatin over the mix and let it soften for a minute. Now heat over moderate heat until gelatin is dissolved, then let mix sit until it is at room temperature. Beat cream until it peaks, then whisk in milk. Fold into the gelatin mixture. Fold in berries, put filling into crust, and chill under plastic wrap for 4 to 5 hours.

VALDOSTA TART

From down in Georgia comes this tart, from a town whose name is really the Italian Val d'Asota, where polenta (yellow cornmeal) is an essential part of life, just as in the Georgian counterpart.

For dough:

⅔ cup yellow cornmeal

Scant 2 cups flour

Scant cup of sugar

1¼ cups chilled unsalted butter,
    cut into pieces

4 egg yolks

For filling:

3 cups dry red wine

6 whole cloves

1 teaspoon grated lemon peel

¼ cup sugar

8 to 9 medium pears (ripe but not mushy), peeled, cored, and cut into thumb-size pieces

Sugar and allspice, for sprinkling

To make the dough, combine cornmeal, flour, and sugar; add butter, cutting in until mix looks like coarse-ground corn. Blend in egg yolks till dough just comes together. Take ⅓ of dough and make a ball; flatten into disk. Wrap in plastic. Repeat action with rest of dough and wrap in plastic. Refrigerate dough for at least 30 minutes. You can do this a day ahead.

For the filling, heat wine, cloves, and lemon peel to simmer. Add sugar, cook 4 minutes, and then add pears. Simmer until liquid is reduced.

Preheat oven to 350 degrees. Now roll out larger disk of dough and place in buttered baking dish, covering sides with a bit of edge hanging over. Put in filling. Then roll out smaller disk of dough and place on top; bring up sagging edge to seal. Put air holes in top and ruffle, rosette, what you like, the edge. Bake for about 25 minutes or until dough is golden and done. Toward end, take tart out of oven, lightly butter crust, and sprinkle with a little sugar and allspice. Serve with ice cream or sherbet.

MRS. HANS CURJEL'S PEAR TART

For crust:

1 stick unsalted butter, room temperature

1 3-ounce packet cream cheese, softened with a drop of milk

1 cup all-purpose flour

Good pinch of salt

For filling:

9 cups ripe but firm pears, sliced

1 tablespoon lemon juice

Dash of grated lemon peel

⅓ cup brandy

½ cup sugar

⅓ cup flour

Pinch or so of grated cinnamon

Pinch or so of nutmeg

½ stick unsalted butter, softened

Cream butter and cream cheese together until smooth and perfectly blended. Add flour and salt; blend till it forms dough. Shape dough into ball, cover with plastic wrap or wax paper, and chill till firm, about 2 hours. On lightly floured surface, roll dough into circle about ⅛ inch thick. Line 10-inch pie plate with dough. Roll out remaining dough and either freehand or with cookie cutters cut into decorative shapes: leaves, shells, diamonds, whatever. Place on cookie sheet.

Anise-fiends like to sprinkle a few anise seeds on these decorations; ginger-fiends have been known to lace finely chopped crystallized ginger. Some dust with powdered nutmeg. To cause raised eyebrows, use cracked juniper berries or cumin seeds.

Preheat oven to 350 degrees. In big mixing bowl, toss pears, lemon juice, lemon peel, and brandy together. Now sift sugar, flour, and spices together and add to pear mix. Stir all well. Smooth filling into pastry shell; dot with butter. Place pie plate and cookie sheet in oven; bake till fruit is tender and pastry begins to turn a nice golden brown, roughly 1 hour. The fancy pieces should only take 20 or so minutes. Cool fancy pieces on rack, then arrange on tart.

PEACH COBBLER

Among dishes that we have inherited intact from the Golden Age of the Can Opener (pre-refrigerator) are a number calling for canned peaches. Rightfully. The best canned peaches from the South have a different texture and flavor from any fresh peach. A grand variation of peach cobbler is the Gulf Coast cantaloupe cobbler, more or less the same recipe but with 4 cups of peeled, sliced cantaloupe instead of peaches and a slight insistence on cinnamon as flavoring. Not unexpectedly, chopped ginger in syrup was often added.

Pastry for 1 double-crust pie
¾ cup sugar
2 tablespoons flour
½ teaspoon cinnamon
¼ teaspoon nutmeg
Dash of allspice
Pinch of salt

2 20-ounce cans sliced peaches
   with their syrup
1 teaspoon of one of these:
   almond extract, lemon extract,
   rose water, orange blossom water,
   Triple Sec
2 tablespoons melted unsalted butter

Preheat oven to 400 degrees. Gently roll out ⅔ of dough on lightly floured board. Line a 6 × 10-inch baking tin with dough. Mix sugar, flour, spices, and salt. Add peaches, extract, and butter and mix well, then spoon into baking tin. Roll out dough that's left and cut thin strips to make lattice topping. Press edges to seal. With fork, flute crust along outside of baking tin. Bake for 35 to 40 minutes or until pastry begins to brown.

LAFAYETTE COBBLER

For filling:

4 pounds Bartlett pears, peeled, cored, cut into ⅓-inch slices

1 cup packed dark brown sugar

⅓ cup best bourbon

2 ½ tablespoons all-purpose flour

1 teaspoon fresh lemon juice

½ teaspoon vanilla extract

Pinch of allspice

2 tablespoons (¼ stick) unsalted butter

For topping:

2 cups flour

¼ cup packed dark brown sugar, plus more for sprinkling

1 tablespoon baking powder

¾ stick unsalted butter

¼ cup half-and-half

6 tablespoons best bourbon

1 teaspoon vanilla extract

Pinch of nutmeg

Pinch of powdered ginger or a bit of finely chopped crystallized ginger or crystallized orange peel

¾ cup light cream

Preheat oven to 450 degrees. Combine all filling ingredients except butter in big bowl. Put into deep baking dish of about 12-cup capacity, dot with butter, and bake about 15 minutes, until bubbly.

While that's in the oven, prepare the topping: Sift flour, sugar, and baking powder into bowl. Add butter and cut in till mixture is like coarse meal. Make a well. Combine half-and-half, bourbon, and vanilla and put in well. Stir till just mixed, but don't stir too much. Quickly drop batter by spoonfuls into hot pear mix, covering well. Sprinkle with sugar, nutmeg, chopped candied fruit, what you like. Hurry in oven and bake 1 minute, then reduce to 375 and go on baking until top is golden and firm, about 20 minutes.

Serve warm or at room temperature, pouring some cream over each serving.

Cookies

BOURBON BALLS

2 ½ cups vanilla wafers

1 cup pecans

1 cup confectioner's sugar,
  plus extra for dusting

3 tablespoons cocoa

⅔ cup best bourbon

2 tablespoons Karo Light corn syrup

Pinch of mace

Smash vanilla wafers to fine crumbs. Chop pecans very fine. Stir together the crumbs, pecans, sugar, and cocoa. Add bourbon and corn syrup. Mix well. Roll into balls 1 inch in diameter, then roll in confectioner's sugar and mace. Store in tightly covered container and age at least 24 hours. This makes 40 to 48 balls.

BETTE DAVIS COOKIES

Who knows why they're called this? Perhaps because two of her greatest roles were southern belles, in *Jezebel* and *The Little Foxes*.

¾ cup solid vegetable shortening

¼ cup light molasses

1 cup sugar

1 egg

2 cups flour

2 teaspoons baking soda

Pinch of salt

Pinches, as you like, of cloves,
  cinnamon, nutmeg, ginger

1 ½ tablespoons dark rum

More sugar

Preheat oven to 375 degrees. Butter big, heavy cookie sheets. Melt shortening and set aside in big bowl to cool, then mix in molasses, sugar, and egg. Combine flour, soda, salt, and spices, then stir into first mix. Add rum and mix well. Cover and refrigerate 10 minutes or so. Shape dough into 1-inch balls. Roll each in sugar, covering completely. Place 2 inches apart on sheets. Bake until cookies are set, roughly 8 minutes. Cool on rack, then store in airtight containers.

EGGNOG COOKIES

These were often made right after a party, to use the nog in the bowl. Nowadays, one can buy ready-made eggnog in the grocery. ALWAYS, in this case, add a good dash of the best Kentucky bourbon whiskey.

1 cup unsalted butter,
softened
2 cups sugar
1 cup eggnog
Dash of bourbon whiskey
1 teaspoon baking soda

½ teaspoon freshly ground nutmeg
(more if you like)
5 ½ cups all-purpose flour
1 lightly beaten egg white
Colored sugar or rock sugar crystals
for topping

Cream butter and sugar; beat in eggnog, bourbon, soda, and nutmeg. Gradually add flour; mix well. Cover and chill 1 hour. Preheat oven to 350 degrees. On lightly floured surface, roll out dough to about ⅛-inch thick. Cut into circles or fancy shapes, as you wish. Place on ungreased baking sheets. Brush with egg white; sprinkle with sugar topping. Bake until edges are lightly browned. Cool on racks. Makes about 16 dozen.

BRITTANY SHORTBREAD

This is better the day after it's made: Let it sit, covered, at room temperature, overnight.

1 ¼ cups softened unsalted butter
¾ cup sugar
1 egg
2 egg yolks
2 teaspoons kirsch (clear eau-de-vie
of cherries, available everywhere)
1 ½ teaspoons vanilla extract

⅓ cup ground blanched almonds
1 ¾ cups sifted all-purpose flour
1 lightly beaten egg
Confectioner's sugar
Candied violets or candied
kumquat peel

Preheat oven to 350 degrees. Beat butter and sugar till light and fluffy. Beat in egg and the other yolks, one at a time, beating well after each. Now add kirsch, vanilla, and almonds; beat well. Fold in flour. Spoon batter into buttered 9-inch tart pan, 1 ½ inches deep with removable bottom, if you have such. Spread evenly in pan. Brush with beaten egg. Bake till top is golden. Cool, then dust with confectioner's sugar and, if you can find them, candied violets. Failing that, candied kumquat peel.

LEBKUCHEN (GERMAN COOKIES)

These are served with any number of ices, custards, and fruit desserts. This is a Kentucky version.

⅔ cup honey	Pinch of powdered mace
1 cup sugar	Pinch of powdered ginger
⅓ cup unsalted butter	Pinch of cinnamon
1 beaten egg	1 ⅓ cups chopped walnuts
¼ cup plus 1 tablespoon best	¼ teaspoon grated lemon peel
bourbon whiskey	½ teaspoon anise seeds,
4 cups cake flour	well pounded
¼ teaspoon salt	2 ½ cups confectioner's sugar
1 teaspoon baking soda	¼ cup boiling water

Heat honey, sugar, and butter about 5 minutes, stirring until sugar dissolves. Set aside to cool. Beat egg and add ¼ cup bourbon. In another bowl, sift flour with salt, soda, and spices. Add, in alternation, egg mix and flour mix to honey mix. Add nuts, peel, and anise seeds and mix well. Cover and chill thoroughly. (Traditionally, the dough is chilled overnight.)

Preheat oven to 350 degrees. Now roll small pieces of dough between your hands and make little ½-inch balls. Flatten them and place on lightly buttered baking sheet. Bake about 7 to 10 minutes or until well browned. Let cookies cool, then dissolve confectioner's sugar in boiling water, stir in remaining bourbon, and cool slightly; spread on cooled cookies.

RUM BALLS

2 cups vanilla wafer crumbs
(1 8-ounce box)
1 cup confectioner's sugar
2 tablespoons unsweetened cocoa
½ cup light corn syrup

¼ cup white rum
Confectioner's sugar as needed
Candied ginger or candied orange
or lemon peel

In big bowl mix crumbs, 1 cup of confectioner's sugar, and cocoa.
Then add corn syrup and rum; stir until well blended. Dust fingers with
confectioner's sugar and form 1-inch balls. Let stand about an hour, then
roll balls in sugar and store in tightly covered container 3 days before
serving. Every version of this recipe says to press the balls a little and
top with a bit of candied ginger or candied orange or lemon peel.

BOOBALOOS

1 cup unsalted butter
⅔ cup sugar
½ teaspoon salt
2 egg yolks
2 cups flour

⅓ cup sauterne or white port
Sugar
Cinnamon
Allspice

Preheat oven to 375 degrees. Cream butter and sugar, add salt and egg
yolks, and mix well. Add flour and wine alternately; mix well. Shape into
small balls between palms. Flatten cookie with the bottom of glass in
sugar and spices. Bake about 10 minutes, then while hot sprinkle generously with more cinnamon and sugar.

RUM BUNNIES

4 ½ tablespoons unsalted butter

⅓ cup fine granulated sugar

1 egg

½ cup unsifted flour

2 ½ teaspoons dark rum

5 ½ tablespoons ground almonds

Preheat oven to 350 degrees. Cream butter well, add sugar, and beat until light and fluffy. Beat in egg, fold in flour, and add rum. Mix in almonds well, then drop dough by half teaspoons onto lightly greased baking sheets. Add a little more flour if dough seems not stiff enough. Flatten the blops of dough with a fork moistened in rum. Bake for 8 minutes or until edges of cookies brown. Cool cookies on wire rack.

LAFAYETTE CRUNCH

The name refers to Lafayette, Louisiana, the presumed origin of this crunch beloved of children, not to the dear marquis.

1 cup brown sugar

1 cup white sugar

¾ cup dark corn syrup

½ cup warm water

2 tablespoons best wine vinegar

Dash of brandy

4 cups smashed unsalted potato chips

1 cup finely chopped toasted pecans

1 tablespoon melted unsalted butter

Combine sugars, syrup, water, and vinegar in saucepan. Cover and cook to soft ball stage over medium heat. Remove from stove; cool slightly. Add brandy, mix well, and pour over potato chips and chopped nuts. Pour into buttered pan. Cool, then cut into squares.

Sherbets & Ice Creams

APPLEJACK ICE

1 ½ cups unsweetened applesauce

1 ½ cups unsweetened apple juice

3 ⅓ cups superfine sugar

¼ cup fresh lemon juice

¼ cup applejack or Calvados

Powdered cinnamon for garnish

In a big bowl, mix applesauce, apple juice, sugar, and lemon juice. Strain if you wish; most like it unstrained. Freeze about 20 minutes, then add applejack or Calvados. Mix and freeze again.

Sprinkle with powdered cinnamon when serving. Cinnamon wafers are good alongside; so are anise cookies.

ARKANSAS SHERBET

1 ½ pounds fresh rhubarb

1 ½ cups Riesling or white port

¾ cup sugar

2 tablespoons fresh lemon juice

1 teaspoon grated lemon peel

Bake rhubarb in covered baking dish about 25 minutes at 375 degrees, or until soft. Dish may be anything but aluminum. When cooked, puree rhubarb until smooth in processor, in blender, or by elbow grease. Mix rhubarb with wine and all other ingredients and then freeze. If in ice cream freezer, follow manufacturer's directions. If in freezing compartment of fridge, freeze to mush, take out and beat thoroughly, and return to fridge. Or: Pour mix into large shallow dish; cover and freeze for an hour. Remove from freezer and beat until frothy, re-freeze for a half hour or until it starts to freeze again, then beat again and return to freezer to harden before serving, say 2 to 3 hours.

Serves 4 to 6. Sounds like lots of trouble, but well worth the effort.

APPLESAUCE SHERBET

1 16-ounce can applesauce
(smooth or chunky)
¾ cup Karo Light corn syrup
¼ cup orange juice
1 tablespoon lemon juice

1 tablespoon grated orange peel
Pinch of salt
Dash of white rum
2 stiffly beaten egg whites

Combine the applesauce, ¼ cup of corn syrup, citrus juices, peel, salt, and rum in bowl. Beat the remaining syrup gradually into the beaten egg whites and then fold this into applesauce mix. Put into a shallow pan and chill until firm.

Serve with paper-thin wafers and a slug of Calvados or cider alongside.

CANTALOUPE SHERBET

7 cups cantaloupe flesh
1 cup water
1 cup sugar
4 tablespoons Pernod

1 teaspoon grated lemon peel
2 tablespoons fresh lemon juice
½ cup heavy cream

Discard seeds, peel, and green part of flesh of ripe cantaloupe. You'll want 7 cups of chopped cantaloupe flesh. Stir together water, sugar, Pernod, and lemon peel. Boil till sugar is dissolved, then simmer about 5 minutes. Stir in lemon juice and put mixture in bowl; chill well, covered. Puree the cantaloupe till it is fairly smooth, blend in cream and the syrup, and then force through a sieve (not a fine one). Freeze the mixture in an ice cream freezer according to manufacturer's instructions. Makes about 6 cups.

MARQUISE AU CHAMPAGNE

In classical French cookery, a *marquise* is any fruit sherbet with whipped cream mixed in before serving.

1 ½ cups water

¾ cup sugar

Grated peel of ½ orange

Juice of 2 lemons

Juice of 2 oranges

¼ teaspoon salt

2 cups chilled Champagne

Strawberries

Boil water and sugar for 5 minutes. Add the grated orange peel, lemon and orange juices, and salt. Let this syrup cool, then add chilled Champagne. Strain the mixture into a shallow pan. Freeze. Serve over strawberries marinated in Champagne and sugar or in Champagne flutes as a simple sherbet. You can use kumquats instead of orange for Something Special.

GRENADINE SHERBET

2 cups buttermilk

¼ cup lemon juice

½ cup sugar

1 ½ cups Karo Light corn syrup

½ cup grenadine with a splash
of vodka

Mix buttermilk with lemon juice, sugar, and corn syrup. Freeze at coldest setting until mushy, then place in chilled bowl and beat smooth, mixing in vodka-spiked grenadine. Return to freezer until firm. If you have any pomegranate blossoms, you might alarm the timid by placing one perfect bloom on top of each serving. Or very pretty is a borage flower. If all else fails, use mint leaves.

JADE SHERBET

2 cups buttermilk

¼ cup lime juice

½ cup sugar

1 ½ cups Karo Light corn syrup

1 cup pureed avocado

1 teaspoon finely grated lime peel

Mix buttermilk with lime juice, sugar, and Karo syrup. Freeze to mush. Place in chilled bowl; beat smooth. Add pureed avocado (remove fibers and lumps) and grated lime peel. Return to icebox; freeze firm.

Variations: In the second stage, instead of avocado, add 1 cup pureed ripe peach and a splash of apricot liqueur, or 1 cup crushed ripe strawberries and a splash of white crème de menthe.

MIDSUMMER SHERBET DREAM

9 teabags of orange pekoe

1 cup chopped mint

Juice of 3 lemons, plus peels

2 quarts boiling water

3 cups sugar

6 cups cold water

Juice of 2 oranges

¼ cup clear mint liqueur

Candied orange peel and mint

   sprigs for garnish

In a big heatproof bowl, place teabags, chopped mint, and lemon peels, then pour boiling water over and steep 30 minutes. Strain through fine sieve into pitcher or whatever vessel; stir in sugar until dissolved. Keep in fridge 24 hours. Stir 6 cups cold water, juices, and liqueur into chilled tea. Freeze until almost solid. Spoon into cold sherbet glasses; garnish with candied orange peel and mint sprigs. Makes about 12 servings. Some prefer to include hard cider rather than mint liqueur in the dish. Thin wafers alongside.

SIMONETTE'S SHERBET

3 pounds black grapes

3 cups sugar

1 ½ cups water

½ cup plus 1 tablespoon fresh

   orange juice

½ cup plus 1 tablespoon fresh

   lemon juice

¾ cup best ruby port

Heavy cream, whipped with a pinch

   of allspice, if desired

A day ahead, puree the grapes and put through a sieve to remove seeds and skins. Cook sugar and water over medium heat till sugar is dissolved. Boil the syrup for 5 minutes. Pour this into a mixing bowl and let cool, then stir in the grape paste and the juices. Whisk till well blended, then pour into molds or metal pans or what you will and freeze to mush state. Now beat the ice until smooth and freeze overnight. An hour or so before serving, remove from freezer, beat once more, and add port, mixing well. Refreeze till firm. Serve in small portions with whipped cream, if you wish.

BELLINI SHERBET

2 ¼ cups peach syrup

1 cup simple syrup

4 ½ tablespoons light corn syrup

3 tablespoons peach schnapps

1 ½ tablespoons grenadine syrup

2 teaspoons fresh lemon juice

1 ¼ cups Champagne or other
    sparkling white wine

Mix all ingredients save Champagne. When well mixed, add Champagne, cover, and refrigerate until well chilled. Then put in ice cream freezer or do the usual freeze-to-mush-then-beat-well-and-freeze-again. This does about 6 cups. Paper-thin cookies or wafers served alongside.

BUTTERMILK SHERBET WITH GINGER SAUCE

1 quart buttermilk

1 cup sweet milk

1 cup sugar

1 tablespoon vanilla or lemon extract,
    as you think

For sauce:

3 tablespoons candied ginger

½ cup bourbon

Drop of molasses

Mix sherbet ingredients together and freeze, adding fruit if you wish. Serve with sauce made of candied ginger soaked in bourbon with a little molasses added.

MELANIE'S REVENGE: WATERMELON SHERBET WITH WHITE RUM

1 20- to 25-pound watermelon

2 ½ cups sugar

2 tablespoons fresh lemon juice

1 egg white

Plenty of chilled white rum

Cut melon in half, scoop out flesh, and press flesh through colander placed over bowl. Squirrels like the seeds; flesh should go into compost heap. Sweeten juice. Here's where judicious taste comes in: Amount of sugar depends on how sweet melon happens to be. Remember, the melon-sugar slush will taste sweeter before being frozen than after. Add lemon juice and mix. Freeze in ice trays just to mush stage, then take out and beat in cold bowl; return to icebox. When mix starts to harden, take out and beat in beaten egg white. Stir every 20 minutes or so until sherbet really begins to harden.

This sherbet will keep weeks in freezer. When ready to serve, put portions into chilled sherbet glasses and pour chilled white rum as you think over all. This dish is worth the trouble, believe me. You can employ this recipe for Persian melons as well as other sweet melons.

SOUTHERN BELLE SHERBET

This sherbet is ALWAYS accompanied by flutes of ice-cold brut Champagne or ice-cold *blanc de blancs* wine on occasion. This combination is sometimes called Happy Day Sherbet. Roses should be sweet old-fashioned kinds, not wild modern hybrids.

1 cup water

⅔ cup sugar

Barest pinch of powdered allspice

2 cups rose petals, torn up coarsely

3 cups white grape juice

Bring water to boiling point; stir in sugar till dissolved. Remove from heat. Add allspice and rose petals. Cover and let steep overnight. Strain syrup and discard rose petals. Mix in grape juice. Put into ice cream freezer and freeze. Can be stored in tightly closed container in freezer up to 2 days. Serve in stemmed glasses.

For a very long time, there was a tradition more honored in the telling than in the observation that southern belles drank no spiritous beverages save Champagne. Perhaps a very occasional slug of dark rum or bourbon in their morning tea or coffee in very cold weather. If they were "feeling porely," perhaps a tiny glass of Sherry or Madeira before holiday or birthday feasts. But everyone has noted females from toddlers to teenagers who demanded a taste of Papa's mint julep, drank, frowned, fled, came back a few minutes later for another taste, drank, fled, returned a few minutes later . . . One line in Lillian Hellman's play *The Little Foxes* brought roars when the play was first performed in New Orleans with Tallulah Bankhead; entire families made a pilgrimage to that city to see Miss Bankhead in the leading role of Regina. Speaking of the character Aunt Birdie (delightfully performed by Patricia Collinge), another character scoffs: "She doesn't have headaches. She drinks, all alone up in her room."

1 cup fresh (morning-plucked)
   pink rose petals
2 tablespoons sugar

1 cup Champagne (*blanc de blancs* or a
   fine white Bordeaux, if you must)
1 quart best vanilla ice cream, softened
8 candied pink rosebuds

Trim off the part of the petals that joined them to the stem, then mix petals, sugar, and Champagne till smooth. Stir this mix into ice cream and pour into shallow pan; return to freezer. Freeze about 4 hours, then take out and give a strong stirring to break up ice crystals. Repeat this an hour before serving. Top each serving with a candied rosebud.

ITALIAN SUNDAE

1 cup vanilla ice cream

½ cup crushed amaretti
(Italian almond cookies)

2 plums cut in 1-inch pieces

2 to 3 tablespoons sugar

2 teaspoons fresh lemon juice

2 tablespoons rum

In metal bowl mix ice cream and cookies well; freeze, covered with plastic, for 30 minutes. Simmer together plums, sugar, and lemon juice about 10 minutes, until plums are very tender. Force mixture through sieve, discarding skins, then let sauce cool and stir in rum. Divide ice cream into 2 small bowls; pour sauce over it.

This serves 2; adjust recipe for more.

SAN FRANCISCO SUNDAE

In spite of the name, this dish comes from the old St. Charles Hotel in New Orleans.

2 ½ cups California Zinfandel

½ cup sugar

Skin of ½ lemon

Good dash of powdered
cinnamon

1 pound ripe, pitted cherries
(Bings are best)

1 tablespoon chopped candied ginger

6 scoops vanilla ice cream

½ cup heavy cream, whipped with
a pinch of cinnamon

Bring wine, sugar, lemon peel, and cinnamon to a boil, stirring till sugar is dissolved. Reduce heat; add cherries. Poach, below simmering stage, very slowly till cherries are tender, 5 to 10 minutes. Take out cherries with slotted spoon; set aside. Bring wine mix to boil and cook till reduced to about 1 ¼ cups, about 8 to 10 minutes, then add cherries and ginger.

Cool a little, then spoon over scoops of vanilla ice cream or frozen plain yogurt. Top with whipped cream and a pinch of cinnamon.

In the kitchen, Mobile, 1980s. Courtesy of Eugene Walter estate.

Fruit Desserts

POINT CLEAR BANANA FRITTERS

4 really ripe bananas, well squashed	1 teaspoon grated orange peel
¾ cup flour	1 teaspoon best bourbon
Pinch of salt	Oil for frying
3 tablespoons sugar	Cinnamon
	Sugar

Combine bananas, flour, salt, sugar, peel, and bourbon in big bowl. Mix well and beat slightly. Take 1 heaping tablespoon of this mix for each fritter. You want oil ½-inch deep in a frying pan heated to 350 to 375 degrees. Fry the fritters, a few at a time, 1 ½ to 2 minutes, turning till they are golden brown on both sides. Drain on paper towels; sprinkle with cinnamon and sugar. Makes 20 to 25.

ORANGE PARFAIT (FANCY NAME)/ORANGE SOG (FAMILIAR NAME)

A great many Bible scholars as well as classical scholars have a certain respect for the orange. Many think it was this fruit, not the apple, that grew in the Garden of Eden. Eve's apple and Erda's apple are much mentioned, but the pomegranate and the peach are candidates for the role of the fatal fruit as well.

The Gulf Coast of the United States has always had oranges from the Caribbean, so the fruit doesn't have the rare (and expensive) aura it once had in other parts of our country. The Gulf Coast South has so many orange-flavored desserts that we'll just take samples from the list for this book. Perhaps a 3,000-page cookbook on the citrus family later.

The use of leftovers, always a high form of art in the rural South, whether in rich or poor kitchens, produced some delightful dishes. The endless pies, gumbos, hashes, and casseroles made of the carcass of the Thanksgiving or Christmas turkey are enough to fill several volumes. But the use of the wreckage of wedding or birthday cakes is less known. Indeed, any yellow cake, light, spongy, even pound, can serve for this.

Leftover yellow cake

6 pasteurized egg yolks

¾ cup sugar

6 tablespoons Grand Marnier or
Cointreau, or anisette for the
anise and caraway crowd

6 egg whites

1 cup heavy cream

Carefully remove all icing and sugar roses or whatever from top and sides of the cake wreckage. Set aside. Cut cake into ½-inch cubes.

Beat yolks and half of sugar till pale yellow. Stir in liqueur and set aside. Whip egg whites till foamy. Gradually add rest of sugar and whip till peaks form. Set aside. Whip cream until stiff.

Fold yolk mix, cake cubes, and whipped cream into egg whites. Pour mix into 4 × 8-inch loaf pan and freeze till firm, about 5 to 6 hours. When ready to serve, wrap bottom and sides of pan in warm damp towel and turn pan out onto service dish. Cut into thick slices and serve at once.

SPICED ORANGES

8 to 9 oranges

¾ cup Madeira or sweet Sherry
or port

6 tablespoons sugar

Dash of cinnamon

Dash of cloves

Remove peel, pith, and centers from oranges. Slice into sections; remove seeds and membranes. Arrange these sections in a serving dish. In saucepan combine Madeira or sweet Sherry or port with sugar, cinnamon, and cloves. Heat mixture, stirring frequently, until sugar is dissolved. Pour at once over orange sections. Ladyfingers or thin anise cookies alongside.

"Madames Orange,
Lemon, Lime, alwa[ys]
stars," Walter sketc[h]
Courtesy of Eugen[e]
Walter estate.

In the South, the lemon is ubiquitous — on every table, occurring somewhere in every meal. The grated or slivered peel and the juice are an acknowledged or secret part of more than half the dishes that come to the southern table.

"Thank God for Florida!" was an oft-repeated and truly fervent cry in the old days. Oranges, grapefruit, kumquats, satsumas, tangerines, citrons, but most of all the lemon.

The fact is that during that deplorable period of Prohibition, a great many people couldn't face using their prescribed or smuggled spirits for the Bananas Flambé they all enjoy, so they just heated lemon extract and set it on fire over the bananas.

Lemon extract might understudy spirits in some recipes, but for those classic southern favorites, only fresh lemons will do. You don't throw them out after the peel and juice have been employed! The sogged-out half lemons sit by the washbasin to deal with fingernails when you come in from gardening. Real gardeners just don't wear gloves. They do yeoman labor with nailbrushes and files after coming in from close contact with the earth.

4 bananas	1 cup brown sugar
Lemon juice	½ teaspoon cinnamon
4 tablespoons unsalted butter	¼ cup rum or brandy

Slice bananas lengthwise and sprinkle with lemon juice. Melt butter in pan; add sugar and cinnamon. Stir until sugar melts. Add bananas to pan and sauté until they soften. Remove pan from heat, add liquor, and ignite, using a long match. When flame burns out, place 2 banana halves into each dish and top with best vanilla ice cream. Spoon pan sauce over.

PEACHES FLAMBÉ

6 ripe medium peaches or
   8 smaller
1 tablespoon fresh lemon juice

⅓ cup raspberry jelly
⅓ cup pine nuts (pignolias)
¼ cup cognac, brandy, or rum

Blanch peaches in boiling water for half a minute; remove and put in ice water. Peel peaches, remove seeds, and rub with lemon juice. Place in shallow heatproof dish. Melt jelly in small saucepan, stirring till smooth, then brush peaches with this and sprinkle with pine nuts. When ready to serve, heat cognac and sprinkle a little over the peaches. Set the rest on fire and pour over peaches, rocking dish so cognac and flames are distributed.

If you can't find pignolias, use slivered blanched almonds. Many like to add minced sugared orange peel.

BAKED PEACHES

In the summertime, we enjoy so much anything made with peaches with that lovely perfume, which reminds us that the fruit is a rich Persian cousin of the rose. But oh, woe, most peaches we can get nowadays from the store left home and Mama all too long ago, before they had learned coquetry, pleasance, and French perfumes.

Peaches
Honey
Orange juice
Powdered mace
Powdered nutmeg

Whole-berry cranberry sauce or
   peach preserves
Rose water and/or peach brandy
   (optional)

Preheat oven to 350 degrees. Peel, seed, and halve peaches. Place peach halves on buttered sheet or pan; pour over peaches a few drops of honey thinned with warm water and flavored with orange juice, powdered mace, and powdered nutmeg. Put a spoonful of either crunchy cranberry sauce or peach preserves into each half. If you are of a mind, add a few drops of rose water and/or peach brandy. Bake for about 15 to 20 minutes. Serve with very cold, very heavy cream.

Without the cream, these can come to table with baked, boiled, or whatever ham or pork.

BAKED PEACHES WITH LIQUEUR TOPPING

6 ripe peaches

1 cup sugar

1 teaspoon powdered cinnamon

1 tablespoon unsalted butter

1 lightly beaten egg

½ cup flour

½ teaspoon baking powder

Pinch of salt

Whipping cream or vanilla ice cream

Anisette or orange liqueur

Preheat oven to 350 degrees. Scald peaches, peel, and stone; slice into 10-inch pie plate. Mix ⅓ cup sugar with cinnamon and sprinkle over. Set peaches aside and make batter: Work together butter and ⅔ cup sugar, then mix in the lightly beaten egg. Mix well. Stir in flour sifted with baking powder and salt. With big spoon, drop this batter over peaches; it doesn't have to be even. Bake 20 to 25 minutes.

If you serve warm, top with sweetened whipping cream flavored with anisette or an orange liqueur. If you serve cold, top with vanilla ice cream sprinkled with any orange liqueur.

PEACH GRATINÉ

3 ripe peaches, sliced and
    soaked in white port

⅓ cup brown sugar

1 lightly beaten egg

½ cup heavy cream

2 tablespoons cookie crumbs
    (any crunchy cookie such as
    Lorna Doone or cinnamon
    crisps)

1 tablespoon confectioner's sugar

Preheat oven to 375 degrees. In a round shallow baking dish, arrange your peach slices in a circular pattern. Put more slices in center. Sprinkle with brown sugar. Mix beaten egg and cream (with a pinch of allspice if you like) and pour over peaches. Sprinkle with cookie crumbs; bake for 35 to 40 minutes. Sprinkle with confectioner's sugar; let cool down before serving. Makes 4 to 6 portions.

ROASTED PEACHES

For dessert, or to serve with roast pork, spareribs, pork chops, sausage, etc. This recipe is for one person.

1 peach, peeled, stoned, and
    cut in half

1 sugar cube
1 teaspoon dark rum

If using a grill, get the coals hot or preheat the oven to 475 degrees. Place peach half, at room temperature, on square of heavy foil. Put sugar cube in cavity and pour rum over; place remaining peach half on top. Wrap peach securely in foil, careful not to spill any rum. Place on barbecue for 5 to 10 minutes or bake in oven 10 to 15 minutes. Serve hot, in foil.

POACHED PEARS

In certain central and north Alabama families, this is a traditional Thanksgiving dessert, always followed by a slug of apple or pear brandy.

2 cups dry red wine

2 apples, peeled, cored, and chopped

½ cup sugar

2 ¾ cups water

1 teaspoon powdered cinnamon

¼ teaspoon grated nutmeg

1 slice fresh gingerroot, or 1 tablespoon
    finely chopped candied ginger

6 firm pears, peeled, core removed
    from bottom, leaving stem intact

1 ½ cups blueberries, frozen raspberries,
    or strawberries

2 tablespoons Mrs. Knox unflavored
    gelatin

Fresh mint leaves for garnish

Bring wine, apples, sugar, and 2 ½ cups of water to a boil, then add spices and gingerroot. Reduce heat to simmer; poach pears until tender, about 20 minutes (or a minute or so longer). Pears are done when fork slips easily into bottom. If overcooked, they mush. Remove pears and place on serving dish or in 6 dessert dishes.

Boil liquid a quarter hour or longer till you have about 2 cups. Reduce heat to simmer; add blueberries or whichever fruit. In small bowl, stir together gelatin and ¼ cup water. Remove liquid from heat and slowly add gelatin, stirring constantly. Return to low heat and stir until sauce thickens and clears. Strain. Pour sauce around pears. Put mint leaf near each stem; chill an hour or so before serving. Serves 6.

For four people, you'll want eight small or four bigger pears. Smaller pears can be left whole, bigger ones halved or quartered as you think, but peel them all.

Juice of ½ lemon

7 tablespoons sugar

2 cups red wine

Good dash of powdered cinnamon

Dash of mace and allspice

2 crushed peppercorns

2 cloves

½ cup crème de cassis (a black currant liqueur made in France; for this dish a blackberry or elderberry liqueur could be used)

8 small or 4 larger pears

Combine lemon juice, sugar, wine, spices, and crème de cassis in a large saucepan. Put pears in pan and be certain they are completely covered by the liquid. Cover; simmer over low flame for 30 minutes. Let cool. Remove pears and reduce sauce by half. Return pears to sauce and chill 24 hours.

Serve with paper-thin cookies on the side.

There are almost as many versions of this dish as there are of mint juleps. This is my favorite.

1 9-inch sponge cake (some use plain pound cake, the old-fashioned kind)

¾ cup cream Sherry

6 cups mixed fresh fruit, such as blackberries, raspberries, blueberries, peaches, apricots, Persian melon balls, kumquats cut in half and seeded

A little grated orange or lemon peel

Good splash of any orange liqueur

Mint sprigs for garnish

Cut cake into little squares and place on dessert plates. Divide Sherry among them, soaking cake. Remove fruit from fridge when ready to serve (the fruit must be very cold).

Top each piece of cake with fruit, orange or lemon peel, and orange liqueur. Garnish with mint sprigs. This makes about 8 servings.

Serve with heavy whipped cream flavored with pear brandy or white rum.

APPLE MERINGUE

1 ¾ cups sugar	8 medium tart apples
1 cup water	¼ cup red wine
Good pinch of salt	2 egg whites
Hint of cinnamon	½ teaspoon vanilla extract

Preheat oven to 325 degrees. Combine 1 ½ cups sugar, water, salt, and cinnamon and bring to boil. Pare, quarter, and core apples and add to hot syrup. Cover, bring to boil, reduce heat, and simmer 15 minutes or until apples are tender. Transfer apples from syrup to buttered 1-quart casserole. Sprinkle wine over them. Beat egg whites till they stand in stiff peaks, then slowly beat in remaining ¼ cup sugar and vanilla and spread over apples. Bake about 15 minutes or until browned.

Serve warm or cold. The cooking syrup, with a little orange juice added, then reduced over low heat, can serve as sauce.

Pineapple:
The Fleshy Flower, Neither Pine nor Apple

That delightfully perfumed chunky, prickly scaled edible object rising above saber-like leaves, with its taste not easily described — not quite sweet and sour, perhaps flowery and tingly, honeyed but astringent — is not a fruit and has nothing to do with either pine or apple. It's a kind of floral middle-age spread. Its botanical name is sometimes *Ananas sativus*, sometimes *Ananas comosus*, and technically it is a sorosis, a form created by the union of originally separate flowers, whose stems thicken and turn into one succulent, aromatic mass, varying in color from almost pure white to a deep golden yellow.

Most people associate the pineapple with Hawaii so adamantly that it comes as a doleful surprise to learn it was introduced there only in the

1880s. It was Cristoforo Colombo's men who first spotted the pineapple, in Guadalupe in 1493. Native to the Caribbean and Central and South America, the pineapple aroused great enthusiasm among early explorers and writers. Gonzalo de Oviedo y Valdes, struggling to define the delightful flavor of the fruit, as have so many writers since, wrote in 1535 that the *pinas*, as it was known to him, combined the flavors of melons, strawberries, raspberries, and pippin apples. Sir Walter Raleigh in 1595 was exclaiming over the "princesse of fruits that grow under the Sun, especially those of Guiana." All who tasted it raved, with the exception of Charles V, king of Spain and Holy Roman Emperor, who refused to taste it for fear of being poisoned.

The pineapple reached China early on, as well as the Philippines, and was in cultivation by 1594. Louis XIV was sternly anti-pineapple because, when offered the first he'd ever seen, he greedily bit into it without peeling it and cut his lips badly on the pineapple's sharp "eyes." Louis XV, on the other hand, ordered a special hothouse for raising pineapples and spent 1,000 francs a year on the project. George Washington, traveling with his brother Lawrence to Barbados in 1751, wrote home that of all the exotic foodstuffs he'd sampled, "none pleases my taste as do's [does] the pine."

Certain initiation rites for Carib and Central American Indian adolescent boys still take place: They are forced to run through parallel lines of the cruelly barbed pineapple plants. Two centuries of work by hybridizers and plant breeders, however, have almost eliminated the prickles, making harvesting much easier.

The Indian custom of hanging a pineapple over the door to indicate that the family is at home, food and wine are being dispensed, and friends are welcomed was seized upon with delight in England and Europe, and the pineapple became the symbol of hospitality, carved, painted, wrought, and cast on sideboards, serving dishes, cups, and punch bowls and over mantles. The image of delicate ladies languishing in big four-posters with exuberant phallic pineapples surmounting the bedposts bears thinking about. Hospitality, indeed! The symbol still obtains: Several new restaurants in the Gulf Coast area have pineapples over the entrances.

Lusciously scented pineapples were comparatively unknown in the United States until well into the twentieth century. The fruit has to ripen on the plant; once ripe, it quickly goes into fermentation. Lack of transport kept it rare until canning processes were perfected. And Hawaii took the lead, oddly enough, even though the plant flourished in Florida. By 1951, three-quarters of the world's supply of pineapples came from Hawaii, but gradually the big canning companies moved their operations to the Philippines, Kenya, Thailand, and other areas where labor was cheaper.

The flavor of the pineapple is, indeed, irresistible. It has been the lifesaver of many a harried hostess whose soufflé has failed or who has to come home from the office and whip up a dinner for eight. For students, bachelors, and fishing campers, it has been a standard. Now that much basic American cookery is being rediscovered or re-explored and the can is no longer held in scorn, the pineapple is definitely "back." And there's a good reason; it preserves its best features when canned, unlike some of the green vegetables, for instance.

Pineapple contains a strong proportion of sugar (between 15 and 20 percent), citric and malic acids, a helpful fermentation agent called bromelain, and a kind of vegetable pepsin, making it a powerful aid to digestion, especially after heavy meat dishes. American cooks and serious eaters, Francophile to their toenails, have always lamented that the French have never truly "coped" with three American basics: the pineapple, the peanut, and the catfish. Personally, I think the French fashion of serving fresh pineapple one of the great table triumphs of all time, ranking with ripe tomato with basil and black-eyed peas with rice. I mean those slices of fresh pineapple, very cold, drowned in kirsch and sprinkled with candied violets. Well, I mean . . . ! Balzac and Dumas *père et fils* wrote with wild fondness for pineapple fritters, so obviously we must include the *recette*, as follows.

PINEAPPLE FRITTERS

Pineapple slices	Kirsch or white rum
Sugar	Apricot jam

For batter:

²⁄₃ cup milk	2 teaspoons baking powder
1 beaten egg	Pinch of salt
1 cup flour	Oil for deep-frying
2 tablespoons sugar	

You must have thin slices of pineapple. Canned is all right, but fresh is 100 percent better. Sugar the slices very lightly and put them to soak for 1 hour in either kirsch or white rum. Dry the slices thoroughly and then coat them with a very thin layer of apricot jam. Make batter by combining milk and egg, then beating into dry ingredients. Stick pairs of slices together and dip into light batter. Fry in deep oil; serve at once on a folded napkin.

PRUNE SOUFFLÉ

1 ⅔ cups pitted and chopped
    moist prunes
2 to 3 strips orange peel
3 ½ tablespoons brandy
½ cup warm water

2 tablespoons sugar
Few grains of salt
3 egg whites
Pinch of powdered allspice
Confectioner's sugar

Simmer first 4 ingredients a few minutes, then remove from fire and cover. Let stand about 20 minutes, then take out orange peel and beat mixture with wooden spoon until you have a lumpy paste.

Preheat oven to 400 degrees. Lightly coat a 2-quart soufflé dish with vegetable oil, then slosh sugar around to coat dish evenly, tossing out excess. Add salt to egg whites and whip until stiff but not dry. Fold about ¼ of prune mix into egg whites, then gently fold in remaining prune mix. Pour into soufflé dish, smooth out top, and run your thumb around edge of soufflé. Bake about 15 minutes until soufflé has puffed up and turned golden. Dust with allspice and confectioner's sugar; serve at once. For 4 greedy-guts, 6 dainty pickers.

Rhubarb

As far as can be discovered, rhubarb (*Rheum rhabarbarum*), also known as pie plant, redbarb, and redstem, originated in Siberia, but the plant was already listed in a Chinese herbal dated 2700 B.C. It was employed in many medicines, usually remedies for intestinal problems. Interesting that most warm-blooded mammals (man and all his unlettered wooly cousins) seek something bitter or acidic for tonics or cures. Powdered rhubarb roots were one of the very earliest laxatives. In the 1600s, the British began to grow rhubarb at home to avoid the tremendous prices asked for imported Chinese roots. They experimented with the plant as food, and one of the first results was rhubarb pie, which came very early on in the States.

Dale Marshall, at Michigan State University, who is known as "Doctor Rhubarb," wrote a monograph on the plant for the U.S. Department of Agriculture in which he describes some fifty species and informs us, surprisingly, that it is a better source of muscle-building qualities than spinach (had Popeye but known: high in potassium and low in calories, too).

In the Deep South, there is still, after over a century of canned goods, and almost that of frozen foods, an enthusiasm for "firstlings"—the first butter beans, the first eggplant, all that—and the ancient favorite, rhubarb pie, makes a welcome appearance in spring or again in late summer. Every household has a variant recipe. Rhubarb is often paired with strawberries in dozens of sweet-and-sour desserts, and the variations of chutney, preserves, jellies, etc., based on rhubarb are infinite.

All southern cooks pride themselves on having some little "secret" concerning their most successful recipes. A great many Gulf Coast cooks like to secretly add a few small ripe, sweet strawberries to the rhubarb mix in these recipes; some add a bit of very ripe peach or apricot or nectarine. This adds a memorable je ne sais quoi to almost any rhubarb dish.

RHUBARB CONSERVE

Serve with poultry or roast meat.

3 ½ cups coarsely chopped
   rhubarb
1 cup apple juice (or cider)
½ cup dark honey
½ teaspoon (or more) chopped
   fresh ginger

1 cup coarsely chopped zucchini
   (with skin)
Good dash or so of freshly grated
   nutmeg
½ cup raisins
¼ cup chopped walnuts

Mix rhubarb, apple juice, honey, and ginger in a big pot. Cook over medium heat until thickened, about 15 minutes. Add zucchini; cook 5 minutes longer. Remove from stove; add nutmeg, raisins, and walnuts. Pour into hot, sterilized half-pint jars. Seal and refrigerate. Some cooks soak the raisins in an orange-flavored drink such as Triple Sec, Grand Marnier, etc.

RHUBARB-PEAR COMPOTE

¼ cup dry red wine

⅓ cup sugar

⅓ teaspoon powdered allspice

Pinch of powdered ginger

2 Bartlett pears, cut lengthwise, cored, and cut into coarse pieces

1 ½ cups rhubarb, cut into coarse bits

In heavy saucepan over medium-low heat, bring wine, sugar, and spices to a simmer, stirring till sugar dissolves. Add pears and simmer 2 minutes. Mix in rhubarb. Cover and simmer till all is just reaching tenderness, roughly 8 minutes.

Spoon into bowls and top with buttermilk sherbet, frozen yogurt, or vanilla ice cream.

STRAWBERRY CRUMBLY

2 pints ripe strawberries, cleaned and cut in halves

1 ½ tablespoons white sugar

3 tablespoons dark rum

1 ½ cups sour cream

½ cup firmly packed light brown sugar

Pinch of powdered ginger

Pinch of allspice

Preheat oven broiler. Mix well the berries, sugar, and 1 tablespoon of the rum, then spread the mixture evenly in 10-inch glass baking dish. Mix sour cream and rest of the rum, whisking well, and spread over the berries. Force the brown sugar through a sieve, spreading evenly to cover dish completely. Place under broiler, about 4 inches from flames, for 5 to 6 minutes, till sugar has melted and bubbles.

Sprinkle with ginger and allspice and serve at once. Some cooks like to add a couple of crushed gingersnaps or vanilla wafers to that last layer, the brown sugar. Along the Gulf Coast, ripe mulberries are sometimes used for this dish.

STRAWBERRIES ROMANOFF

2 pints ripe strawberries

⅓ cup plus 2 tablespoons sugar

⅓ cup Grand Marnier or Cointreau

1 orange

¾ cup heavy cream

Remove stems from berries, rinse and drain, and pat dry with paper towels. Place berries in bowl with ⅓ cup sugar and orange liqueur. Peel orange very carefully: You want only the thin outer peel, not one bit of white. Cut peel into thin shreds; add to berries and fold gently. Cover and refrigerate. Whip cream with remaining sugar; serve alongside berries. 6 portions.

KENTUCKY COMPOTE

½ ripe honeydew melon

A combination of summer fruit:
cherries, strawberries,
whatever you fancy

About ¾ cup chopped mint

½ cup cold water

½ cup sugar

1 cup bourbon

1 tablespoon lemon or lime juice

Mint sprigs for garnish

First prepare your fruit: With a baler, scoop out half a ripe honeydew melon, pit and halve cherries, and slice strawberries. Add ¼ cup chopped mint. Chill. Mix water and sugar in a pan over heat until sugar dissolves. Stir in ½ cup chopped mint, bourbon, and lemon or lime juice. Set aside to cool.

In chilled bowl, gently mix fruit and syrup. Chill 1 to 2 hours. Garnish with mint sprigs before serving.

This is a breakfast dish or a dessert after heavy meats. It's a do-it-as-you-like dish, basically a thick, crunchy crust over the chopped fruit flavored with molasses and spice.

1 scant cup smashed Triscuits

2 cups smashed gingersnaps
    and/or graham crackers

½ cup brown sugar

Spices as you like: pinches of
    powdered allspice, ginger,
    and mace in crust; powdered
    cinnamon and clove in apples

3 tablespoons unsalted butter

1 tablespoon warm water

6 Granny Smith or Jonathan apples

½ cup molasses

¼ cup Calvados or dark rum
    or bourbon

Preheat oven to 375 degrees. Smash together the Triscuits, cookies and/or crackers, brown sugar, and whatever spices you wish; add the butter and warm water. Set aside. Scrub and core your fruit; chop in thumbnail-size bits. Don't peel! Butter a shallow baking dish or pie pan and arrange the fruit, sprinkling spices of your choice over them, then evenly pour the molasses and whichever liquor over them.

Spread the crunch crust evenly over this. Bake half an hour. Good as is or can have vanilla ice cream, whipped cream, sour cream, or yogurt served with it. Pears can be used instead of apples. If you use peaches, choose the harder ones. Can also be made with not-quite-ripe muskmelon or cantaloupe.

2 ½ cups unbleached flour

1 ¾ cups sugar

2 teaspoons baking powder

½ teaspoon baking soda

½ teaspoon salt

2 cups buttermilk

½ cup vegetable oil

2 big eggs

8 cups bran flakes cereal

½ cup jam or marmalade

Preheat oven to 350 degrees. Put paper muffin cups into your muffin tins. Mix first 5 ingredients.

Separately whisk together buttermilk, oil, and eggs. Add dry ingredients and cereal; stir all together. Put ½ cup batter into each muffin cup. With a little spoon, make a little hole in center of each and fill with 1 teaspoon jam or marmalade, then top with remaining batter. Bake until tester comes out clear, about 25 minutes. Pour muffins out onto racks. Cool a minute or so; serve warm.

The delight of this recipe is in the infinite possibilities of the choice for what goes into the center: orange marmalade with a few drops of Triple Sec, fig preserves finely chopped with a splash of bourbon, raspberry jam with a bit of red port, apple butter mixed with some finely chopped candied ginger or citron peel and a splash of Madeira, dried apricots soaked in port and honey then drained and chopped, etc., etc. Have fun.

Dessert Sauces

HARD SAUCE FOR FRUITCAKES AND PUDDINGS

2 sticks unsalted butter

3 cups sifted confectioner's sugar

¼ cup Grand Marnier

Cream butter and sugar until light and fluffy. Add Grand Marnier and process until smooth. Put in serving dish and refrigerate until firm. Bring to room temperature before serving with fruitcake, nut cakes, or English-style puddings.

For ice cream, buttermilk sherbet, pound cake, etc.

¼ cup sugar

Slivered peel of 1 orange

½ cup water

2 pints strawberries, hulled and sliced

1 ½ tablespoons fresh lemon juice
    or more to taste

2 tablespoons Grand Marnier or
    Cointreau

Mix sugar, orange peel, and water and bring to a boil, covered; boil 5 minutes. Remove peel and toss out; cool mix. Puree the strawberries, by blender, processor, or elbow grease. Force the puree through a fine-meshed sieve, banging down on the solid bits. To the berry juice add the syrup, 1 ½ tablespoons lemon juice, and 1 ½ tablespoons Grand Marnier or Cointreau.

Chill, covered, for 2 hours, then add additional lemon juice and liqueur; serve sauce over ice cream, cake, whatever. Some cooks add, as a "secret ingredient," a small ripe peach or apricot.

MANGO SAUCE

2 tablespoons unsalted butter

2 tablespoons sugar

1 cup water

1 teaspoon cornstarch

3 tablespoons cold water

2 cups mashed ripe mango pulp

5 tablespoons best dark rum

Pinch of ground nutmeg

Pinch of ground allspice

Mix butter, sugar, and 1 cup water in saucepan; bring to boil. Dissolve cornstarch in 3 tablespoons cold water, add to syrup mix, and stir well. Bring back to boiling point, stirring well. Add mango, rum, and seasonings; stir well.

Serve over frozen yogurt or vanilla ice cream or pour over buttermilk biscuits for a sticky-finger delight.

BOURBON SAUCE

½ cup buttermilk

½ teaspoon baking soda

6 tablespoons (about ¾ of a stick)
    unsalted butter

1 cup sugar

1 tablespoon light corn syrup

1 teaspoon vanilla extract

¾ cup best bourbon

Combine buttermilk and soda in small bowl. In a saucepan melt butter over medium heat; stir in sugar, corn syrup, vanilla, and the buttermilk mix. Bring this mixture to a boil, whisking constantly, and boil about 1 ½ minutes. Remove pan from heat, let sauce cool 10 minutes, and then stir in bourbon. Serve sauce warm. Makes just over 1 ½ cups.

Serve over ice cream, frozen yogurt, pound cake, sponge cake, or chilled cooked fruit. Variation: Make the sauce as above but with dark rum, then add currants (white raisins) or dark raisins and chopped candied orange peel.

WHISKEY CREAM

⅓ cup sugar

5 egg yolks

½ cup milk

¾ cup heavy cream

½ teaspoon vanilla or almond extract

¼ cup best bourbon whiskey

Whisk sugar into eggs yolks; beat till mixture is pale and somewhat thickened. Heat milk and cream almost to boiling, then add to egg-sugar mix very slowly, whisking the while. Put all back into saucepan over low heat and cook until thick enough to coat a spoon. This takes 6 to 8 minutes. DON'T let it boil. Strain into clean bowl and add vanilla or almond extract and bourbon.

On some occasions, you can add bourbon in which minced orange peel and minced candied ginger have marinated.

At home, Mobile, 1997. Courtesy of Jerry Siegel.

Index